PENETRATING
THE
TERRORIST
PSYCHE

by Nancy Hartevelt Kobrin

©2013

PENETRATING THE TERRORIST PSYCHE

MultiEducator, Inc.
Publishers since 1994
New Rochelle, NY 10805
www.multieducator.net

In memory of my mother and father

"The emperor marched in the procession under the beautiful canopy, and all who saw him in the street and out of the windows exclaimed: "Indeed, the emperor's new clothes are incomparable! What a long train he has! How well it fits him!" Nobody wished to let others know he saw nothing, for then he would have been unfit for his office or too stupid.

Never were an emperor's clothes more admired.

"But he has nothing on at all," said a little child at last. "Good heavens! Listen to the voice of an innocent child," said the father, and each person whispered to the other what the child had said. "But he has nothing on at all," cried all the people at last. That made a deep impression upon the emperor, for it seemed to him that they were right; but he thought to himself, "Now I must carry on."

The Emperor's New Clothes
by Hans Christian Andersen, 1837

Table of Contents

Acknowledgments

My first association with Osama Bin Laden was the famous fairy tale of *The Emperor's New Clothes*. This inspired me to write my first book, *The Sheikh's New Clothes: The Naked Truth about Islamic Suicide Bombing,* which was later changed to *The Banality of Suicide Terrorism,* with the same subtitle.

I first heard the fairy tale as a little girl and was relieved to know that out of meaningless and senselessness there was meaning and purpose and that the little child was believed. Those whom I acknowledge here understand the importance of the story and how it inspired the child in me, giving me courage to write about what has been ignored in the literature. This book has been a most daunting task, perhaps the most difficult writing task I have ever faced. I am profoundly grateful to my friends and colleagues, who supported me throughout this endeavor.

I must thank Dr. David Van Dyke, who read this narrative in process several times and told me, "I want to say after my second reading that you have found your Moen faucet, and I'm not sure you realize how beautiful and challenging it is." He was referring to the TV commercial in which a woman plops a Moen faucet on her architect's desk and tells him to build a house around it. (The hard object of the Moen faucet providing life-giving water seemed a most positive image for this book as I talk about how terrorists use and misuse objects, including us.) It was David who identified this text as falling within the genre of a psychological anthropology.[1] He further added that this book challenges many long-established and alienating paradigms of thinking and forces the reader to see how even violence and manipulation can be the only contact a person has when he or she is in an extreme situation.

As a psychoanalyst, I go beyond genre or scope to integrate my highly specialized training in semiotics and languages, including Semitic languages. I found this comprehensive training crucial as a link to understanding the complex nature of global, and more specifically Islamic, terrorism. I learned to speak the language of terrorists. I came to understand their pantomime of inflicting pain, and equally important I came to understand how I internalized their terrorism into my internal terrorist. To know the terrorist within is the first step toward the exit to freedom. In this book, I share my learning process to reveal the birth of the suicide terrorist in a culture of shame, sexism, unspoken fantasies of violence, all mixed with penetrating yet unmet need for empathy and nurturing merger. I will show you how much of the path I have shared with the suicide terrorist over five decades of my own middle-class domestic violence and child abuse. They are interlocking and potentially negatively synergistic if one chooses to live in denial and to identity with the aggressor.

Dr. Joan Jutta Lachkar, who has authored numerous books and has extensive clinical experience treating cross-cultural couples from a psychohistorical/psychodynamic perspective in therapy, has guided me every step of the way, urging me to write in the first person, even though it runs the risk of this book falling into the category of a memoir, which is not my intention.

This book would not have been possible without the superb care and editing of Joanne Freeman, my editor. I am profoundly grateful for her excellent eye and outstanding work.

I wish to thank Amy Erani, from the MultiEducator, Inc. design team, who brought this book to life. I am profoundly grateful.

Special tribute goes to Merry Prose, my next door neighbor in St. Paul, Minnesota, who read this manuscript in its earliest and roughest form and called it a page turner. I hope that readers will experience the same excitement.

My colleague Dr. Kathy Seifert—author of *How Children Become Violent*, as well as a columnist for Psychology Today—also read the manuscript and validated the importance of this text for counterterrorism studies, saying that nothing like this book has ever been written before and should be brought to the awareness of those in government and homeland security.

Dr. Sander Breiner, professor of psychiatry and scholar in the area of counterterrorism studies as well as a leading authority on the history of child sacrifice focused primarily on the psychological mentality of Arab Muslims, read this manuscript and wholeheartedly encouraged me to find a publisher. Unfortunately, he died before seeing it published.

I am especially grateful to my life partner, Professor Yitzhak Reiter, who read an early draft and was concerned about the risk of the tell-all aspect of this psychological anthropology for fear of what others might think of me. He is a profound and highly respected scholar of Islam, particularly in Sharia law, and had the unique experience of being the only Jew ever to spend extensive time in the archives of the Sharia court in Jerusalem. I am extremely indebted to him. He has taught me not only to understand Islam but to understand its "secret" codes of behavior that go beyond terrorism. When I first immigrated to Israel, he helped me become absorbed into Israeli society by speaking only Hebrew in our home. The confluences of these experiences contributed to the integration of this psychological anthropology approach as I viewed Israeli culture through these new lenses.

As a new immigrant, he helped me understand the degree to which Israeli culture is in fact a microcosm of the Arab shame–honor culture. While individualism is highly cherished and valued in Israel unlike in Arab Muslim culture and there are virtually all the freedoms seen in the West, the group is still venerated over the individual and to a degree dominates. The group comes first, and along with it a special concern over one's behavior. This is motivated to a degree by the concept of *l'fargen,* which in Yiddish means to speak well of someone or, more broadly, "Will you be praised for your behavior?" If not, you had better understand this honor code. In my opinion it runs the risk of pressuring people to avoid being shamed.

I am also indebted to my family, my children, and my grandchildren, without whose understanding and patience, this book would not have been written. Forgive me for the time that writing has taken away from you, and for any pain I may have caused you over the many long, difficult years.

Introduction

We must always take sides. Neutrality helps the oppressor, never the victim. Silence encourages the tormentor, never the tormented. --- Elie Wiesel

Zeh sippur lo kal/ Hadhihi al-qaddiyya laysat bisahle—This is not an easy telling.

I translated this sentence from the Hebrew and then the Arabic, which is a real challenge for me. In Hebrew it is *kasheh al ha-panim,* literally "hard on the face." In other words, it sucks. I began my narrative in the first person, but the words wouldn't come. Later, switching to the third person allowed my words to flow like a wild stream. I had experienced this rushing of words just once before, four months after 9/11, when composing a psychological analysis of Islamic suicide bombing because I began to find meaning in all of the chaos and terror. It had taken me only a few weeks to develop the initial theory for my first book, *The Banality of Suicide Terrorism.* The first book is a professional take on terrorism; the second explores the parallels and interlocking aspects and conflicts that I saw and experienced within the light of terrorism and examines the parallels between Judaism and Islam, unfamiliar territory for most.

I showed the first draft initially to a colleague, who chided me about writing in the third person." But what was wrong with speaking of myself as "she"? I thought of Mullah Omar of the Taliban, who speaks about himself to others in the third person." Perhaps this one-eyed Taliban spiritual leader and terrorist is also dissociated and detached from himself. Speaking in the third person rather than embodying and owning one's own voice is an indicator of trauma because until one's internal terrors are dealt with, it is just too scary to own them and the accompanying vulnerability.

However, after contemplating my colleague's advice and being inspired by the honest eloquence of Jessica Stern's *Denial: A Memoir of Terror*, and Ursula Mehlendorf's *The Shame of Survival—Working Through A Nazi Childhood*, I found myself needing to translate what I had written back into the first person because my theory and insights on terrorism were based on events in my life. Like a detective I was drawing parallels and searching for clues that are often hidden, conducting a "forensic examination" of domestic violence and the political violence of suicide terrorism.

This easily could have been a memoir allowing a stream of consciousness in a work of fiction. Instead it is a psychological anthropology designed to understand the cultural and social relations of the Middle East by putting myself into the shoes of the other, especially the female in Arab Muslim societies. It may seem like a double bind to use the first person narrative, but how else can we know the other without knowing ourselves first? Ironically, this is the beauty of analytic work. As much as we deplore the aggression and the heinous crimes terrorists commit, we can show empathy toward what motivates them. It is through empathic understanding and empathy that we can understand the fears and terrors they project into us. Furthermore, in order to understand the mind and mentality of terrorism we have to examine the terrorist within, our own internal terror and terrors that have been inflicted upon us. Say, for example, you are standing in line and the person ahead of you is taking an extraordinarily long time and being exceedingly aggressive to the cashier; suddenly you become aware of your own violent fantasy about this person who is taking up your time. This is your "momentary" internal terrorist, but you do not act out your murderous thoughts. You process them and become aware of them and then move on. If not, you may swallow your own rage and not be aware of it, acting it out inappropriately on others, mistreating them and behaving in miniature like a terrorist, threatening and aggressive. This is your own projection. One does not have to live in a Muslim country to know about the fears and terrors that get projected into us; we may know them because we have experienced abusive parents or an abusive partner. I have gleaned the interlocking links of terrorism denoted in this volume from firsthand experience. To understand this you have to search for the interlocking links of terror in your own life. Perhaps, you have known them all along.

I no longer allow what people may or may not say influence me, or what they may think stop me from telling that which is not easy to tell. I have written this book to inspire those who have been the object of longstanding hatred, who have been pushed around and chronically disregarded, so they might also begin to recognize how and where terrorism abides. By naming the rules of terrorism, which are interspersed throughout this text, people may begin to put together pieces of their own puzzles more easily. My aim is to help people recognize not only what terrorism is, but what causes it, who is behind it, and how it works. People need to demystify terrorists and understand that terrorists, both domestic and international, are basically all the same. They are predators and therefore cannot be reasoned with. They can look normal, but they are not normal. They lack complete empathy for the other. The key is exposing the behavior and setting boundaries.

Life can become one big out-of-body experience that is too scary to accept. Each one of us has an internal terrorist and it is scary to get in contact with this aspect of our self. But in order to understand the nature of terrorism we must! This is why it is important to remain in contact with our own internal terrorist. Everybody has one, composed of the terrors that are part of ourselves, from which we dissociate. When you are abused, one can't really grasp how the person whom we depend on could hate and treat us so horribly. This creates ambivalence because the abuser who can be cruel and sadistic can also be loving and kind. This is a function of the paranoia shown by terrorists, who trap us into their delusional systems. While their storm rages, you are at its center, flooded with anxiety and terror. You are an object to be hated rather than a person to be loved.

In this parallel study, I attempt to unlock the interlocking links of terror, tracing trauma from early childhood through adulthood in order to make the seemingly unexplainable explainable—the Islamic suicide attack. This psychological anthropology approach intertwines the tenets of terrorism with my experiences. I could not have understood what lies behind the Islamic suicide attack without having lived every page of this book, extracting rules about the terrain of terrorism from a lifetime of living with terrorists. This is a book about the psychological dynamics of being constantly hated, absorbing the projection of the hatred by those who dominate the other, the female. At the base of political terrorism, the singular problem that has failed to be addressed is the underlying gruesome hatred of the female.

You may be wondering: Who am I to claim to have cracked the code? Who am I to know about the unveilings of Arab sheikhs—or terrorists for that matter—that deal not with new clothes but with age-old trappings beyond which few can see? I give credit to the tools that psychoanalysis offers. This includes the study of people's unconscious motivations, denial, dissociation, delusions, grandiosity, enactments, splitting, violence, aggression, "unthought thoughts" or thoughts without a thinker, Freud's life-and-death instincts, and life and death in and of itself.

I wondered if people would really believe the connections that I draw. As the first-person narrator I wondered if I were even justified in drawing them. A function of terrorism is that it sucks us into its delusional world, and the force of these delusions begins to erode our own internal cohesiveness. We start to feel it is better to live in denial, dissociated from the truth. Once we are able to extract the self from the world of paranoia and its identification with the aggressor, we develop immunity from getting sucked into this whirlwind of violence and terror. We see the emperor as naked. We call his bluff.

However, integration into a different and better existence post identification with the aggressor is an ongoing process. It is like constantly re-entering the reality of having been abused. The patterns are so deeply ingrained in one's DNA that no matter what one did and no matter how hard one may try to do something better, to remain hopeful and optimistic, the patterns keep repeating. It is arduous to constantly be forced to set boundaries for terrorists who will try to erode them and dominate.

Perhaps counterterrorist experts are still not quite ready to examine their motivations for pursuing their line of work. Yet if we do not know our own subjectivity well, or as best we can, it will skew and affect the outcome of our research on terrorism, creating blind spots that, unrecognized, can limit our comprehension.

The theme of being dissociated runs throughout this psychological anthropology. So how can we think about dissociation? To paraphrase a leading trauma expert, Bessel Van der Kolk, what happens in dissociation is that the levels of emotional arousal (i.e., anxiety and fear) are so high that it causes an inability to create semantic constructs, to derive meaning from what the body is experiencing, precisely because the information is so terrifying that it overwhelms the hippocampus and the cortex in the brain where meaning is created.[2] Howell adds another dimension that helps us understand why attachment, bonding, bondage, and relationships with others is key: "Dissociation is the one way that the psyche modifies its own structure to accommodate interaction with a frightening but needed and usually loved, attachment figure."[3] This figure is most often the mother, our first attachment figure in life.

This book applies a metapsychological approach to explore the links existing in global, Islamic, and domestic terrorism. It is unlike Robin Moore's *The Demon Lover*. The purpose is not the search for a root cause; rrather, it is an in-depth study to explain how the intimate relationship with the mother becomes fertile ground for terrorism and how terrorism is inextricably interwoven with the mother. The bitter paradox is that as much as she is needed and depended upon, she must be repudiated and destroyed. The female, little girls, little boys, infants, and even the feminization of the other become irrational stand-ins for the mother. They are targets for the terrorists, whether global, Islamic, or domestic. This is the well-kept secret in terrorism: the maternal platform from which terrorist attacks are launched.

I stumbled upon the code of the "maternal" when contemplating terrorism—reading volumes of material that refer to the mother or the female, listening to terrorists in prison, talking with colleagues, especially Joan Lachkar, and recalling my own life experience. It entailed all these different aspects to crack the code. If we understand this hidden, violent relationship, which arises early in childhood, we will be able to better contain all forms of terrorism, especially global. We will call out the terrorists on their bullying behavior as mama's boys. We will profile more accurately, fashion better interventions, and save a lot of money as we become more able to nip the problem in the bud.

Cracking the code entailed my suddenly realizing how similar Osama bin Laden was to Shakespeare's character Othello, the Muslim military captain who killed his Italian wife. Both men loved and felt dependent upon their women, and so had to murder them. Osama bin Laden actually loved America and all her freedoms, which he was never able to experience. Later in this text you will read about his love story and witness this dance.

This book's unique psychological anthropology approach to examining Islamic suicide terrorism shares what I have learned about terrorism from living with domestic terrorists and finding parallels between abusive parents, spouses, and global terrorists. Although not everyone is married to or living with a terrorist, there are striking similarities between domestic violence and terrorism, including suicide bombings. The Centre for Social Cohesion in the United Kingdom used geomapping to determine where the jihadis lived and discovered that their presence was more dominant in areas in which victims of domestic violence resided. Yet the head of the project refused to acknowledge the connection for want of "hard" proof. The connection is under our noses but people do not want to see it because it is too terrifying.

I blogged at the *Times of Israel* on April 20, 2013, in the aftermath of the Boston Marathon bombings, that the FBI must take domestic violence seriously in its profiling of jihadis. Domestic violence is a manifestation of traumatic bonding. It means that the abusing partner lacks empathy. In the East there is honor killing. This traumatic, lethal attachment to people derives from the first template of maternal attachment in life. The relationship to the mother sets the tone for all other relationships, especially that of the couple. It even affects how terrorists use weapons. As the news reports about the Boston bombings came in, I kept wondering when we would hear from the mother. We finally did. She is convinced that her sons were set up. We hear this repeatedly from other mothers of jihadis.

One of the worst things for a little boy is to witness his mother being beaten because he experiences his mother, on whom he is dependent, as an extension of himself. One wonders if this happened in the Tsarnaev home. Did Tamerlan turn to boxing and his little brother turn to wrestling unconsciously in order to protect the mother they could not protect as little boys? Both boys were also given names that glorify Islamic warring. They wanted to become an engineer and a doctor—both essentially technical professions, one of hard objects and the other of soft objects—i.e., the human body and its body parts.

Did Tamerlan choose the Boston Marathon because he held a particular grudge for his failure to be chosen for the U.S. Olympic boxing team? Could this explain the unconscious tactical choice of placing the bombs at the finish line? By putting these weapons in or near garbage cans, the brothers literally projected their rage at how they felt about themselves. We became the unwitting containers for their "garbage selves," which then were made to explode. They wanted us to feel the pain that they could not feel or express through language. Interestingly, their uncle called the brothers "losers."

Unfortunately, the ideologies of the Quran's Sura 4 on wife beating are a particularly good fit with this underlying configuration. The Chechens were converts to Islam, which spread through conquest. Tamerlan Tsarnaev "conquered" his wife, who converted to Islam. Furthermore, there was a history of domestic violence. *The New York Times* reported how the father minimized Tamerlan's violence and blamed the girlfriend: "Because of his girlfriend, he hit her lightly, he was locked up for half an hour," Mr. Tsarnaev said. "There was jealousy there." Also, according to a senior law enforcement official, Tamerlan was interviewed by the FBI in 2011 when a foreign government asked the bureau to determine whether he had extremist ties.

In March 2012, I was interviewed by two French Canadian filmmakers for a documentary they were making, *The Body Does Not Lie*, concerning airport security at Tel Aviv's Ben Gurion Airport. These women had read my first book, *The Banality of Suicide Terrorism*, which has been translated into Hebrew. A psychoanalyst colleague of theirs also read it and concurred that what I described was spot on. They told me after interviewing a series of specialists and neuroscientists that my theory and descriptive analysis of the problems stemming from maternal attachment dovetail with and are supported by scientific findings.

Decoding the unconscious symbolic meanings, the family psychodynamics, and graphic nonverbal communication of the Islamic suicide attack necessitated making connections between the global and the personal and intimate. This is an aspect of terrorism we seem to forget; yet it is central to how terror works. Through my studies in the Middle East, I came to understand how terrorism accesses our feelings and traumatizes us, appearing as if it is distant when it is the most intimate of death threats. All cultures have different religious practices; different standards, laws, regulations, taboos, ideologies, and treat women differently. But basically we all share the universal need for love, bonding, and attachment. We are more alike than we are different. Nevertheless, we are aware of our cultural differences, especially when they are as diverse as those between the West and the Arab Muslim world. As the renowned Egyptian sociologist Halim Barakat has noted, the family is a microcosm of society.[4] If the family is dysfunctional so will the society be. Jonathan Matusitz, in his *Terrorism and Communication* textbook, repeatedly drives home the point that culture shapes how we view the world. He stresses that jihad is mentioned 41 times in the Quran and, hence, it is a value that is inculcated into the culture.[5]

Shereen El Feki, in her *Sex and the Citadel: Intimate Life in a Changing Arab World* [6] writes something similar: "It's hard to see how democracy can flourish in a society if its constitutional and cultural cornerstone in the family is so undemocratic. Bringing the values of democracy to marriage, including equality of personal freedom, will be the work of a generation at least." We have seen the great hope of the Arab Spring turn into the Arab Upheaval because the family system remains dysfunctional and unable to support democratic institutions.

Simply put, terrorism stems from the devalued female in the Arab Muslim families as well as other highly patriarchal or highly disorganized families from which the converts come and which spawn terrorists. Yet I do not blame the devalued female, precisely because she is the object of such relentless hatred that she internalizes male hatred of herself as self-hatred. *The Banality of Suicide Terrorism* and many of my other writings are currently being used by the U.S. Army and by experts residing in other countries, including, I have been told, Iraq and Afghanistan. This has helped focus attention on the female and the need to teach women how to read and gain access to medical care, as well as the necessity of building shelters for abused women, etc.

A few points to keep in mind as you read this volume:
- The suicide attack is key to understanding the primitive mindset of terrorists.
- The suicide attack explicitly mirrors murder–suicide and its terrors.
- The three types of murder–suicide combinations are political violence, crime like the Virginia Tech mass shooting, and domestic violence.
- Violent bonding, a traumatic bonding of early terrors related to maternal attachment, constitutes murder and can lead to murder–suicide. The first bonding experience is with the mother. An "X-ray" of global terrorism looks at this first bonding experience with the mother, the first site of terrors.
- Intermediary bonding occurs in other relationships, especially that of the couple; hence intimate terrorism and domestic violence.
- Terrors from childhood recycled in a couple's relationship, and then recycled again when there is a political terror attack such as 9/11, are interlocking and make it hard to see how the first set of terrors in life continue to resonate and shape later violence. Together they are synergistic.

In an April 2013 online article written after the Boston Marathon Bombings,[7] Dr. Kathy Seifert quoted my work and describes what poor maternal attachment means in psychological terms:

When attachment bonds are disrupted, it can interfere with:
- Skill development
- Interpersonal relatedness
- Self-concept
- Self-management
- Theory of mind
- Emotional regulation
- Development of pro-social values
- Brain development
- Family cohesiveness and relationships to others

Therefore, if the world is to stop terrorism, part of the effort must be in examining the effects of maltreatment of women and girls and the lack of development of pro-social interpersonal relationships of children in the family. A culture that does not respect women and girls cannot respect outsiders that are different from themselves.

Global terrorism theoretically would not exist if we understood our respective early terrors and if bonding were more optimal in the maternal relationship. The secret to cracking the code of terrorism is inextricably linked to early terrors, trauma, and horrors in childhood, especially when the maternal bond has been compromised. Terrorists bond through violence although they claim they are men of peace. For them bonding is confused with bondage. Global, and specifically Islamic, terrorism could be demystified and its impact deflated if this knowledge were exposed and the interlocking links between the infant's bond with the mother could be dismantled. These links are carried over into other bonding and attachment relationships during childhood, adolescence, and intimate domestic partner relationships, laying the groundwork for political violence.

This volume can be thought of as a kind of instruction manual on the psychodynamics of Islamic suicide terrorism, with a corresponding sidebar on domestic violence. Hopefully, it will help spawn a sub-genre in the field of terrorism studies. Putting aside my own emotions, terrors, and fears and trying not to be too grandiose—even though grandiosity and omnipotence play a crucial role in all forms of terrorism—I hope this will open a door. Although I am properly circumspect, I have complete confidence that this narrative is both a link and a departure point into the study of political terrorism. There are those who may say that my experiences do not justify extrapolating rules for political terrorism. But power, after all, is political by nature. It is never shared; it is negotiated. Isn't everything inherently political? Freud felt that one's professional work contains a kernel of the autobiographical and an evolving sense of self. This kernel begs not to be reduced to the status of a memoir.

Prologue

Kansas City, 1970. Motown music blasting. I lie on a table, legs spread, feet in stirrups, in a ghetto clinic for a "legal" abortion. In Chicago, where I was from, this was not legal. All the other patients were younger, poorer, uneducated, black. The doctor and nurse were white, as if that made less of a difference. Maybe it did, their sameness and safety making me feel a little less vulnerable. It wasn't as if I didn't know black people. I knew about race since I had been born in Evanston, Illinois, a relatively racially integrated city, and had volunteered in the Chicago ghettos in high school, tutoring kids on Saturday. This is not to say, though, that Chicago was not a segregated city back then.

I could not explain to myself how I got there—the only white girl, let alone Jew, although my Jewishness didn't matter much then. It was more like a curiosity. On the one hand being Jewish made me feel "special," perhaps in the sense of being one of the "chosen" people. Of course, I did not know then that "chosen" meant observing the 613 commandments in the Torah— the book that non-Jews call the Old Testament. I knew nothing about being special in the sense of being egotistical, narcissistic. In fact, I knew very little about Judaism, Hebrew, or Israel and even less about Islam and Arabic at that time. But being Jewish made me feel different, and in my innocence and ignorance I felt ashamed of that. However, I was not aware of how deep the shame was, where it came from, and how debilitating this emotion is.

Only after I became a psychoanalyst did I learn and understand that rape and abortion are linked to male rage against the prenatal mother and that this is at the base of Islamic suicide bombing. Think of the abortion terror (a form of domestic terrorism not to be confused with domestic violence's partner, political terrorism) that has occurred in the United States—Alabama, Atlanta and the Centennial Olympic Park Bombing in 1996 by Eric Rudolph. The theme of the prenatal mother is the unconscious stream that ties together the threads of global terrorism. By examining interlocking links of global terrorism, we can disarm and dismantle the mushrooming violence, learn how it works, and raise questions that haven't been asked.

The abortion was a nightmare. I was terrified but couldn't admit it. My anxiety became so great that I dissociated from the horrors of the abortion. Nonetheless, I felt myself shivering and sweating, feeling hot and cold at the same time. The pain and cramping during the procedure grew increasingly intense. Yet I could remember no word of consolation or caring from the blue-eyed, blond-haired young man I had married less than a year previously, no gesture of affection or comfort. His silence was astounding. He never said anything, not a word, not even that he was sorry.

At first I made excuses for him. This is a typical response among high-functioning women who idealize their godlike husbands. My colleague and close friend Joan Lachkar wrote the book on the subject, *The Many Faces of Abuse: Treating the Emotional Abuse of High-Functioning Women*.[8] He was a doctor in training, so I figured he was just preoccupied but that he really cared about me. Or maybe he was just reserved. This was a rationalization for how terrified I was of him. Ayn Rand wrote that rationalization is a process of not perceiving reality, but of attempting to make reality fit one's emotions. But as time went on, I got psychologically stronger, hence wiser, and became more suspicious of that rationale. In fact, later on as I became engrossed in my studies on terror and terrorism, I began to understand that I was living life as if I were a little Arab Muslim girl. It was, in part, my attempt at mastering all the trauma. Out of revenge, he continued to choose not to speak to me or to answer questions. Or he would wage an emotional jihad and vengeance against me. Still, in spite of all my pain, it was made clear to me that I deserved the abortion with all of its punishing agony and pain. He would relish the fact that I deserved to be punished every moment that I breathed. I was living the fate of a female Muslim. It was my destiny and I had it coming. I was an object of unrelenting hatred and rage, but at the time I could not understand this because I was too terrified and highly dissociated.

Terrorism at the symbolic level communicates the destruction of and rage against the prenatal mother. Think of Lacey Peterson, the pregnant woman killed by her husband, or Sharon Tate brutally murdered by Charles Manson and his Creepy Crawlers, his serial killers by proxy. Or the female suicide bomber who is portrayed as pregnant, masking all those bombs under her faux pregnant belly. Or Sara Jane Olson, the Symbionese Liberation Army member who kicked a pregnant woman in the abdomen during a bank robbery. Olson as a female terrorist had simply internalized male rage of the female as self-hatred and then chose to project this lethal rage onto an innocent pregnant women whom she envied.

Often pregnant women or post-partum women holding babies have been killed in suicide bombings. Attacking the other occurs because of feeling enormous shame and envy. The works of psychiatrist Dr. Keith Ablow concerning shame for the male, denial, projection, as well as his book profiling Scott Peterson, Lacey's husband, helped me clarify the intimate connections between domestic violence and political terrorism. But it was his book *Living the Truth: Transforming Your Life through the Power of Honesty and Insight* that shows us how these traits are the keys to unlocking the grip of terror.

Many others argue that "other cultures spawn suicide attacks, not just Islam, so how can you criticize?" The difference lies in the polarization of ideologies that uphold and endorse black-and-white thinking in a love–hate relationship, coupled with a unique position vis à vis Judaism and Islam. Islam is the fastest growing religion in the world; thus, the radical Muslims who are willing to participate in suicide attacks outnumber those of all other groups. The majority of terrorist acts are caused by Muslims. So does the religion have something to do with it? Is there a kind of attraction for those who want to engage in suicide–murder that allows them to find their way to Islam? These are questions raised in this anthropological inquiry. It will be for you, the reader, to decide.

My allegedly legal abortion was over in an hour. We flew back to Chicago from Kansas the same day. Until recently, I had no idea if the abortion took place in Missouri or in Kansas. I couldn't remember. Only recently did I learn that abortion was legal in Missouri at that time. That day remained lodged in my mind and soul as one of unbearable, unspeakable pain. For years I didn't know how to describe it or name it because I couldn't recognize it for what it was. It was more than humiliation. It was shame. Even though I really had nothing to be ashamed of, I had unconsciously taken on the shame and rage of my medical student husband.

That day of shame so unnerved me that for years I never talked about it to anyone. I did not feel safe enough to tell even my closest friends. I went through the motions, living a kind of half-life. I had flashbacks now and then, but I didn't know how to contextualize what had happened to me. I threw myself into my studies. I existed through my studies, my work, and eventually my children. The shame of it all kept me walled off, apart, like a shrouded Muslim woman dressed in black." I was always "the bad guy" and relentlessly blamed.

When I finally did say something, it was only after I had been granted "permission" by my husband, the doctor, to see a therapist. I wound up on the couch of a training analyst from Yale, who helped in many ways but who somehow missed what was going in my marriage.

My childhood had been no better.

PART I

CAPTIVITY
SAUDI ARABIA STYLE

CHAPTER 1

Childhood Terrors: Where It All Begins

I am fluent in the language of terrorism. I was born in the shadow of my oldest brother's death. I had two brothers. The first was dead and the second was as good as dead. This proved to be the impetus for my later identification with Palestinian and other Muslim children born after the death of a sibling through suicide bombings. Most people are unaware that terrorism ignites death fantasies. The children left behind are predestined for an existence of guilt and shame, with little chance for a "normal" life. It is not unusual for these children to feel like replacement objects for the dead sibling, especially when parents cannot come to grips with the premature death of their offspring.

In my experience, my brother's death precipitated a crisis that propelled my father, a Jew raised in a traditional Jewish home, toward an unrelenting hatred of the Jewish God. My mother colluded with my father's rage, envy, and hatred toward me. So now I had a disaffected and ineffective father, whose sadism I could not yet recognize, and a mother with her own brand of terrorism. Their identity crisis would cause a lifelong inquiry into what went wrong and why all this hatred and rage was aimed at me. It is not uncommon for a child to wish that someone would die; that wish is a death fantasy. However, when the person actually dies, the child feels as if he has caused the sibling's death, even if he or she is born after the event.

There was no traditional Jewish naming ceremony to mark my birth. This namelessness was reminiscent of what happens to many females born in the Arab world. Their names are not recorded, only the names of their brothers. As the female in the family, I had no Hebrew name. Back then many people, especially Jews, were trying to fit in after the trauma of the Holocaust and World War II. My parents followed the traditions of European culture rather than the traditions of their Jewish parents and ancestors. My assimilated Jewish family had elaborate celebrations of Christian holidays, right down to dyed eggs and ham for Easter and reindeer juice left for Rudolph on Christmas Eve. They never went to synagogue and were not observant of Jewish holidays except later, at my insistence, when I lit candles for Hanukkah. The message was clear: the family was supposed to look, act, and be all-American. We were not to live in a parallel, unintegrated community, meaning insular and all Jewish.

My mother was beautiful, a natural blond with green eyes—a Geraldine Ferraro look-alike who prided herself on not looking Jewish, although her own parents were in fact Jews from Romania. My father was tall and dark, yet fair-skinned, like the Sephardic Jews who fled to Holland during the Inquisition. Although my mother told me that my father looked Italian, more than likely he was part Dutch Jew. He looked a lot like Cary Grant, who I found out later was Jewish. With my dark hair and brown eyes I looked like my father, so much so that when I traveled to Israel for the first time as an adult in 1972, everyone automatically spoke to me in Hebrew.

My father didn't just want to blend into a gentile culture. He wanted to separate himself from his Jewish past. He hated being a Jew, but I didn't understand that at the time. Later on I understood that he hated Judaism—actually that he hated himself and, above all, was terrified of the female, from which spawned this self-hatred. "I hate religion," he often ranted. "It is the most destructive force of mankind." Yet in the same breath he would quote the New Testament. It was difficult and confusing to reconcile these disparities.

When I had questions about Judaism, they were answered by "Aunt" Florence, who lived across the street, and Bubbie Becky, Aunt Florence's kindly mother-in-law, who filled their home with warm, wonderful aromas of cooking and baking. Aunt Florence, bless her soul, somehow talked my parents into letting me go to Sunday school at Niles Township Jewish Congregation in Skokie, Illinois. But I never felt part of the congregation because my parents weren't members and because I couldn't read Hebrew. However, I remembered the melody of a fragment of a prayer—*Sim shalom,* translated often as "grant peace." Only years later when I finally learned to read Hebrew did I realize from what part of the service it came. The melodies were soothing to me.

My father schlepped me to a Christian Science Church in Evanston, Illinois. Its Sunday School smelled like PineSol and felt like a cult. It was odd then and it is even odd to me now since the *Christian Science Monitor* newspaper that my father kept on his nightstand and read religiously is also considered to be one of the best news sources for the subject of terrorism. One day at Sunday school, the teacher pointed to a funny looking letter in the Bible and asked me what it was because she must have been told I was Jewish and thought I could read Hebrew. I felt mortified that I was called upon and didn't know the answer. I felt a huge surge of anxiety and nearly started to sweat. In retrospect, I realize I had a mini-panic attack. I was maybe seven years old. It was a long time before I decided that Christian Science was not my kind of Christianity. They don't believe in appropriate medical care or doctors. This would also be a repeated theme in my life, getting poor medical treatment or none at all when needed. It constitutes abuse.

Besides going to Christian Science Church, I was exposed to Catholicism early on through my little neighborhood friend, Ann Shannon Marie Teresa Baxter. I was mesmerized by all her names and intrigued by the holy water mounted on the wall going upstairs to her room. I asked her how she got so lucky to have all those names and she said: "You get them if you are Catholic." She was great fun and, like me, a bit of a tomboy. She had a lot of brothers. We always had a good time together, and it was a relief to be in her home and away from mine.

When I went on to delve into Spanish, I came to learn a lot about Catholicism and preferred it to Christian Science. I loved midnight mass at Christmas. When I studied at the Jesuit university La Universidad Iberoamericana in Mexico City, I felt like a portion of these older ties were rekindled. Much later I learned that the Jesuit order had been founded by *conversos*, Jews who were converted to Catholicism. The Jesuits are considered scholars, having inherited the Talmudic tradition of legal arguments and close textual analysis. Later on I would study Talmud, Mishnah, Halakhah and Biblical Hebrew.

This exposure to various sects of Christianity helped me when I found myself drawn to study the so-called Abrahamic faith communities of medieval Spain: Judaism, Christianity, and Islam. I deliberately chose to study Arabic and Islam to round out my understanding of these religious communities. This allowed me to see how religious ideologies can be co-opted by extremists to form cults and to contemplate the dynamic relationships between the three diverse religious faiths, especially regarding the order of the revelations and the giving of the law at Sinai, the moment where divine will is made manifest in human discourse. It is the generator of the political legal code. Law, lawyers, and the court form the crux of a civil society. These academic studies were critical in helping me understand the nature of Islamic Sharia law.

Often we casually talk about the Abrahamic faiths, lining them up one after the other—beginning with Judaism, then Christianity, and finally Islam—as if the three are on a level playing field. Rarely do we consider that they are very different. It is a disservice to the respective adherents to reduce these religions to the fantasy of the children of Abraham. In *The Banality of Suicide Terrorism*, I demonstrated that because of the sequence of the revelations and their relationship in historical time, they should be viewed vertically as if they were a stack of three books, with the Torah on the bottom, then the Gospels, and on top the Quran since Islam appropriates both revelations and claims that the prophet Muhammad is the prophet of the seal, so revelation ends with him. Muhammad also argued that Islam superseded Judaism as the first religion and that the Jews perverted the holy text. This is the Islamic *fitre*, belief. In football, we call this maneuver an end run.

Given this verticality, Islam becomes like a big, fast-growing mushroom, and in its grandiosity and omnipotence pushes out the two other religions and their peoples. Islam's history and track record of conquest play well to victimology, deprivation, and the underdog that ultimately wins, attracting millions of new converts through its unique sadomasochistic appeal. While Christians and Jews are called *ahl-alkitab*, "People of the Book," as well as infidels or *kufars*, they find themselves in the "protected class of dhimmi," meaning they are not on equal footing with Islam or ever truly free. Islam is a hybrid of religion and a political movement that seeks to spread through demographics and conquest and to impose Sharia law, which subsumes all other laws. Eric Hoffer in his 1951 book *The True Believer: Thoughts on Mass Movements* described Islam as an authoritarian–totalitarian mass movement. If we are going to talk about the Abrahamic faiths, Judaism is really like the early mother to both Christianity and Islam, not a sibling or a cousin as many would like to think. Judaism, Jews, and Israel are superficially loved as people of the book, yet simultaneously hated as the infidel; hence Islamic anti-Semitism. The

Muslims have a love–hate relationship with Judaism; it speaks to their painful dependency needs. They cannot acknowledge their debt and vulnerability so they envy and attack.

Terrorism is a cult. To fit in you must be willing to drink the Kool-Aid, in some cases literally, as did followers of Jim Jones before the Jamestown Massacre in Guyana, South America. A cult is a fused, regressed, destructive group that externalizes and projects its shared rage onto the weakest of the group. There is always a lot of scapegoating and denial of truth and reality. A cult leader will not hesitate to kill off his own, especially the children, if they do not agree with him.

Paradoxically, the Christian Science Church had the same peculiarly medicinal odor of the office of our family "doctor," a quack with likely ties to the Mafia. I later found that to be ironic since Christian Scientists don't believe in doctors. I remember waiting for hours in Uncle Willy's office (that's what the family called him), listening to his patients proclaim how "Krebiosen"— his medical treatment for cancer—was saving their lives. I am not sure how it was spelled and when I tried to Google it, it proved "unGoogleable." I'm also not sure how Uncle Willy ran his practice alone, without a nurse. It just didn't seem kosher. I grew up in a cult with a resident charlatan but didn't realize it at the time.

Like my mother's father, my father's father died before I was born. According to my father's narrative, his father was a native of Latvia—Riga and probably part of the Hanseatic Trade Union. I found out later that my grandfather was actually born in Lubawa, Poland, but was raised in Riga. During World War II the town "hosted" a Nazi concentration camp for children. Yet on my grandfather's gravestone, the *matzevah,* is written the word *rav,* meaning not rabbi but learned. I never heard my father talk about his father's Talmudic knowledge. I never heard him talk about his father at all. Only after the death of his mother, did I find out that my grandmother had kept a kosher home.

My father graduated from Northwestern University with a degree in journalism and became a prominent publisher. In fact, you know him if you receive advertisements in the mail. He helped developed the concept of direct mail advertising—junk mail—after World War II. That was his startup. He was a relatively well-to-do man, buying his Mercedes in Stuttgart, Germany, and having it shipped back to the States. He would kick its tires while yelling at it in German. It sounds funny, but it wasn't. Everybody loved him, but that was his public persona. He may have looked like Cary Grant, but at home he was a quiet Nazi, a sadist. I think of the Grand Mufti of Jerusalem, Amin Effendi Amin el-Husseini, who was in alliance with the Nazis. My father was a Dr. Jekyll/ Mr. Hyde, but I didn't see it while I was growing up. I realized it only after I tried to reconcile with him. And then he died. This same kind of splitting between his beloved public persona and his private sadist being occurs routinely in media reports about the terrorist living next door. "He was such a nice guy. How could he have been a terrorist?" And yet he was.

My mother was uneducated, yet brilliant in her own perverse, paranoid way. Her favorite words were "Mike, make her stop it," as if I were always doing something terrible. I never knew exactly what "it" was, but my mother's unconscious projection was so clever and effective that I wondered just how bad I must have been. After all, I was a little girl and I needed her. I was dependent on her. Was I as defective as the serial-killing child in *The Bad Seed?* I felt like it, as though I were some kind of criminal. Yet she was the terrorist, the abuser. No matter how good I was, I had done something wrong and therefore I was punished. Like Saudi Arabia, where the female is utterly held captive. No matter how good these women are, their behavior will never measure up, and they are unconsciously raged at by the male majority.

Serial killing is something that runs throughout Islamic suicide bombings. The bombers are killed off, but they are only proxies. The senders, bomb makers, and other terrorist members are the serial killers. Yet through their aggression and terrors, they enforce or enslave you through identification with them, and you feel guilty and ashamed for the violence.

My mother was a classic hysteric, flirting with every man who came into the house, including my boyfriends and eventually my husband. My mother even contaminated the occasion of my birth with a perverse narrative: that the doctor wanted to seduce her during the birth. My mother was also often obsessive. One Christmas, she spent days scraping the color off mercury ornaments just so her aqua blue flocked Christmas tree would have all-silver ornaments. My mother was more overtly vicious than my father and could easily have killed me during one of her many psychotic episodes. Mothers do kill their children.

After all, don't mothers of suicide bombers essentially kill their children by sending them to their death as suicide bombers. Take, for example, the following excerpt from *Honest Reporting*:[9]

> *Mariam Farhat, who was known around Gaza as "The Mother of Martyrs" died. Farhat (a.k.a. Umm Nidal) became famous for proudly sending three of her sons to "martyrdom."*
>
> *In 2002, she recorded a farewell video with her 17-year-old son Mohammed, giving him her blessing the night before a shooting attack in a Jewish settlement. He killed five seminary students before he was shot dead by soldiers.*
>
> *A fourth son's in an Israeli prison. Farhat's prominence was extraordinary; ABC News said she was Hamas' most popular candidate in 2006 parliamentary elections; it was said criticizing*

Farhat was "Like Attacking Mom and Apple Pie." But the acclaim debunked the idea that popular support for Hamas didn't mean Palestinians endorsed terror. Unlike the sons she sent to die, Farhat passed away in a hospital of lung and kidney problems.

What would keep my own mother from killing me? Had it happened already? After all, my brother, the firstborn son, was dead, and his death was a long-held secret. Obviously my parents must have harbored huge guilt and shame about his death to cover it up for so long.

For the first seven years of my life, I didn't even know that I had a dead brother. I discovered his baby book one day while snooping around in the basement crawl space. I didn't know whose book it was, but the boy in the photos looked exactly like me. I timidly asked an older female cousin who the boy was and learned that he was my oldest brother and that he had died when he was four, after a quack doctor did a tonsillectomy that went wrong. My mother had pushed for the surgery in Florida, where my father was stationed in the Navy. This was in March 1945. There had been a polio epidemic, and my mother decided that my brother had to have his tonsils out immediately. My father wanted the surgery done in a larger hospital back in Chicago, but my mother became obsessed with having the surgery done right there, right away. My mother always got her way. My brother died. At the very least my parents failed to protect him.

I was mystified when first seeing his photo. I couldn't put my feelings into words, but I felt comforted to look like him, to have a "twin." Knowing he had existed made me feel less alone, less isolated. He loved me and protected me. I fantasized that he became my personal archangel, hovering around me, accompanying me everywhere. I told no one about him. He was my secret.

Children, like adults, have elaborate fantasy lives. Yet I felt guilty, as if I had caused his death. Much later, I wondered whether the experience planted the early seed of my awareness of the significance of imagery and nonverbal communication—a kind of deception detection device to decode the unconscious significance of Islamic suicide terrorism as a pathological form of bonding with others. The mother is the platform that is so deftly hidden from sight in unconscious behavior. Who would think that the underlying problem of Islamic suicide bombing is one of maternal attachment? It is a kind of passionate, perverse mothering of the son and daughter because of her own history of extensive misuse as the chronic object of extreme hatred in the Arab and Muslim patriarchal cultures. Might not Mariam Farhat of Gaza, the Mother of Martyrs, fit this bill of goods, which the Palestinian people have been sold hook, line and sinker?

I wasn't sure what my dead brother's name was. My girl cousin had said it started with an M, for Murray perhaps, although others called him Murphy. The idea of a nickname was confusing, but no more so than having a brother who didn't exist.

In jihad one has many nicknames, and the mother in Arab Muslim culture receives her new nickname, her *kunya*, when she gives birth to her first male son. For example, she becomes Umm Osama, Mother of Osama. Actually, they will never say this, but before the birth of her son, the Muslim woman is essentially nameless and insignificant. Name changing is a way of trying to gain a more stable sense of personal identity and a sense of honor because the shame is so great.

These were hard concepts for me to understand because I was so young at the time. It took me years to sort out the story. But the one thing I *did* get was that I was not supposed to talk about him, my dead brother. I was supposed to go along "with the program" and participate in the collusion.

The trauma of losing their firstborn son was huge for my parents, but they never publicly mourned him or spoke about his death. Their conspiracy of silence grew out of their shame that my mother had pushed for the surgery and my father did nothing to save him. The inability to mourn loss yields rage and violence. This lies at the heart of the problem in Arab Muslim culture. They claim to mourn, but it is not genuine because they are obsessed with death and venerate it. While they create posters of the martyrs in the Palestinian territories and hang them on their boulevards as if it were the Hollywood Walk of Fame, it is overcompensation for having sent them to their deaths. Just like bin Laden said, "You love life, we love death." My parents were like Arabs. They tried to deny that my brother ever existed. But there I was, like a bad *yahrzeit* (memorial candle), reminding my parents daily of their loss. It was my curse to look like him. They blamed me for his death and took out their rage on me, taunting and abusing me. I was the designated *Azazel*, the scapegoat, from the moment I was born. It became a double dying.

The littlest female in the Arab Muslim family is the target of rage. She is free game to be attacked. The female in general lives under the death threat of honor killing, which makes murderous impulses concrete, normalizing within the culture that murder is acceptable and okay. Even though the suicide bomber is venerated and "remembered" in a more explicit way than my brother was, there is still an unconscious undercurrent of fantasies swirling around his or her death.

Terrorism centers on the inability to mourn loss. It becomes obsessive about the inability to process the concept of death and dying—the persistent denial of death. Terrorists deny death and even claim to love it. In reality they are terrified and taunt death like bungee jumpers who taunt heights because they cannot accept their terror, their vulnerability, and their own mortality. The suicide bomber is the terrorists' death-anxiety emollient. It is a bizarre kind of counterphobic activity.

Terrorism becomes the celebration of death. Terrorists communicate their obsession with death to their children through peculiar rituals. Think of Hamas and Hizbollah and their death parades, dressing children in suicide bomber uniforms. Or selling little doll suicide bombers as toys, making the bizarre practice of killing off one's own acceptable. Or consider the thousands of plastic keys that the Ayatollah Khomeini ordered from Taiwan to be placed around the necks of Iranian children who went to their death as human mine sweepers during the Iran–Iraq War. The "nice" Ayatollah slaughtered these innocents while telling them and their impotent, terrorized parents that this plastic key guaranteed their entry into paradise. The terrors of the terrorist's "inner child" are literally and concretely projected into their own children. Terrorists feel dead and want others to feel what they feel. But they cannot put their feelings into words. In the world of terrorism everything is the opposite of what it should be.

This is what the Ayatollah wrote about it being permissible to sexually abuse an infant:[10]

> *A man can obtain sexual pleasure from a child as young as an infant. However, he should not penetrate, sodomizing the child is okay. If the man penetrates and harms the child then he should be responsible for her sustenance all her life. This girl, however, does not count as one of his four permanent wives. The man will not be eligible to marry the girl's sister.*

In another part of his book he wrote:

> *It is better for a girl to marry in such a time when she would begin menstruation at her husband's house rather than her father's*

home. Any father who would give his daughter into marriage when she is so young will have a permanent place in paradise.

One wonders how this horribly abused little girl—who grows up under a death threat and sees all these other children killed off by her own leaders and in some cases even her own family—can grow up to be a healthy, functioning mother who can bond effectively with her children? Why is the Iranian regime so obsessed with chemical weapons and nuclear warfare— as in wiping Israel off the map—and in short, completely paranoid? The abuse of the child within the family preprograms the future terrorist to rage and hate the enemy. It is not rocket science, but most people in the West do not want to hear this because they are too terrified, to the point that it has caused identification with the aggressor. It is not politically correct to think about these matters; just turn a blind eye.

Years later, when I was studying the Holocaust, I could relate to those survivors who had created a second family without ever acknowledging their first one. It was just too painful. Yet these Holocaust survivors did not become obsessive about death like the Islamic terrorists or, for that matter, my parents, who turned to abusing and terrorizing me. They did not send their children to become suicide bombers. Israeli Prime Minister Golda Meir said once that when the Muslims stopped killing their children, there would be peace. She knew what neuroscience is now proving. It involves the question of empathy. Why don't terrorists have empathy?

Many of my friends were children born to the second families of Holocaust survivors. Skokie, where I attended high school, had the largest number of children of Holocaust survivors in the country. I remembered seeing tattooed numbers on the forearms of my friends' parents on hot, muggy summer days. Yet no one spoke about those first families that had been wiped out by the Nazis. The generation was still too traumatized. Years later the neo-Nazis would purposely choose to march in Skokie, which they could do because of freedom of speech in America. They chose to do something that was clearly outrageous, and Hizbollah and Hamas have taken notes.

It was like that with my oldest brother: he had died, yet he was part of the first family. I remember that on Memorial Day, after marching in the Veterans of Foreign Wars parade with my Brownie and Girl Scout troops, I would be taken by my parents to another cemetery, the one where *he* was buried, and I would stare at his grave. I had no clue who he was or why we went through this yearly obsessive ritual. It was never talked about.

In Arab Muslim culture suicide bombers are proclaimed as martyrs, and the killing and murdering has become normalized, acceptable. The burial marches in the West Bank and Gaza, for example, play out in the media as heroic. There are instances, caught on surveillance video, where the burial procession has literally fallen apart as the bottom of the pseudo casket dropped out and the alleged dead person walked away. While not all funerals are staged, there is an element that speaks to the cultural hypocrisy about life and death—that life is cheap and is not celebrated.

CHAPTER 2

Brother Bully:
The Intimate Terrorist

I had another brother, an older brother who was a replacement child, born immediately after the death of the first son. He was as good as dead to me. He was a bully, mean as hell, cruel, sullen, and surly all the time. He never chose to be nice. He chose to be vicious. Few people knew it—although perhaps more than I realized because some knew he was picked up by the police on more than one occasion. Nevertheless, none of these authorities, relatives, or neighbors ever asked me if I was okay or safe living with a juvenile delinquent bully of a brother. I have chosen to call him Brother Bully. I prefer not to name him, following the tradition of blotting out the name of Haman, who wanted to destroy the Jews in the *Book of Esther*.

Terrorism is a psychologically layered affair. Do you remember those transparent overlays in biology textbooks that showed the different systems of the body? Using that image, we could hypothesize the first layer as the bonding with the mother. This would be the bedrock for the infant's terrors, along with the building of the baby's brain in utero until age two. The next developmental layer would concern the environment factors for the young child. If the male child is misused by the mother, rage develops and early signs of it can be seen in the developing bully. Bully-ness can be detected as antisocial behavior early on, along with subtly manipulating, coercing, and pushing. Bullies have no boundaries.

They are predators who obsessively target their prey. Such was the case with my older brother.

Later on the terrorist reveals his envy of the little girl who embodies vulnerability and tenderness, and in doing so becomes an easy target for the bully's rage. Think of Miriam Monsengo z"l (z"l is the Hebrew abbreviation for "of blessed memory"), the precious little blond Jewish girl who was executed in Toulouse, France, at point blank range by Muhammed Merah while he held her by her hair. He claimed he had ties to Al Qaeda. His brother said that he had been raised on anti-Semitism, but a recent television program in France made Merah out to be the victim not Miriam. The bully seeks to destroy the female because he actually hates his mother and feels emasculated by her. Little girls who grow up in homes where the female is devalued and chronically blamed are at particular risk for being targeted by terrorists.

All I wanted back then was to understand how I could live in peace and be protected from Brother Bully and my parents while the ghost of MurrayMurphy lived among us. Because his ghost remained, however, the atmosphere could never be peaceful. Because of this unspoken reality there was no tranquility, only relentless yelling, punishment, screaming, tamping down terrors into phobias. Yet it was my dead brother who was the nicest to me, at least in fantasy. Can I extrapolate from here to what it was like for a little girl growing up in an Arab Muslim family where, say, her older sister was the victim of an honor killing or her cousin was sent to her death masquerading as an heroic female suicide bomber? After all I had my own rage.

I loved to see what kind of weather there would be on my birthday. Weather was one thing my parents had no control over. A beautiful spring day with a gentle breeze seemed like a gift from God. There were so many prohibitions about what I could and could not do while growing up that it was as if I lived in the Swat Valley of Sharia law or in Saudi Arabia. I could not speak unless spoken to. I had to serve food first to the men in the family, starting with the eldest, and then to the male children; only after that could the women be served, with the insignificant females the last. I was forced to eat alone at a separate table on occasion. All of this nonverbal behavior communicated to me that I was faceless and worthless. Slowly they wore me down mentally. I became brainwashed and did not know it. It was worse than Cinderella; at least in that childhood fairy tale there is a happy ending. I was forced to scrub floors and clean the house, including my brother's room because I found hard-core pornography under his bed when I was ordered by my mother to change his sheets and iron his shirts even though a "cleaning lady" came once a week. It was terrifying and yet exciting to me.

Funny thing, my husband, the Man without Empathy, got into pornography, too. Many Muslim terrorists are also involved in pornography though this is not talked about by the ummah, the Muslim community. It was a slow process of being infiltrated, similar to how the seemingly "non-violent" Muslim organizations like CAIR, the Council on American-Islamic Relations, have infiltrated America, although they don't really care about Americans.

While researching my book on *The Banality of Suicide Terrorism*, I discovered that the narrative of the suicide bomber was the reverse of a fairy tale. Fairy tales are about teaching children that it is okay to separate from the family and go out into the world and return safely. Muslim children are taught that it is bad to go out into the world, that if you do, you will probably be killed off. So death becomes normalized. On the one hand, people don't want to or can't separate from their Arab mothers and families, and on the other hand an extreme leaving develops into a new kind of honor killing, the shahid, or martyr. Adam Lankford[11] in his brilliant book *The Myth of Martyrdom* proves that the majority of, if not all, suicide bombers are in fact suicidal. So why not commit suicide under the guise of honor and bravery? They die, kill others, and in fantasy get to return to their mothers in death. The fairy tale is a fundamental cultural experience shaping the identity of a child, giving him or her hope. In the end Cinderella is saved. She does not die. Such fundamental security is lacking in Arab Muslim culture. A security blanket for them is not like it is for Linus in the Peanuts cartoon. A security blanket for them is a hard object—explosives, a suicide bomber vest, rocks to throw during demonstrations, or rockets to fire from Gaza. This is how they try to separate and release their rage at being tied in.

Terrorism is infiltration. Terrorists infiltrate your mind and every aspect of your body. They want to completely colonize you and dominate you. Yet, as in the case of the Palestinians, they will scream that they are ones who are colonized when in fact their occupation is about the mother. What they fail to understand is that they were "colonized" or "occupied" by their mother's misuse of them as a narcissistic object, which left them with almost no self-identity. When you live with a terrorist, you don't realize how terrified you are—terrified because you begin to sense that next comes your murder, your death. Colonization is the terrorism's concrete attempt to conquer and control. Consider that the Palestinians are enraged about being "conquered" and "colonized" by the Israelis. When the Israelis withdrew from Gaza, the entire society fell apart and then into bloodshed, with the autocratic Muslim Brotherhood taking over in the form of the terrorist organization Hamas because the members of society had no individual psychological–emotional infrastructure to run a country.

Too many had been under the influence of brainwashing since childhood and were easily susceptible to Hamas' bullying.

As a teen I was rarely allowed to wear slacks, let alone blue jeans—too unladylike. My family mocked me and made fun of me. They hit me, they beat me, they sent me to bed hungry. They shoved me into closets and kept me captive there. They raped me. There are no personal boundaries in a paranoid family. No one has his or her own internal, independent, healthy infrastructure, called a functioning personality.

When I was little, my father, the suave, debonair Cary Grant look-alike, used to call me "shithead" when he was angry. When I saw *The Wizard of Oz* for the first time, I was convinced I didn't have a brain, like the Scarecrow. I worried that if I tipped my head to the right or the left, diarrhea would literally run out of my ears. Because my father always played the nice guy so convincingly, there was never any doubt in my mind that if I had told others of this terror, they would not have believed me.

Much of terrorism has to do with shit. The terrorists project their shit onto you. The graphic Arabic saying "The wolf comes for the sheep, and the dog defecates" underscores its predatory terrorist role. The feeling of terror is visceral, implying a loss of bodily control like a dog, an infantile, humiliating incontinence.

The leading Israeli counterterrorist expert, whose portfolio was that of Osama bin Laden and who informally recruited me to study terrorism after 9/11, called my work "shit." I realized that he was terrified of what I was proposing, that the earliest template for terrorism is grounded in the maternal bond. Because he felt he could not control me or my work, he had to demean it. This is part of the countertransference in counterterrorism studies that the macho counterterrorist experts do not understand, that they are basically dealing with "the shit" of the terrorists and that they have their own. When they feel terrified, the majority resort to projecting their shit. And when someone works in their macho field who is not like them, this other poses a threat. I was much more highly credentialed than my recruiter was. Besides, I had had patients in treatment for years and had undergone my own therapy, whereas as far as I knew, he had no therapy and no adequate formal training in psychology. Yet, he was granted admission to the "sacred" inner circle of the few who got to interview foiled suicide bombers. Therefore, he called my work "shit." Freud got the anal stage of development right. But this Israeli wasn't the only one.

Another colleague who actually helped me at first turned on me when I said that I was making *aliyah*, immigrating to Israel under the Right of the Law for Jews to return. This person screamed at me and reprimanded me for immigrating to Israel. If I were looking for help to get settled when I arrived, it wasn't going to be there. But I never asked for help. Often Israelis say they love immigrants, *olim,* and offer to help. But this is mostly talk. I realized that this colleague was completely terrified that I was invading a professional space. Competition. Because of this level of terror, I knew that this individual really did not understand either psychology or suicide terrorism. Since Israel is essentially a shame–honor culture in miniature in comparison to the Arab Muslim world, I thought that perhaps this person thought that I would not have the balls to make *aliyah* because I was told not to. I said to myself as I sat there taking in the diatribe, "Watch me." I gathered, too, that this individual thought I could be intimidated and would never write about such an incident. This is what I came to call "sideswiping," someone trying to bully you out of the game—the hidden politics of counterterrorism that doesn't make it into books.

I mention this incident here because it reveals the lack of awareness that pervades the entire subject matter. In Israel I was warned not to write about this because this person would not "*mefargen oti*," speak well of me. I would not be praised. *Mefargen* comes from the Yiddish and refers to group dynamics of shame–honor. In the online dictionary *Morfix* it is defined "as to treat favorably, to treat with equanimity, to bear no grudge or jealousy against." Such pressuring is classic in a shame–honor culture. I really don't care what people think at this point in my life. It is this kind of shabby treatment of the other, an attempt to terrify, that ultimately backfires and, worse than that, inhibits investigation of the truth. It is political. This incident spoke volumes about this person's worst fears—to be found lacking in understanding psychology. This person suffers from the Queen Bee syndrome—one who rises to the top but will not help. There are other Queen Bees. The main one, an American, probably has set back terrorism studies at least 50 years by denying that the unconscious exists at all.

I have to add that there were three Israelis in particular who did help me. Rafi Sela, Professor Amatzia Baram, and Professor Gideon Kressel extended a hand, and I will remain eternally grateful for their tuning in and valuing my work. On the other hand, there was a prominent individual, whom Adam Lankford in *The Myth of Martyrdom* describes as one of the leading counterterrorist experts in Homeland Security. If there were a King Bee Syndrome (and why not?), this individual would be at the top. This so-called expert is one who engages in sideswiping. I know so because he did it to me at a conference in Berlin at the International Society for Political Psychology. I presented my paper, drawing a parallel to domestic violence—intimate partner terrorism— and the murder–suicide template. Women in the audience sat silently nodding their heads in agreement with me. Afterwards, a prominent alleged authority on paranoia came up to me and said: "That was an interesting paper, but you are entirely wrong." His comment and nonverbal communication, his facial rage, betrayed his psychological demeanor and behavior. I noticed while writing this book that I describe a number of people yelling at me or reprimanding me. The reality of this points to targeting someone on whom to vent rage. It was an attempt to silence the person who has discovered that the emperor isn't wearing any clothes. Ironically, he and his coauthor wrote a book on paranoia, but they never once explained that paranoia arises in the mother–infant relationship, that the mother experiences the baby as attacking. This feeling is communicated unconsciously to the baby, along with the feeling of being misused as a maternal object. This causes the baby to grow up feeling persecuted and the victim. In the book, the gender issue is completely missing, as is maternal attachment and discussion of the devalued female.

Sideswiping is not only envious, attacking behavior, but it is part of the countertransference undertow. It can be acted out, most especially around a psychoanalyst. They can hurl their inadequacies and their terrors at you because the analyst has an x-ray view of behavior and can detect the problems—most of the time. Although one has to be careful to analyze only those one has on the couch. Yet it is hard to take off one's psychoanalytic "glasses."

My parents once became so enraged at me that they forced me to eat my dinner off a toilet seat. I was barely five years old. Think about it: My father developed the concept of junk mail. If that isn't anal, what is? Again, terrorism is an anal thing. Almost sixty years later, I can still see what was on that plate: meat loaf, mashed potatoes, green beans, a glass of orange juice. They ruined the pleasure of food for me. To this day, I don't like to drink orange juice. It would be decades before I could learn to savor a good meal again. By this nonverbal sensorial experience they chipped away at pleasure to force me to submit to their rule. All the little punishments become compounded and often turned into phobias.

And still I had no idea what I did wrong. I was the proverbial good child who got punished for trying to be good. It was very confusing, terrifying and disorganizing. I was flooded with anxiety, swallowing my own rage. The toilet seat/table incident became a turning point for me, even a bizarre kind of blessing. Although I could not articulate it back then, I knew at my young age that a toilet seat was not a proper table. Even I knew that my parents had broken some kind of socially accepted code. They had communicated to me nonverbally. I called it a "semiotic moment."

Terrorism entails the need to spoil your fun and pleasure. Just think what the Chechen terrorists did during the Boston Marathon. They had to destroy our pleasure. Terrorism is having the last word while twisting around the words of others. Terrorists only understand when we draw a line in the sand, set firm boundaries, and say, "No more. We do not accept this aberrant, horrific behavior. "

I learned through the toilet incident that terrorism is the nonverbal communication of the predator. Even law enforcement can fail to respond appropriately because they, too, are terrified by the nonverbal communication expressed. All too often they take the criminal terrorist bait and go to the opposite extreme, as in police brutality. The terrorists are slick talkers, but their behavior bespeaks a thousand words that are way slicker than those they verbalize. The terrorist communicates so effectively by tapping into these unrecognized universal human terrors left over from our childhood. The terror web, our preexisting communicative network of terrors from early childhood, lays the groundwork for political violence. If there is a bully in your family, you have grown up with a terrorist.

More than ninety per cent of what we communicate, we do so nonverbally. It is more than just talking about religious extremist ideologies. We often forget that we are animals with a human overlay of verbal language that gives us the illusion of thinking. But in the case of terrorists, they have unthought thoughts, ensuring that their actions will be motivated by the unconscious and fantasy rather than rational ideation.

Other childhood incidents of cruelty reinforced feelings of being terrified and terrorized. I talked late, they told me, not until age three, and they ridiculed me for that, too. Since I was not permitted to speak unless spoken to, it was a wonder I spoke at all. Terror is not fear; it is nonverbal and preverbal. It happens early. When I was very young my Grandma Rosie spoke to me in Yiddish and Romanian. If I answered in either language, my mother washed my mouth out with soap. I was supposed to be an American, not a Jew. Think of all those little Arab, North African, or Pakistani Muslim girls in England or France who do not want to wear the veil and how they are must abide by what the parents want.

When I was about five years old, I became very excited and animated about something that I no longer recall. In a rare moment I tried to share my excitement with my mother, who was busy in the kitchen. My mother told me to shut up. At first I did not notice that my mother was slicing a calf's tongue. My father liked to eat tongue. My mother warned me again that if I didn't stop talking, she would cut out my tongue on the spot. Having had my mouth washed out with soap, I took this threat seriously. I sensed that if she engaged in one concrete behavior, she could engage in another. It was safer to watch and listen and not talk. After that I shut down for a long time and felt myself to be mute.

In 2013, when I went to Iftar, the breaking of the fast for Ramadan, they served tongue. I was momentarily startled. The knife and sword have a very special place in Islamic culture. Slaughter is the proscribed manner of killing in the Quran—the slitting of the throat, hitting the carotid artery and beheading. The butchery of the British soldier in London in May 2013 by the Al Qaeda affiliate terrorist Nigerian Boko Haram took place in this manner. Slaughtering is embedded in Islamic culture, and is part of the holiday ritual of Eid al-Adha, the Festival of Sacrifice. The slaughter of a goat takes place in the presence of children, who often are forced to hold the legs of the goat as its throat is slit. Nor should we forget that the honor killing often entails slitting of the throat. I am reminded, too, of my eldest brother's tragic and needless death as the quack physician slit his carotid artery, and he bled to death.

Think of all those flags that have the symbol of the sword in the Arab Muslim world, especially Saudi Arabia where finally they are discussing execution by shooting instead of beheading by the sword. Terrorism is concrete and literal behavior. The punishments have a perverse logic to them. In *A Thousand Splendid Suns* by Khalid Hosseini, an Afghan Muslim husband becomes outraged with his wife because, in his opinion, the rice she had cooked was too hard. So he goes outside and brings in some stones and forces her to eat them, which breaks all of her teeth. The terrorist husband punishes by substituting stones for rice. A simple but important pleasure such as food is targeted and ruined by the terrorists. The wife's body is attacked as well. Childhood punishments prime the pump for later abuse. Terrorism's punishments never fit the "alleged" crime. They far outweigh any human justice system.

Another thing: I could not read English. I had dyslexia, but back then the diagnosis did not exist or, if it did, it was not talked about or tested for in the schools. I suffered in silence, dreading the spelling bee and being called on in class to read. It would take years to get over my anxiety about public speaking. Later I would identify with the mute in Holocaust literature. To this day I understand what it feels like to be illiterate, like females in half the Arab Muslim and Afghanistan/Pakistan world. Literacy is key to defeating brainwashing and breaking its master—slave bondage, especially for little girls.

Studying Spanish in primary school was my salvation. Spanish gave me a window onto English: how letters had sounds and how words could be sounded out. Because I never felt confident, however, I resorted to memorizing everything. Had I been a Muslim boy, I would have easily become a *hafez*, one who memorized the entire Quran. Memorization is extremely important in Muslim culture. Yet it has a downside because one can use it as a crutch, clinging to memorizing to avoid serious thinking and contemplation. This happens when one has been traumatized and flooded with anxiety. Furthermore, memorization is a kind of concrete literal imitation. The Muslim concept of *taqlid* involves memorization as a form of imitation as well as control.

In first grade the class was charged with drawing a series of pictures in art class, using the theme of the popular television program "This Is Your Life." One of my pictures was titled "What I want to be when I grow up." That was easy: I drew myself as a ballerina dancing between two trees with my arms by my side. It was a new position for arabesque—a zero arabesque, like a jet plane or bird preparing for takeoff. I loved ballet since I had started taking lessons at the age of four. I was *en pointe* early, perhaps too early because it may have ruined the structure of my developing feet. But I could not have been happier. I danced until I was twelve, which is when my mother realized how much I loved it and stopped the lessons. She had wanted me to study ballet in order to lose weight. My mother could not tolerate that I was enjoying something.

Dancing is a unique form of nonverbal, emotionally expressive communication. Dancing is liberating, and that is why Western dancing has been banned by the Taliban and where Sharia law has been imposed. However, the Taliban terrorists just can't seem to be able to give up watching the dancing young boys, whom they anally rape. Terrorism is devoid of pleasure. Terrorists seek to destroy what they cannot experience—that is, pleasure and a sense of hope—because they are so fixated on death and locked into the sadomasochism of violence.

My ballerina drawing is further revealing. There is a black hole in one of the trees. This, I was told by a psychoanalyst, represented the abuse I was enduring. I had a hole in my soul because I did not feel whole, validated, and appreciated. But more than that, in the picture I drew, I have my back to the audience as if I were filled with shame and could not face them. I am faceless, like a Muslim woman shrouded in a full black veil, although the back of my head and my body are fully exposed. I am alone in the picture placed between two trees, perhaps two marginally functioning parents who were emotionally vegetative? A picture speaks a thousand words.

At age six I became hugely fat. Brother Bully had raped me at the Edgewater Beach Hotel. I never told anyone when it happened. Just like I never told anyone when I had the abortion for the repetition of rape. Later some would minimize my brother's behavior as child's play. I do not agree. Years afterward, my analyst and I would conclude that after the rape I had thought I was pregnant. It was horrible and terrifying. I felt so unloved that even this disgusting interest in me did not assuage the pain that I felt.

My brother was just like some Arabs; he had no boundaries. He owned everything. I was fat because I developed what is called a pseudocyesis, a false pregnancy. The theme of the prenatal mother appears once again.

Of course not all Arabs rape their sisters but it has been known to justify the honor killing of a sister because her brother forced upon her an incestuous relationship. The honor murder is merely a cover-up of his crime.

My brother and parents would tease me and make fun of my size. When Brother Bully and my mother walked past me they would moo like a cow. Think of it as terrorism's envy and attacking—the viciousness of the family dynamics that became familiar. How ironic is it that the word "familiar" comes from the word "family"? I may not have looked svelte in my red velvet ballerina recital costume, tutu and all, but I felt proud and alive. At least for the moment. At least until I came under attack again and was ridiculed and laughed at. It was a no-win situation and ever predictable. I was always waiting for the other shoe to drop. Always walking on egg shells.

Like all children who are adrift, I started writing my own script to make sense of my world, the psychotic unreality in which I was trapped. For what is sane in an insane family? What is sane in an insane society such as Nazi Germany or in most of the Arab and Muslim countries where there is suppression of the female? To protect myself, I tried to be good. If I were, it would be better for me—or so my thinking went. I desperately wanted my family to really love me. I became so accustomed to obeying my parents and brother in the hope they would stop being cruel to me that when I was older and finally understood this, I would jokingly say that if you had told me to go stand in the corner of the kindergarten classroom for being bad, you could have returned 40 years later and still found me standing there.

But what I did not realize or understand was that I had developed a kind of "'reverse'" superego, a self-punishing one. Everything was my fault, and I deserved my family's treatment. I was their relentless object of hatred. I was there to be raged at, to be constantly blamed. Allah willed it; this was my destiny. I repeatedly asked for help. No one listened or believed me. I begged my parents to send me to boarding school. They refused. I begged my aunts to talk to my parents. They patted me on the head and said everything would be okay. Those whom I told minimized the abuse—in fact, exacerbating the trauma. They were participating in it in a most insidious way.

Terrorism includes passive–aggressive bystanders, like my aunts and many others. Indeed, Tawfik Hamid, the Egyptian reformed terrorist, calls these bystanders passive terrorists.[12] They vicariously participate in creating the effectiveness and the reach of the terror. The bystander derives a perverse pleasure from watching others be victimized. Their thinking is, "There go I but for the grace of God. Better you than me." Enmeshed clans like my family are run like terrorist organizations. So here is an interlocking link, so to speak, to the terrorist entity. They make it difficult for anyone to assume responsibility for the abuse. Scapegoating is the rule of thumb. There is always a proxy who is eliminated through the attacking and is killed off. This killing off of one of their own purges the group, the cult, the clan, the family of its toxic rage.

I cried myself to sleep. I contemplated suicide every night from the age of eight until eighteen. I thought that this was normal. My method of choice would have been carbon monoxide in the car—gassing myself à la Auschwitz. When I was sixteen, my parents went out of town. During the time I was home alone, I drove to the family doctor, not knowing he was a quack. How could Uncle Willy be a quack when he was a friend of the family? I begged him to refer me to a therapist. He told me to go home and stare at a candle and everything would be better. One of my classmates from grammar school, who also had dark hair and was Jewish, actually committed suicide. Years later I bumped into a mutual friend from grammar school who said, "I thought you killed yourself." He had confused me with our dead classmate, but he must have sensed unconsciously my severe chronic depression.

The unspoken, unacknowledged rage that circulated in the family and that targeted me specifically was the wish to kill me, which I internalized as the wish to kill myself. That was their twisted honor code. The person who ultimately commits suicide becomes the "dead" end for familial rage. I had picked up on their unspoken, unconscious message. I did not acknowledge their murderous rage, or mine for that matter, until much later.

Becoming a suicide bomber provides the perfect camouflage for committing suicide without exposing the shameful dysfunctional family dynamics. "Honor" for one's self while hating the enemy displaces hatred of the suffocating mother and the absent passive–aggressive father who is supposed to protect and set healthy boundaries and limits, but does not out of his perverse pleasure and his own pathological maternal fusion. This kind of dynamic also perfectly facilitates identification with the aggressor at the global level. Probably the majority of people across the globe live in fused clan-like groups. As Osama bin Laden said, they like the strong horse—i.e., the abusive, violent one.

One might inject here, "Okay, so you experienced violence in the home." It is more than that. Domestic violence intersects and interlocks with political violence. The early dynamics in the home are carried over into political violence. Terrors and their traumatic bonding accumulate within us like a series of Matryoshka dolls that nest one inside the other, but at the same time are all interconnected through the complexity of biology, fantasy, and trauma, becoming encoded into crippling interpersonal relationships. The Matryoshka dolls fit snuggly with the idea of traumatic bonding with the mother; the name derives from the Russian, *matriona*, traced back to the Latin *mater* or mother. Domestic violence helps hide the psychodynamics and facilitates an identification with aggressors because it does not name the reality out of which it grows. Domestic violence is still an extremely difficult subject to treat within Western society and all the more so within developing societies. Hence, political violence can flourish more readily because the connection between the two is denied.

I became a hardworking student, which only made my mother hate me all the more. She envied me. My parents repeatedly and disparagingly called me an "overachiever." My mother, who had not gone to college and was too paranoid to hold down a job, had an inferiority complex. They accused me of being "oversensitive." This is often what abusive parents do– dismiss the reality of the abuse they inflict on their child and then accuse the child of being oversensitive, thereby minimizing the pain they have inflicted and denying their reality. A pervasive wall of denial.

My mother was a 1950s stay-at-home mom, not a *Revolutionary Road* mom who aspired to more adventure. I thought my mother was a witch when I was really little. While some would say that was extreme, and my analyst would later try hard to get me to see that I didn't have to hate my mother (and I actually didn't), that did not mean that my mother didn't hate me or would not have murdered me. I had the impression that my mother could have killed me, and that my father would have been an accomplice in his unique passive–aggressive way. After all, I had a dead brother.

Terrorists keep their women in check by coercing them to live under a death threat. In the shame-honor culture of a terrorist group, the female is always at risk to be "honor murdered." Counterterrorist experts are unwilling to connect the dots between the killing of one's own in an honor killing, like the Palestinian mother who sends her child to his or her death as a suicide bomber. These are interlocking circles of disavowed rage. Living under a death threat is paralyzing, with the victim slowly losing the capacity to be proactive. The practice of keeping people under a death threat runs through Arab and Iranian Persian culture. Take, for example, Egypt. In *Sex and the Citadel,*" El Feki relates the story of Amany, who went against her parents and married secretly.

> *"My parents, if they find out, they will kill me. Really. It happened in my family. The sister of my grandmother she had a relation, and they took her and one day..." Amany drew her hand across her throat like a knife [the theme of slaughter reemerges]. Honor killings are a shadowy subject in Egypt and no one is quite sure of the scale of the problem...but for Amany, it is far from a dying practice; the story is kept alive in her family to keep the girls in line (p.131)."*

Furthermore, terrorism and its threats must always be taken seriously, no matter how outrageous they may sound to the Western ear. Terrorists tell you through their threats what they are going to do and then they do it. Just think of Iran threatening to wipe Israel off the map. They intend to do it, given the chance. After all, this is a culture whose leader, the Ayatollah Khomeini, sent the country's children to sweep mines during the Iran–Iraq War with plastic keys to paradise (made in Taiwan) hung around their necks. Since it is nothing for them to kill their children, they will not hesitate to kill you next. Aggression breeds aggression if it is not stopped.

I had my mother's facial features, but she never allowed me to identify with her. Although she named me after Nancy Sinatra (the thought of which made me want to throw up, no offense to Nancy Sinatra), I identified with Nancy Drew. I read every Nancy Drew book in the series (the Hardy Boys, too) and worked at figuring out the mysteries. My deep-seated need to understand myself and what was going on must have stemmed, in part, from my desire to forgive myself. I had taken on negative identifications with my parents' criminal behaviors. It had left me feeling like a criminal.

By seventh grade I became severely anorexic after a bout with the Asian influenza and getting my period at the end of sixth grade. I lost more than 40 pounds. Unconsciously, this gave me a kind of relief from my constant fear of pregnancy as Brother Bully's abuse continued. Yet I swung to the opposite pole of abusing myself through starvation. My sixth-grade teacher was shocked by my thinness after that summer break and asked if my parents had sent me to Auschwitz—a name that I didn't fully understand then. But even my teacher, one of many who became my surrogate mothers, did not really want to know how or why I had become so thin. There was no word for anorexia back then, or if there was I didn't know it. It seemed like nothing bad had names, not even me. I was a faceless worthless "she" in the family.

This namelessness is similar to Arabic culture. Technically, there is no word in Arabic for "honor killing," just as there is no word in Arabic for "suicide bombing." The idea is that if there is no language to describe a slaughter, then murder has not been committed—nothing has happened. This is magical thinking in the extreme. The murderer who carries out the so-called honor killing is proclaimed a "hero" for cleansing the shame and restoring the honor of the family. To give a slightly different example of the effect of Arabic terminology, El Feki relates that during a rare sex education course in the West Bank "some participants were simply unaware that there are indeed Arabic words for female genitalia, having been taught to consider such subjects shameful beyond discussion" (p. 150).

My eating disorder worsened in high school. I remember identifying with the pictures of the Nazi death camps in *Life* magazine. All those Jews, starved to death. So I starved myself, too. This is the intrapsychic drama and hysteria that emanates from the need to be recognized, to have an identity. Yet I did not understand my own masochism. Anorexia became my tool of power. I could control my own body. I was hospitalized for a week several times but never diagnosed or given the help I needed. That was back when a young male intern could do a pelvic exam without a female nurse being present. For a young girl who was being abused at home, this was an utterly terrifying and mortifying experience. I associated with the Egyptian virginity test done on brides, who have no say in the matter.

My parents even manipulated my anorexia. Rather than talk about the problem, exhibit empathy for my severe chronic depression, or allow me to see a therapist, they bought a mirror that made me look thinner so that I would eat more. They resorted to "gaslighting," a form of psychological abuse named after the 1944 movie *Gaslight,* in which Charles Boyer plays a husband who manipulates the environment of his wife (Ingrid Bergman) in order to control her and drive her insane. The distorted mirror my parents put in my room was definitely crazy-making. I already had problems looking at my reflection in a regular mirror, so when I looked at my warped image, it was something of an out-of-body experience. I wasn't sure if it was real or not. It made me think of the mirrors in a carnival funhouse. And now it makes me think of the depth and degree to which the psychotic reality in the Arab Muslim world is so effective and terrifying to onlookers—also sadomasochistically enticing because the female is so controlled.

By the time I sought out one of my parents to complain that my brother was hurting me, my brother had already run to them to claim I caused the problem. Just like the Arabic expression—"He hits me and cries and races me to complain." My brother would come out smelling like a rose even though he was bigger, stronger, older, and the bullying terrorist. Everything was upside down and, like all good paranoiacs, my parents would twist my words around. It was excruciating and insanity inducing, but that is the nature of living in a psychotic household. The terror and the destructiveness of the psychosis should not be underestimated. We live within a hair's breadth of psychosis all the time when we witness violence.

Terrorism in a psychotic household is a perversion. Terrorists have a lust for complete submission and for imposing it on the targeted victim. They are control freaks because of their terror of death, as much as they claim that they love it. They perversely bond with and love the sadomasochism of their own submission. Their cruelty makes them feel "occupied," as if they are the victims. Yet the terrorists do not understand that they themselves have caused the occupation because the defective smothering bond with their mother has impeded maturation. Their bad behavior has become normalized within the dysfunctional culture.

My father connected with me through his own denied rage and disavowed depression. He manipulated me. At times he appeared to be nicer, but only when I behaved like a tomboy, causing me to identify even more with my dead, look-alike brother. It confused me. I was nothing more than a support prop, an object. My father never took me seriously when I asked him numerous times to intervene on my behalf with my psychotic mother. I did not understand their complicity and their perverse codependency. They needed to hate me together. Their hatred of me kept their fragile personalities together. When I begged him to get me professional help, he just kept telling me that my problems were of my own making and that they would go away if I would just think more positively, the Christian Science way. He minimized and denied my experience. But like everyone else I loved him. Or at least I felt that I needed the fantasy of having at least one parent to love in order to make life seem normal. In retrospect, I realize that he, too, had psychotic episodes.

Did I really think my parents would help me? Get me therapy? Love me? If they had, it would have changed the entire family dynamic. No, they needed to hold me hostage as the scapegoat for their rage. They needed to see me as the problem. I had to be their target, their prisoner. The house was a mental torture chamber. When I finally got to high school, I remember shutting my locker door at the end of the day, feeling overwhelmingly despondent that, "Oh shit, I have to go home now." School was an island of freedom. That is why the little Muslim girls in Afghanistan desperately want to go to school. They taste freedom while they are in school, unlike being little "slaves" in their families. This is why the Taliban can't stand females being educated since they will lose control over them and have no slaves. Malala Yousafzai, the Pakistani girl who was shot in the head by the Taliban, became a target because of her demand that girls be educated. These are interlocking links in the long chain of terrorism.

My father manipulated me through intimidation, physical as well as psychological. When I was seventeen, my mother picked a fight with me just before leaving on a business trip with my father and would not speak to me. In retrospect, I realize that she obviously had separation issues and was very confused about her own identity. She always became enraged when leaving. My parents abandoned me to the "care" of Brother Bully. My father then sent me an airsickness bag from the airplane, on which he had scrawled: "To my darling daughter, for your charming personality. Love, Dad." He was sick, yet oh, so charming—Cary Grant the Sadist. His barf bag communication was really about his feelings about himself; he could not contain them and had to project them onto the most vulnerable in the family, in part because he could get away with this mini "soul" murder moment. There were endless moments like that.

When I was little my father beat the dogs in front of me, and then beat me with a belt and also his hand. Do you remember the Al Qaeda videos of their testing chemicals on dogs to kill them? In Islam dogs are considered unclean because of a series of hadiths, traditional narratives, recorded concerning the Prophet Muhammad. He hated dogs.

Once my father tied a sled to the back of his car and forced me to ride on it as he whipped me around, driving erratically. He terrified me with his brutality. He also over-stimulated me, as well as my mother, sexually through the abuse. It destroyed me.

My mother and father laughed and pretended the barf bag was a joke. Even now when I am on a plane and I see the seat pocket in front of me, I remember the message he sent me. The reach of terrorism is beyond the grave. It is forever. So in a way, one can only diminish the effects of such sadistic bonds through consciousness and mourning the loss of what was not—mourning the deprivation rather than being stuck in the role of perpetual victimhood like the Palestinians. It is too easy to be the victim. One has to move on. In Christianity the sense of forgiveness facilitates moving from victim to being proactive. I found it more complicated being Jewish, and I had to search in order to achieve a sense of gratitude. It took me a long time.

When I went to my friends' homes, I would try to read between the lines to figure out what was really going on. Were their parents really kind and loving to their kids? I was always skeptical. It was hard for me to believe that they could be, and it probably would have made my sense of loss greater and more painful. My friends were not really welcomed in my parents' home—a classic paranoid household with no freedom to bring friends over because their presence would open the "closed circle" of family/tribe/clan paranoia. Pryce Jones wrote a book titled *The Closed Circle: An Interpretation of the Arabs,* which deals with the suffocating Arab tribal/clan culture. As time went on, I didn't want to subject any of my friends to this. I was so ashamed of my parents and myself for not being able to change the situation.

One of the turning points in my relationship with my father came years later, when he refused to come to my son's bar mitzvah. My son was his only grandson, and yet he couldn't be kind enough to attend. My father must have been terrified to confront his own delusional hatred of Judaism and his own self-hatred and the fact that I had bucked the system and had chosen to do things differently. After that I had no desire to see either of my abusive parents. I spent hours in analysis to come to this painful conclusion. Ultimately, my decision to break off with my parents was my attempt to protect myself and my children.

Years later, after my mother died, I attempted to reconcile with my father before genuinely realizing how truly mentally ill he was, though he looked so normal. He had hidden behind my mother. It is harder for me to write about my mother because the abuse was so pervasive and chronic. It took place daily. It is as if all the memories run together, and it is hard to find good memories. I have looked back and explored so much of the relationship in stark detail, and find no good memories, just terror and dread of my mother. She was so crazy, although she also looked pretty normal most of the time.

My father launched into his familiar diatribe about how he didn't attend my son's bar mitzvah because he hated religion. I had heard this ad nauseam growing up. My father would rant about religion and then turn around and call his Christian Science friend, his "reader." "Uncle" Jack would come over and brainwash him into thinking positively. Talk about internal dissonance and denied emotional conflict! It was my father's way of dealing with his depression, although it never worked. Every five years he would wind up in the hospital for a week with some kind of relapse. But it was never called depression, and he never saw a psychiatrist—at least not that I know of. He would then return to reading back issues of his *Christian Science Monitor* and Mary Eddy Baker's *Science and Health* and *The Manual of the Mother Church*. It is always about the mother in religion one way or another; in Islam the theme of the mother is significant, but the cry of Allahu Akbar, like crying out for the absent father, comes to the fore.

My father went on and on with his harangue, asking how I dared to have my son bar mitzvahed. This time, though, I got up the nerve to ask, "Dad, don't I have the right as a parent to decide how I want to raise my children?" My father fell silent, but I had sealed my fate. Two years later he, too, was gone, having disinherited me and my children. What had my children ever done to him or my mother? Brother Bully, who inherited everything, never stopped to consider that my children received nothing while his daughter did. Had I been a Muslim girl I would have fared better, receiving at least half of what my brother had received.

When I was five or so, I remembered hearing the child's rhyme about how Lizzie Borden took an axe and gave her mother forty whacks. I found the rhyme not unusual. I understood how a child could murder a parent. But I never talked about that with anyone while I was growing up. When I finally did confront my family about the abuse, they could not accept what I intuitively knew. Once again my sense of reality was routinely, consistently, and endlessly denied by others. This is another interlocking link between a terrorist group and the family—deny the reality, the truth because they will kill you. So if you grow up in a family where you were abused this compounds a predisposition to identify with terrorists—and in many cases repeat the trauma by becoming a terrorist.

Throughout my childhood it was implied that I was supposed to forgive my parents for being so mean to me because they had lost their firstborn son. It was their unspoken excuse. They never had to own their behavior. I was supposed to honor them according to the Ten Commandments. However, one day I read a passage in the *Shulkhan Arukh*, a compendium of Rabbinic discourse, in which its author, Rabbi Yosef Caro, stated that if the yoke of the child–parent relationship becomes too burdensome, it is permissible to leave the relationship. "The yoke"–couldn't this be read as traumatic bonding? It was a relief to read this passage. At least someone got it. I have not been able to find anything similar in Islam.

My doctor–husband, the Man without Empathy, never had to own his behavior either. Funny how it all fit.

CHAPTER 3

The Maternal "Occupation"— Her Accusatory Evil Eye

When I was in the seventh grade, I was sent to the Illinois State Science Fair at the University of Illinois in Champaign-Urbana. The focus of my project was photosynthesis and the effects of growing black-eyed-pea plants in the dark. Plants seemed to be safer than animals or people. My science project allowed me to gain insight into the concept of heliotropism, by which a plant tracks the sun as its source of power. This was a kind of bonding between plant and environment, which transferred easily to the concept of an infant who heliotropically searches for its mother as the sun of its universe. This unique relationship to the power source also occurs in therapy during transference, as the patient bonds with the analyst. I should know; I wrote the article. It also gave me insight later on to the nature of malignant bonding between a charismatic leader like Osama bin Laden and his terrorist followers. They look to him even after his death as if he were the sun, the power source for their fragile lives.

Only years later did I tumble to the notion that my science project represented my intuitive attempt to master the trauma of being kept in a dark closet as a child, further compounded by the traumatic maternal attachment. My sin? Maybe I was too inquisitive? I really don't know. One could say that this abusive parental punishment was a concrete attempt to make me experience the terror of my parents' own psychotic darkness and probably the poor traumatic attachment that they had with their own mothers, while literally "keeping me in the dark" about them abusing me. It was another nonverbal communication that was terrifying at first and begged to be made sense of later in life.

At the fair I took first place in botany, but even more exciting than winning was my stay in the campus dormitory. The prospect of going to college someday gave me a glimmer of hope, a taste of freedom, a means to an end: escape. School again, but you got to leave home and stay away. Hopefully it would be a safe place.

I began reading the big college guides and dreamed of going to Cornell, Sarah Lawrence, or Middlebury in Vermont. I was a topnotch student and graduated from high school with honors, yet I scored below the national average on my SATs. My undiagnosed dyslexia interfered with my performance. I also had too little self-confidence, too much anxiety, and wasn't aware of either. I assume in retrospect I suffered from chronic PTSD, on which I would become an expert. Some counterterrorist experts claim that terrorists commit terrorist acts because they suffer from post traumatic stress disorder. It is not enough of an explanation, in my opinion. Their psychopathology is much more malignant than that.

My parents took me on a car trip out East to visit the colleges that I fantasized about. But paying private school tuition and traveling expenses was out of the question as far as my father was concerned. He was cheap and always complained about money. Those who are cheap are also stingy with their emotions. So once again I was enticed and then pulled up short. My parents would not allow me to separate from them. They had to keep me close by so that the enmeshed family dynamics could continue.

When I got braces as a teen, my father would parade me around like a horse, opening my mouth to show people how much he was spending on me. I was nothing more than an object to him. Terrorists are like that; they have no empathy and treat people as objects. There is nothing worse one can do than to treat another as an object. I sometimes fantasized about being a slave sold at auction. My father would berate me and accuse me of being a JAP, a Jewish American princess, though I never was financially

—or otherwise—indulged. I internalized his diatribes, convincing myself that I didn't merit his financial support. I felt entitled to nothing. Most women in the Arab and non-Arab Muslim world know virtually nothing about handling money. Not only are the majority unable to read; they are also financially illiterate, which keeps them in economic bondage.

Terrorists do bait and switch. You will never get what you want. Terrorism is about persuasion. Terrorists say one thing but do another, always claiming that it's in your best interest. They lie easily. Things are never what they appear to be, that is why it is so important to understand their nonverbal predatory behavior.

My father forced me to begin to work at the age of fourteen, doing market research for the advertising company that he created on the side. It was an abuse of child labor, just as terrorists use children inappropriately, like human shields, doing the dirty work of adults. I had to go door to door with questionnaires and interview people. It was horrible since I was so shy and suffered from social phobia. I felt, too, as if the value of the dollar had been shoved down my throat.

After my father died, Brother Bully received all the nice stuff—the Mercedes, acres of rich land in southern Indiana, the house in Rancho Mirage, the car, the retirement portfolio etc. I received virtually nothing because I was the devalued female: the consummate object of hatred. At the insistence of a financial advisor, my husband went to my eldest cousin of "the clan" to negotiate that I get something. I did, but it was a laughable pittance. Any brother in his right mind would have split the inheritance down the middle. More than that, he would have wondered what my grievances were and would have seen and addressed my abuse. But not Brother Bully. He was the perpetrator. His unwillingness to do the right thing is an indictment of his crimes in all of this. But this was not a court of law, and I never had any rights in the first place.

My parents decided that I would go to a state school close to home. I ended up at Indiana University—the same school where my older male cousin went. He was expected to look after me, not unlike a nineteenth-century chaperone. The arrangement was reminiscent of how the Arab family designates a male to supervise the female's sexual purity. The most powerful person in the Arab family is the eldest brother—the one charged with guarding the family honor by obsessively monitoring the "purity" of the female's pelvis. My cousin introduced me to his fraternity "brother," my future husband, and so it was like *bint am* or cousin marriage—considered to be the ideal marriage in the Arab Muslim world. The son marries his father's brother's daughter. He is the *ibn am*, the uncle's daughter.[13] This keeps the blood, fantasized as pure, within the closed circle of the family.

Sharaf and 'Ird: Male and Female Honor

The Arabic word for male honor is *sharaf*. Male honor, if lost, can be reinstated. Pryce-Jones[14] defines honor in the Islamic world as: ". . .what makes life worthwhile: shame is a living death, not to be endured, requiring that it be avenged. Honor involves recognition, the openly acknowledged esteem of others which renders a person secure and important in his or her own eyes and in front of everyone else. . . . Honor and its recognition set up the strongest possible patterns of conduct, in a hierarchy of deference and respect."

On the other hand, female honor, *'ird*, which literally means pelvis, can never be regained if lost. The woman must be put to death. An Egyptian proverb phrases it succinctly, "The honor of a girl is like a match. It only lights once." As A. H. Ali notes in *The Caged Virgin: An Emancipation Proclamation for Women and Islam*, "Nowhere is the denial of Muslim individuality felt more strongly than in the relationship between the sexes.

Islamic sexual morality places a heavy emphasis on chastity." This is how the shame of the family is cleansed and purified through blood vengeance. The closed circle of the clan is maintained through blood relations.

There are a series of Arabic sayings that underscore the importance of blood. The most famous is "My brother and I against my cousin. My cousin and I against a stranger." In other words, blood is thicker than water. The female cannot compete with the male as far as blood relations, which the following Arabic sayings show: "The son of a son is dear; the son of a daughter a stranger." A variation on this theme is: "The son of your son is yours; the son of your daughter is not." Allegiance and trust are blood related and only involve the males. However, the family sense of honor weighs heavily upon the female and what happens to her pelvis. The little girl grows up living her life under a constant communal death threat—the honor killing, as the following excerpt from Elizabeth Fernea's online article on Muslim childhood details: [15]

> *Any breath of gossip impugning a girl's sexual behavior was cause for her to be severely punished and ultimately could result in her death. No such restriction was placed on the boys. For a girl, the intention to protect her honor was stated by modest behavior and by wearing of modest dress. Carried to its extreme in some contexts, it meant the wearing of the veil by girls after the age of puberty and seclusion of women after marriage.*
>
> *The concept of honor is found in societies around the Mediterranean basin, including Greece, Spain, and Italy, as well as in nomadic Arab societies from the Mediterranean. So-called honor and shame societies stress the responsibility and the reputation of the group, and the maintenance of a public image, free from dishonor. The moment of testing honor came at the climax of the marriage*

ceremony, the consummation. A man's honor and that of his family required him to be virile enough to consummate the marriage; a woman's honor and that of her family required that she be a virgin at marriage. To provide evidence of that virginity, a bloodstained sheet, which family members traditionally publicly displayed, was offered as tangible proof that the groom's honor and the bride's honor were intact. Small children were present at weddings from their earliest years, so these tests of honor were made clear through observation and example, and through admonition and discussion of honor by parents, grandparents, siblings, and cousins. Honorable as opposed to shameful behavior was one of the strongest values for which male and particularly female children were socialized. Parental admonitions categorized much of children's behavior as either honorable (good) or dishonorable (bad).

The female pelvis is socially regulated and controlled by prescribed gender roles simply because of fear of the biological difference that the female sex represents, and her ability to give birth, which is a threat to male authority. Speaking in Berlin in 2006, British author Salman Rushdie said that the West has failed to grasp the extent to which Islamic extremism is rooted in men's fear of women's sexuality. This is bound to inhibit a little girl's fledgling sense of self, a question examined by Breiner:

What might a little girl's reactions be if she experiences the depreciation and denigration of females and sees a contrasting relationship to the males in her environment? What would her perception of reality be if magical thinking, denial and projection are the adult modes of functioning in reality? What would her reactions be if her genitals are attacked emotionally, morally and then physically as well? What might her reactions be to sexuality in general and to the product of her sexuality, her children, and the relationship to her husband be if sex is seen as an attack by her husband? What might her reaction be to herself, to children, to childbearing, to the world if her genitals are so traumatized not only in her childhood but as a result of the various genital complications due to related diseases and injuries? How can she be expected to respond to her children? What happens to all her turmoil, rage, confusion, and conflict?

One could ask similar questions about the male. What might a little boy's reaction be if he is raised in such an environment, with such an experience about women, and such an experience about his own genitals? What might this little boy's feelings be if his genitals are repeatedly fondled and touched and then they are attacked later in a circumcision? What might this little boy's reaction be to being a male as well as his response to a female if he is terrified of his father and at the same time threatened by the seductiveness of his mother? What might his response be to his mother, to women in general with this kind of confusion and lack of protection from injury of women are also depreciated? How will he respond to his children? . . ." when an Arab couple marries each will bring to the marriage all the results of these previously described external experiences, particularly a sense of body mutilation and a hurt (fragile) sense of self. It is likely that the wife will become the repository of her husband's projections of hurt self image and poor control of aggressive sexual impulses.[16]

Terrorism is a part object operation. Terrorists do not see women as whole human beings with real feelings and needs. They diminish women to body parts, like the 'ird, to devalue and diminish her. They are so terrified of her because she can give birth to a baby and can create life. Terrorists can't understand how they can be born from such a devalued female body.

I have heard that there are Arab Muslims who believe that the prophet Muhammad was not born from a woman. This is hearsay, but it was told to me by an Arab Muslim. Just think of it, in Christianity you have the immaculate conception; the female is the nurturer, as in the Madonna and Child fusion image. In Islam I could not find one well-known image of a nurturing female, although I searched to the best of my ability. Islam is devoid of peaceful imagery though it claims that it is the religion of peace. Maybe there are peaceful images but those are not what is conveyed through the mass media, on Islamic flags, and at their peace conferences.

Terrorism is targeting the victim and putting her under surveillance of the glazed, paranoid eye. When victims have been under surveillance for a long time, they are slow to realize it. They only feel it in an unspoken, creepy way. Victims will vacillate between freedom and terror until finally freed physically and mentally. It is a lifelong process of two steps forward and one step back. The victim begins to see herself not as a victim but as an agent. The terrorist will seek and find another woman to victimize as soon as the first is able to leave him because he cannot be alone. Terrorism murders the hand that feeds it. Terrorists won't hesitate to kill you if need be.

So there I was at Indiana University, separating from the "clan," which decided that since my eldest brother was dead my cousin could provide a kind of unconscious surveillance. Of course, none of this was spoken about directly, but it was intimated in a series of ways. I was the female baby of many male cousins in this clan, this *hamula* as it is called in Arabic. I was resigned to being under surveillance without the freedom of my own initiative, although I didn't realize it at the time.

I did not want to go to Indiana University. I was accepted within ten days of submitting my half-hearted application in August 1965, before beginning my senior year of high school. I was awarded a Chicago Alumni Scholarship and then a series of merit scholarships, so I paid virtually no tuition for my college education—though my father complained bitterly about the cost of college. Once I was flown back to Chicago to attend an alumni dinner on the private jet of the president of Indiana University. I was terrified that I would have to speak publicly, worrying the whole way. The effects of having been silenced during my childhood lingered into adulthood. I had become programmed not to be seen or heard, not speaking until spoken to or given permission to speak.

I first visited the Indiana University campus on the weekend of my cousin's fraternity mixer when I was a junior in high school. That is when I met my future husband, a pre-med student, the Man without Empathy. At least this is what he claimed. I had no memory of meeting him at all, probably because I was terrified of him so early on. But he always liked to tell people that. He looked nothing like my tall, dark, and handsome father. The pre-med student was fair like my mother and Brother Bully, with blue eyes like my Grandma Rose. He also had a prominently hooked Semitic Jewish nose, about which he always complained.

He creepily told others that he watched me from afar during my freshman year of college and part of my sophomore year. He was stalking me, waiting to make the right move. And like a heat-seeking missile he found his prey. It was a stealth attack though I did not realize what was happening, that I had been under his surveillance. At least, not consciously. He must have smelled my terror. He said he waited for me to date around during my freshman year and then joked that he "went in for the kill." What I didn't understand at the time is that he meant it. Here then the joke was not a joke, just like Freud wrote; rather it was seemingly benign, and masked his rage. He revealed his lack of empathy, to which I was completely oblivious because of my own vulnerability, which stemmed from the abuse I had suffered. I was completely blindsided by his aggressive threat.

I felt something was wrong when I began dating him, but could not put my finger on it. I felt constantly agitated and pressured. Only once, by accident, did I see his rage. We were moving a rocking chair I had brought to his apartment, and it tore the interior of his car. He lost it, and blamed me. But it was really he who had put it in the car incorrectly. Years later I would see him have another melt-down over "his" car. It was terrifying. Obviously it was his inadequacy. The car represented his imagined perfect, non-defective self, so I had thought. I had destroyed that, according to him.

Terrorism is tantrums. Terrorists show their own terrors by placing them on others through blaming and intimidation. When their defective self emerges suddenly, they resort to high drama. They scream, stomp, demand, threaten, and even murder because they cannot put into words what their real terrors are: terrors of abandonment, vulnerability, loss of control, impotence, death. They cannot stand that they are not perfect. This is because they have been born from a devalued female, and thus have to deal with their prejudice. They are traumatically bonded to their defective mothers, which means that they are not separated from them psychologically and remain in a fusional state intrapsychically. It is as if they are one.

When the early mother herself is deprived of love and nurturing and is viewed as a "bad," defective object, it has an impact on the child's healthy development. The lack of empathy, nurturance, love and compassion leads to sadism as a form of perverse bonding. The mother is flooded with anxiety, and as an object of longstanding rage she cannot bond healthily with her baby. Such maternal attachment is now believed to be so traumatic that the mother cannot facilitate the creation of vital mirror neurons for the baby's brain to develop adequately to experience empathy. Terrorists are symbiotic; they must cling to their hated object, which is part of their sadomasochism.

This partially explains why terrorists lack empathy, concern for others, and the ability to form healthy attachments. You can see the disrupted attachment in a number of ways—through the violent image, the need to exist in angry crowds, and a penchant for chaos, instability, and controlling the female. In short, nothing works in Arab countries. The industrial infrastructure reflects the weak psychological personal infrastructure. If they were to form healthy attachments or bonds, love would become the replacement for violence. Rarely do counterterrorist experts discuss the meaning of their own life experiences; nor do they have the motivation or the insight to understand what makes them the way they are.

For me this new relationship, this new "bonding" felt like I was drowning, constantly fighting to come to the surface, struggling to breathe. I tried three times to get out of the relationship while it was still new. I tried to say no to more dates, and I even did say no. But he would not take no for an answer. Later on I would have to remind myself that I did fight back and that I did, in fact, assert myself. I had said no, but it was to no avail. He kept pushing. I was "it," the object in a game of tag, and he was determined to capture and control me.

None of this could I have put into words at the time. Young women did not speak about trying to get out of bad relationships back then. He was fixated on me and had developed an obsession with me. On the one hand, his obsession afforded a perverse sense of attention for me; yet, on the other hand, I was a "goner." It is hard to describe or explain what that was like. I was mentally enslaved and physically in danger, but I remained oblivious to all of it. It was simply too terrifying to acknowledge. This kind of suffocating feeling runs throughout terrorism, and it connects to strangling and the Sharia practice of death by hanging, as in Iran. It is the perverse attachment to the umbilicus at an unconscious level. In America strangling a partner is considered a felony, a crime of domestic violence, intimate terrorism. Terrorists slowly infiltrate your mind. You are not even aware of it, of how totally and utterly vulnerable you feel, until you start to feel like you are suffocating. Then you have to choose to seek freedom or to die a slow, painful death. Terrorism is insidious.

The man without empathy stalked me relentlessly. On a psychological level it was like Chechen Muslim bride-stealing, where one targets a certain female and goes after her. Before he finally captured me, I had another taste of freedom from my family after my freshman year in college. That was the summer I went to Mexico City to study Spanish at La Universidad Iberoamericana. Despite my dyslexia, or perhaps because of it, I had become fascinated with languages. My command of Spanish especially was so good back then that I had been put into senior-level courses during my first year of college. Yet I didn't really understand that this was an accomplishment to be proud of.

The Mexico experience felt like Girl Scout summer camp. After a four-day bus trip from Indianapolis with a group of fellow IU students, I began to feel freedom—at least temporarily. I attended wonderful literature courses with the poet Sergio Mondragón. With my dark hair and eyes and singular Spanish accent, I could pass for a Latina. However, my Spanish professors inevitably would ask, "Where are you really from? What are you?" When I would say, "soy *judía*," a Jewess, their next query was, "Do you know Hebrew?" I had to confess that I didn't, but it wasn't all that long before I decided that one day I wanted to be able to say yes to this question.

One more semester at Indiana University would pass before my future husband would go in for the kill. He kept pressuring me for sex and took my virginity during my junior year. No doubt he thought of me as damaged goods. He knew that my family had abused me while growing up. Often you provide information about yourself in confidence, with a sense of trust. But your abusers will hit below the belt and throw it back in your face.

Brother Bully remained obsessed with me, too. He followed me to Indiana University, pursuing his master's degree in photojournalism, so that I would not remain outside his orbit of power. He would probably deny this because of his total lack of psychological awareness. Perhaps photojournalism was yet another attempt to handle his obsession with being a voyeur and his perversion with pornography. It was a way of putting the world under surveillance, including me. Perhaps it was even an excuse to justify photographing nudes.

One day during my sophomore year Brother Bully pressured me into sitting for a series of photographs. I was scared, but I had been taught that I had no right to say no, so I complied. I also thought that if I went along with it, he would not be mean to me. I remember being on the verge of tears but not understanding why. He kept trying to provoke me in order to capture some kind of look. It was creepy. His obsession with me would persist well into my adulthood. When he married his third wife, everyone told me how much she was like me; she was an academic too, blah, blah, blah. It terrified me so much that I wanted nothing to do with them because it was a kind of shadowing me, verging on eradicating my sense of identity. Isn't identity theft something that terrorists and criminals engage in all the time?

Brother Bully was a mama's boy. Terrorism is an institution for mama's boys. Hysteria is for emotional babies. Male terrorists are really mama's boys, bullies who present themselves as the victims. Brother Bully had only one testicle, a topic that my parents discussed in my presence. Did I really need to know that? He was impotent emotionally and psychologically and took it out on me. He had never separated from my mother. He had to follow me to Indiana because I was a substitute for the hatred that he held for our mother. This was also the case for my ex-husband, the Man without Empathy.

>-~ ⊙ ~-<

Terrorism entails a perverse attraction to the female. They first give a false sense of hope, later betray your trust, then attack and destroy. They lure you into thinking that their show of attention and kindness is genuine, when it is not. They toy with you, waiting for the right moment to attack. Sometimes you get fed and sometimes you don't. The unpredictability of it makes it more confusing. Terrorism is predatory behavior toward the female as an upshot of the perverse traumatic bonding to the mother. Terrorists prey on their sisters, little girls, and other females. Tamerlan Tsarnaev was described by a high school classmate as constantly "following" his little sister around as if he were really there to protect her; rather, he used her presence to support his fragile psychological self. Because they lack family support, women are easy targets for the terrorist predator, who probably smells their terror. The traumatic bonding sets up a master–slave sadomasochistic mentality with all females.

While the mama's boy syndrome cuts across all cultures, it is particularly relevant to the Arab Muslim world, with five percent of the terrorists coming from within this population group. The percentage is probably even higher than that because of the group's passive terrorists, who collude with and facilitate the terrorism machinery. But why are they mama's boys? Because the father is absent from the family as a result of practicing polygamy. The half brothers are pitted against one another, in competition for their father's attention and the benefits arising from that. Furthermore, it doesn't help that the father is chronically absent as he obsessively pledges his allegiance to country and Allah, which plays a role in the further abandonment of the mothers of his children

Being the first born and hence the favorite male son entails his being figuratively wedded to his mother. This grandiosity causes a peculiar sense of entitlement, which propels the violence. There are no limits to his omnipotence, no safeguards concerning power. The famous Tunisian psychoanalyst Abdelwahhab Boudhiba wrote in his *Sexuality in Islam* that the males suffer from their own cultural kind of Oedipal complex called the Judar complex[17], named after a protagonist in one of the stories in *One Thousand and One Arabian Nights*.

The mother of a terrorist attempts to protest again her own powerlessness through the abusive power of her terrorist son. A mother most often will defend her terrorist son to the end; the terrorist would sell his mother down the river while praising her as the most wonderful person in the world. Her terrorist son is generally the mother's only source of power. Consider the fact that often Al Qaeda and Hamas members, along with other Muslim terrorists, have been tracked down by following their mothers. This was the case for Osama bin Laden's messenger, who kept calling his mother, as seen in the movie *Zero Dark Thirty*. Rohan Gunaratna, the Sri Lankan Al Qaeda expert, was quoted in an issue of *Playboy* magazine explaining that the Pakistan police would haul in the mother and strip her naked in front of her terrorist son to get him to talk. The mother is their Achilles' heel, to mix cultural metaphors.

Terrorists are dependent on their mothers. They are fused to them mentally and they hate their mothers for that very reason. They not only turn their rage against the mother outward onto other women, but the other becomes feminized. The Jew is the female. The mother is so much larger than life in the mind of the terrorist that she is almost in a category by herself. She is "heroic," which is nothing more than a defense against hating the female and the devalued little girl in a shame–honor culture. Like being attached to a "nuclear" maternal power plant, the terrorist vacillates between fusion and fission, wanting to remain fused while at the same time gripped by conflict over separating from his mother and seeking a fission. Separating for terrorists is tantamount to the splitting of their "atom." That is why the terrorists claim that they are "freedom" fighters. Ironically, their fascination and draw to nuclear power harkens back to this core problem of maternal separation. The fusion causes cognitive impairment because they are too fused to their mothers to see reality clearly—to see "the forest from the trees." And they are confused about their identity. It is part and parcel of their paranoia.

During my third and last year of college (I finished in three years in order to save money), I was determined to go to Brazil to study Portuguese. I had already received a Fulbright-Hayes Scholarship to study second-year intensive Portuguese at the University of Wisconsin at Madison. I had also been accepted on full scholarship to Georgetown University and New York University to do a doctorate in Portuguese. I never went there because I had no self confidence.

I had planned the trip to Brazil after the summer I spent in Mexico City. But the pre-med student was becoming more needy, more demanding, and aggressive, and he started pressuring me not to go to Brazil. He felt that I was abandoning him, that I had no right to go. After all, I was his property because he had had sex with me. It would have been a threat to his fusion. Sex is a concrete fusion.

He was losing control of me, but he was struggling for other reasons, too. His applications to medical school (which I had typed) had been rejected by a series of schools. With many doctors in his family, it seemed as if no other profession existed or mattered to him or to them. With a lot of family maneuvering, he finally got into medical school after his father paid $5,000. His family clan had previously done that for his older cousin—male of course. Just think of all the females who were rejected seemingly for not having the credentials. It was a travesty; there were only a few females in his class. When I found out about this I was horrified because I had worked so hard and was an accomplished student while he weaseled his way into medical school. I never felt that I was in a position to say anything. It was as if it was matter of fact.

Yet I freed myself of him and went to Brazil. I had to. And from that safer distance, I made the separation official with a Dear John letter. Mind you, this was the sixties. A couple of times I even slept with another student, someone I had met on the plane to Brazil. Some years later I realized that sleeping with the other student was my unconscious yet concrete attempt to break the chains of the sexual submission to my future husband. The Dear John letter had not been enough; I was desperately trying to physically break the mental bonds of bondage and enslavement.

I had hoped to stay in Rio de Janeiro for a year, but by the end of the summer I was back in Chicago. I was in crisis too. I felt guilty about the pleasure I was having; I was not supposed to enjoy myself. I was worried as well. My father had threatened to cut me off financially once I turned twenty-one (which he would ultimately do anyway). Although I didn't quite believe him, I felt rushed to finish school by the end of my junior year. I could never fully comprehend that my father hated me as much as he did. But terrorists tell you what they are going to do, and they will do it. There was something so surreal, so bizarre about his complaints about me spending money. I existed on virtually nothing in college, living not only as a physical anorectic, but a financial anorectic as well. So why did he continue to complain?

Tired and terrified of my father's threats, I fled one disaster for another: I married the pre-med student. I had caved in to my guilt about experiencing pleasure in Brazil and its terrors. I had gone back to him. Yet I had a hidden sense of heavy shame. I took my vows on December 27, 1969, in a wedding gown with puffy medieval-style sleeves à la Romeo and Juliet, along with a mantilla because I still thought I was Latina. Didn't Romeo and Juliet commit suicide? I wore no face veil, which was scandalous for a traditional Jewish wedding, but back then I knew nothing about religious customs. My father knew but he refused to observe. He would not wear a *kippah*, a yarmulke, at my wedding. My father initially refused to sign the *ketubah*, the marriage contract, and it wasn't because my father feared for me entering an abusive marriage.

I thought I was marrying a traditional Jew from a traditional Jewish family. By marrying differently, I thought I was marrying better—a better man than my father. The truth was the opposite. The reality was too terrifying to acknowledge, let alone feel. I had gone from the proverbial frying pan into the fire without realizing it. Unfortunately I did not know the Egyptian Arabic saying that "Marriage is like a watermelon; you only know how it is inside once you cut into it."

What I did feel was what I had felt when I had first tried to walk away from the relationship: that sinking feeling of someone who has been thrown into the ocean with concrete blocks tied to her feet, a mafioso-like murder. Terrorism has to do with visceral gut reactions. My gut reaction was that once again I felt like I was suffocating.

Terrorism is the suffocation of the other. This is the terrorists' projection of being tightly bound to their devalued mothers. Terrorists suffocate or strangle their object/subject through power, domination, and control. They will do anything to devalue women and keep them in a submissive position, even engage in pornography, although they insist that women be covered from head to toe, creating a suffocating, autistic environment. They do this because they themselves feel smothered by their mothers.

How the mothers feel about themselves, how they raise their children, and how religious ideologies learned in the home early on inculcate the likelihood of terrorism and child sacrifice build the political terrorism's infrastructure of hatred. The Chechens have a proverb: What is learned in childhood is like carved in stone. It is too bad that the five per cent of Chechens who are terrorists refuse to understand how abusive their shame–honor culture is to their own children. The home and the world meet, even though the experts would like to keep them discrete.

Davis and Davis[18] describe the difference between Moroccan child-rearing practices leading into adolescence where interdependence is the norm as opposed to Western notions of autonomy, individuation, and separation. Timimi, in his book *Pathological Child Psychiatry and the Medicalization of Childhood,* argues that since Western cultures value different child-rearing practices than do Eastern cultures, "psychological theories describing adolescence as a stage of involving autonomy and independence bear only limited relevance to the common patterns of psychosocial maturation encountered in Arabic culture." Yet, too close a maternal bond in conjunction with child-rearing practices involving shame may hold the key to the nature of suicide terrorism's psychological warfare. What if child-rearing practices move beyond shaming and involve the use of terror and abuse, and what if they violate accepted universal standards of care? Couldn't these questions shed light on the molding and shaping of the personality, which may contribute to producing terrorist operatives?

Lawrence Sager wisely posed the question of child-rearing practices and culture difference: Who is to judge if child-rearing practices are healthy or unhealthy and how culturally relative they are?[19]

"There are some matters—for example, some aspects of child-rearing—that connect to things that groups of people understandably value, but that are not necessarily portable between or among groups. Whether or not children sleep with their parents at various ages, whether or not parents spank their children, whether parents encourage independence and free choice or demand strict obedience and narrow conformity, whether parents are open or closed about nudity, encourage or discourage physical touching of various body parts, etc. – some or all of these may be matters of what a group is comfortable with, of how a group thinks people should live, rather than questions of what is morally required. But other matters are not like that: slavery is not like that; the historic treatment of women is in many particulars not like that; the physical or psychological injury of children or the radical foreshortening of their life options is not like that."

So what does it matter if you grow up constantly stalked, incessantly under surveillance, or have a brother who is a bully? Does the paranoid glaze of the bullying terrorist impact your growth and development? Does it make you a better, fully functioning citizen for a democracy. Or does it leave you on your knees, unable to keep your head above water? Childhood with the mother becomes the launching pad for adulthood. Terrorism is bred in the home and is taken out into the world. It becomes problematic when men without empathy dominate and rule the planet.

CHAPTER 4

"Father is Great"— His Mosque As Mother

The great Islamic crie de coeur—and the Muslims contend, also their cry for peace—is *Allahu Akbar,* God is Greatest. This cry has always struck my ear as a reaching out to an impotent, absent father figure, searching for him like an orphan in a crowd looking for his daddy. Might not they be saying, "Oh, my father is the greatest, greater than your father!" I thought of my father like Allahu Akbar, as someone who would rescue me from my persecutory mother. But it never happened. Both of my parents in their own unique ways exceeded the cruelty of the other. Then there came the Man without Empathy.

Like my father, my husband was a mastermind at impression management, presenting a cheerful, likable public persona that made everyone love him. Like my father, the Man without Empathy also was quietly passive–aggressive, denying my reality, opposing me at every step, controlling me. Passive–aggressive behavior is particularly difficult to catch in the act and to call by name. Gaslighting is one example, but if you point out this behavior to passive–aggressive personalities they will not own it. They will deny it or remain silent.

Like my father, my husband ranted and complained about everything, especially money. But always behind closed doors. No one ever saw this side of him. As I write now, I think of polygamy. This might seem tangential at this point in the narrative but it is a perfect example of a seemingly benign cultural practice. Below its surface is manifest passive–aggressive behavior. The way to deal with a female is to pit her against other wives.

This manipulative behavior is a kind of divide-and-conquer technique. While my father and the Man without Empathy did not practice polygamy, they were manipulative in their unique passive–aggressive ways.

Three months into the marriage, my husband began to hound me about what had happened in Brazil. "Did you sleep with anyone?" he asked again and again. It was always the same. He was relentless and desperate. I was repeatedly interrogated about my behavior. But his behavior could never be questioned. This would fit with a polygamous man: his harem of females would be under his scrutiny.

Even though in my mind I had broken up with him before I left for Brazil, even though my sexual history was my own business and he had no right to ask about it, I told him. I confessed out of guilt, terror, and exhaustion; I caved into his hounding me. I didn't realize that I had rights, human rights. It was as if he had infiltrated my mind since the day I had met him, although I did not remember meeting him. I felt that I had no control or say, that I was not entitled to any agency at all. He did not own me as if I lived in the Arab Muslim world. Yet this is what he thought. And he made me think like that, too.

"Why don't you love me? You have betrayed me!" he kept on yelling. The so-called betrayal was his problem, not mine, I thought. But I became his paranoid whipping post anyway. I did not yet understand that he suffered from delusional jealousy, and that he had this fantasy that I was his whore—that he needed me to be his whore. My mother had called me a whore too. It was her projection, but I had not understood this at the time. I was told to believe it, and so I did. It became my self-perception. That was what I had become wasn't it?

Enraged, my husband raped me. Rape is a tool of terrorism. Rape is a forced, concrete, sexual fusion with another, the feminization of the other—symbolizing the early maternal fusion. It is an ugly maternal cameo.

I had developed a theory of imagery and coined the term maternal cameo to express this perverse traumatic bonding with the enemy–the female. The traumatic bonding takes place in the first relationship of life. I came to realize that the perversity of my relationship with my husband had a lot to do with the tortured relationship with my mother and the added factor of having a sadistic father, very similar to the Arab Muslim culture of violence. When you are tortured as a young child, the parents in fantasy and in reality become a kind of amalgam of one persecutory being.

Terrorism is a perverse thrill of hurting the innocent. Never assume that all doctors are caring or that they take care of their families. Medical neglect by physicians is a known problem expressing passive–aggressive sadistic behavior. Think, too, of all the physicians involved in jihad and the Nazi doctors. Think of Nidal Hassan, the psychiatrist who perpetrated the mass murder at Fort Hood.

It was all oddly familiar, and sadly ironic. After all, I had been raped by others before. If I had been Roman Catholic, the marriage would have been annulled. I did not know that I had the right to divorce, although he still would have had to "grant" me the divorce according to Judaism. Islam is like that too, very patriarchal. The male can say three times "I divorce you." And, presto, you are divorced. I was too terrorized and shut down to formulate a plan to get out of the marriage. There was no name for this bad thing, this rape. I had no family to turn to for help. I was completely alone. He knew I was isolated. It worked to his advantage.

My husband never answered for his behavior. He never admitted the rape and never apologized for it, ever, in the course of the marriage. Perpetrators don't apologize; they remain silent. It is as if someone has read them their Miranda Rights: you have the right to remain silent. Such an effective strategy, saying nothing. To me he became the Man without

Empathy, of which he was devoid. No criticism ever stuck to him; he was like teflon. He was so clever in his projections and blaming.

Terrorism means never having to say you are sorry. The terrorist's cover is silence, massive denial. Or blaming when confronted, projecting the rage onto the victim. In fact, like Erdogan, the head of Turkey, the perpetrator wants you to apologize to him because he is the victim, not you.

I still have flashbacks. I remember the rape occurred in our first apartment on Aldine Street. A blue-and-white toile print wicker chair sat next to a round end table skirted in blue, which was alongside the brass bed. The Man without Empathy attacked me on my side of the bed. I struggled but could not get him off of me.

Currently, it is the custom in Afghanistan and other countries for a man to rape his wife. Back in 1970, the United States had no laws against spousal rape, let alone a term for it. Again, it appeared to me that nothing bad had a name. The legal term, spousal rape, didn't appear in the scientific literature until 1980. I learned this later, when I researched it in order to master the trauma of it all. But at the time it happened, I didn't even know that it was rape. I just knew my husband was having his way with me against my will.

I know that sounds strange, but in his family he was the beloved only son, the favorite. He was the middle child, sandwiched between two sisters, his mama's golden boy. He was the Jewish version of the Arab first-born male. His bad behavior had become normalized and permissible within his traditional Jewish family. He simply had no boundaries and got away with reprehensible behavior all the time. He had admitted to me early on that he almost flunked out of his freshman year of college because of poor grades and bad behavior. As the favorite child, his mother had tried to entice him out of going away to college by buying him off with a car. In the end, he left and got the car anyway. His mother extended his childhood.

Did he act out because he no longer had title to being the baby of the family after his younger sister was born? I could only imagine how pissed he was at that. Did the fact that I myself was the third and last child in my family compound his feelings of displacement by the third and last child in his family, thereby making me a prime target of additional irrational rage? Other members of his family seemed to have boundary problems as well, although they manifested in other ways. His mother, the youngest of fourteen from a Hasidic family, was born in Munkasheva, Hungary. She seemed emotionally needy, always inappropriately touching others as if they were some kind of pet. Years later, in couple therapy, the Man without Empathy recalled how his mother and older sister painted his fingers with nail polish, probably because he didn't fit in as a boy.

His mother's family paralleled that of a larger Palestinian family. There is no way that a mother with ten children can adequately nurture emotionally all of her children. I had seen in clinical treatment a series of patients who came from very large families with more than ten siblings. They had a variety of religious backgrounds—different Christian denominations, Muslim, and Jewish—but they all shared one thing in common: the description of what it was like to grow up in such a large household. The most striking aspect was the utter chaos; household upheaval showed the lack of object constancy, the lack of ability to create stable relationships and appropriate bonding within the family. These patients struggled to relate to the other as a person in his/her own right. They could not even find a shelf to call their own where they could put their clothes. Their sense of place was completely dictated by who had more power. It was brutal. Think of the Arab spring and its societal chaos as a reflection of unstable social bonds with people and institutions. You can imagine what the interiors of some of these homes looked like, though I do not say that all are like that. I am reminded of an incident when we went to stay at the

Man without Empathy's sister's home. She started reprimanding me, saying that the guest room in which we were staying was messy. First of all, it was not. Second, when I looked around her house, there was total chaos. I was appalled by her yelling at me. I was maybe all of twenty-three but the Man without Empathy said nothing.

I always wondered if the Man without Empathy's older sister suffered from Munchausen's by Proxy, a psychological disorder in which mothers fabricate illnesses and injuries in their children to get attention for themselves. That is how I got to thinking of the familiar feeling of the suicide bomber as a proxy. Often their rage is the result of unresolved hunger for a father who was absent in the child's early years. Often the father is a physician. It all fit: the Man without Empathy's father was a doctor; he had been absent during the first two years of the older sister's life while serving overseas during World War II; her adopted kids were constantly sick and hospitalized. By the Man without Empathy's own account, his older sister was a pathological liar. Talk about the pot calling the kettle black. Had this sister abused him as a child? He repeatedly related how this older sister threw an alarm clock at him. Clocks are beloved hard objects by the schizoid personality.

In any case, the abortion was the direct result of the rape. It was forced upon me because having a baby would keep me from working, and therefore keep me from supporting the Man without Empathy through medical school. But the abortion was even more than that. It was an unconscious psychological strategy to shame me and thereby slowly erode the little confidence I had. He was my pimp, and I was his whore. As smart as I was, I handed my hard-earned money over to my husband. But all he did was complain and demand more. He made only a small contribution to our household income by earning extra money working in the ER, or as a sperm donor, and by delivering babies. For years, especially after I had my own kids,

I lived in fear of his genetic children tracking him down. He never gave me a say in the matter. His part-time jobs as a sperm donor and delivering babies exposed his obsession with the prenatal mother and women in general—which he hated. I could not as yet put together his rage against the hated other—the female—whom he needed to suppress, manipulate, and control. He was confused about who he was. He remained enraged at me for years. I remembered how he would come home from medical school and talk about "that bitch," always complaining about women. He would always say that I forced him to marry me. In every argument, he would pick on me about my alleged infidelity in Brazil, even though I had broken up with him at the time. In retrospect, I see it was always about leaving or separating. His mother had never allowed him to separate from her. He was completely emasculated by and dependent upon her. She, in turn, had no power, coming from the ultra-orthodox family she grew up in.

I came to understand how this paralleled the Arab Muslim family involved in terrorism, although in the Jewish Haredi family it played out in miniature. There was no institutionalized honor killing, but they could cleverly commit soul murder through chronic daily abuse and by targeting the female as the scapegoat in the large family. I would try to explain, even though there was no reason to explain. I had done nothing wrong, but it didn't matter. He directed all of his diatribes at me just like my parents had; it was part of his strategy to keep me under control and brainwashed. He was relentless. Yet it was all familiar to me and hence had become normalized in my dissociated existence.

Terrorism is an obsession and fixation with the feminized other. An obsession becomes an excuse for not having to grow up. The fixation serves to anchor a poorly put together personality, which basically lacks an identity. A fixation is a delusion because it warps reality. It is a way of inappropriately attaching to another. It was during this time frame that the

Man without Empathy attacked me in bed while we were both sleeping. I woke up suddenly in pain to find that he had locked his jaw into my shoulder and would not let go of it. It was very painful. I had to literally fight him off. I remember mentioning this to my analyst, who didn't say anything in particular that I recall. Now I think of it as revealing how enraged he was unconsciously. The Man without Empathy would deny this, as well as that his way of attaching to me was by concretely attacking me. It was bonding through hatred on his part, and no one saw it. By glomming on to the other in a pathological, hateful way, the terrorist feels like he has an identity, albeit by parasitic means. It's like an unwanted Siamese twinship. Terrorism is at its core a kind of psychological identity theft. Think about it: Terrorists steal other people's identity because they have no stable identity of their own. It is not just about criminality since it also serves a psychological function. Terrorists seek to destroy the "evidence" that you are a real person. They deny your very existence.

It would be the same when he who was without empathy sodomized me. It would be more devastating and remain unspoken, so traumatizing that it is hard for me to write about it. I debated whether to reveal this act. But it fit with his sadism, power, and control. It is important to understand anal rape and the destruction of the other by complete, humiliating submission. Later, it fit with his penchant for pornography. His rage was escalating.

Doctors say that it is hard for people to talk about anal cancer, let alone anal rape. I think of Farrah Fawcett and how brave she was to be forthcoming about her painful terminal battle with anal cancer. Even *The Joy of Sex,* which I read years after its heyday, explicitly warns against anal intercourse. But pain became confused with pleasure. I already had formed an addiction to terror and its sadomasochist aspects. I felt so dead that the cycle of being berated—"fucking and fighting" as the Man without Empathy loved to call it—enlivened me. But ultimately I found it so tiring and repulsive. I did not like getting sucked into his arguments, which he provoked. It would take me years to work my way out of this excruciating mental as well as sexualized physical bondage. It is a kind of sadomasochism, which fascinates and draws many into its circle—part of the unspoken, disavowed attraction of suicide terrorism.

Terrorism and rape become a systematic strategy that dehumanizes the female and little boys. Rape is a severe form of that fusion, and sodomy speaks to the anality of terrorism and its shit. Terrorism is an anal cult. Terrorists relentlessly and anal retentively clutch at and cling to their ideologies, as if they were on a sinking ship. They are not developmentally capable of moving beyond this limited phase of relating to others as objects.

Anal rape also fits with Arab and Muslim cultures. In Afghanistan there is the "thirteenth man," a young boy called the *Bachi Bazi* whom the male group routinely rapes. If, as a child therapist, you saw a young child in play therapy take a toy car and repeatedly ram the car into the back of a toy truck like a suicide car bomber, you would wonder if the child had been anally raped. This is the nonverbal symbolic language of terrorism. Terrorists have no boundaries. They form a malignant twinship with you, and project their terrors into you, and in turn victimize you. Sexual abuse, to the best of my knowledge, has not really been adequately factored into explaining the Islamic suicide terrorism. Yet I believe that the quality and quantity of the rage speaks to that kind of abuse.

Terrorism is about shame, not honor. Anal rape is a subject that counterterrorist experts, the majority of whom are male, are extremely uncomfortable talking about. If anything, they make jokes about it. To be a male and be raped is the ultimate sign of submission, of being made into the female through this violent act. Perhaps it is the ultimate shame. Anal rape occurs frequently in Arab Muslim cultures and in Afghanistan and Pakistan as well. The sense of physical and psychological submission cannot be dissociated from the visual concept of submission in Islam, as concretely made evident by its prostration in prayer. Indeed, in reviewing El Feki's *Sex and the Citadel,* Maslin quotes an Egyptian woman cited in the book as saying: "Men in Egypt and the Gulf, they always want to have sex in the wrong place," and she was not referring to geography but to anal intercourse. They also wash their face with their hands as if to remove the stain of impurity.

It should not be surprising then that terrorism is an anal entity. Terrorists are obsessed with shit because at some level they identify themselves with shit. I am not sure that they can even feel like shit. They compensate by seeking to rid themselves of their impurities through projection and purification. That is why they are obsessed with immolation as purification through bombings. As a victim you are the designated holder of their shit. To them you are shit. Similarly, a toilet seat is not a tabletop. Even though it can be used as one, it is a perversion of the concept of table and eating, and it is linked to shit. It is the misuse of an object. Terrorists have even hidden bombs in their anus like drug mules. Abdullah Hassan al-Asiri, an Al Qaeda suicide bomber, hid an improvised explosive device in his anus as he tried to assassinate Saudi Arabia's Deputy Minister of Interior, Muhammad bin Najef, in August 2009. He died but the prince lived.

Besides the nonverbal communications at a psychological level of submission in prayer, it is important to consider that they are not just submitting to their "Father" Allahu Akhbar; the submission unconsciously is really to the mother. The father is like a transparent overlay of the unconscious maternal fusion. It can be accessed through the veneration of the mosque. It is really a statement and testament to the mother; the mosque is defended as if it were their mother.

Shahin Nafaji, an Iranian rapper living in Germany, came under a death threat like Salman Rushdie for defaming Islam when he published the jacket cover of his album, which I blogged about at Family Security Matters:[20]

> *Our current Salman Rushdie is the young, courageous Iranian rapper Shahin Nafaji, now in hiding in Germany who has received a death threat because he wrote lyrics to his song Naqi. However, I contend it is the album cover, which broke the proverbial camel's back of the Mahdists [Islamic messianism in Iran and hence radical Shiite Islamists]. The cover depicts the dome of the mosque of the 8th Shia Imam as a female breast with a rainbow flag "à la sexual diversity" as a thin impotent phallic minaret arising out of the nipple! A picture speaks a thousand words.*
>
> *In an interview by the BBC, Shahin spoke about sex and Shia Islam—"how transparent Islam is with regard to sexuality."*
>
> *What exactly did he mean by "transparent"? I take him to mean that a perverse sexuality lurks below the surface of Mahdist culture, which hates the female. The dome of the mosque is an unconscious representation of the female breast of the nursing mother. This is the essence of a shame–honor culture signifying that there is maternal deprivation and paranoia. They go hand in hand. The little girls and women are abused. With shame, comes blaming the other but hardly ever the mother because the mother is the object to be protected by the little humiliated, shamed boy who witnesses his mother being abused. The little boy feels his mother to be an extension of himself. To see her hit is for him to feel her pain. He must protect her at all costs. Picture a frightened little boy clinging hysterically to his mother's skirt.*
>
> *This same little boy harbors an erotized rage that in many instances exceeds murder itself. It is not just enough to murder; it*

must in order to redeem honor through blood violence. The hatred and violence is an erotized hatred—the intense hatred of the female that is not satiated by merely murdering.

The Mahdist regime is perpetually stuck in an infantile mode of shame, regressed to defending their weak mothers who live their lives through them and they hate it. It is a vicious cycle for which we pay the price as the rage is projected outwards in the vessel of political violence and nuclear war. Remember too, that it was Shia's Hezbollah who initiated Islamic suicide truck bombing on a grand scale in southern Lebanon in the early 1980s. It was readily adopted by Arab Muslim cultures because they too are shame/honor. The mosque is their mother too. Indeed this transparency of symbol and obsession for the mother can be sensed in the word "umma" meaning the Muslim community, derived from the same root as the Arabic ummi or "mommy."

Learning Hebrew

While working to support this man without an ounce of empathy, I managed to complete my master's in Spanish and Portuguese at Roosevelt University in Chicago. There was no celebration. He didn't even take me out to dinner. Marla—whom my kids would later call their "love aunt"—encouraged me to take beginning Hebrew. Marla had studied Hebrew and thought I would enjoy it as well. I began a night course in Hebrew at Chicago's Spertus College of Judaica, taught by Mar (Mr.) Kahana, a wonderful teacher who was Romanian. As I placed the binding of my Hebrew book on the left side like an English book on the first night, Mar Kahana said, "You really don't know anything about Hebrew, do you?" But by the end of the term, I had surpassed the Man without Empathy's bar mitzvah Hebrew. Hebrew is a Semitic language like Arabic, which I would study later.

My conversion to Judaism, which also helped me understand the converts to jihad, made me realize that, as a Jew, I had to choose a Hebrew name. One night in a different class several years later, while sitting next to the daughter of Israelis, I heard the girl say her Hebrew name: Atzmaut. I thought it was such a terrific name that I chose it as my own, particularly after learning that my birthday, like this girl's, fell within the thirty-day period leading up to *Yom Ha-Atzmaut*: Israeli Independence Day. I was born in the same year as the State of Israel, 1948. While my life may have been more on the order of the Palestinian *Nakba*—"the catastrophe," in Arabic, as the Palestinians prefer to call Israeli Independence Day in their narrative—my yearning to be free was cast with and bound to my identification with my people and Israel, as corny as that may seem. Nonetheless, it is true.

Like a freedom fighter, I was struggling for my independence, albeit in a nonviolent way. Nationality often functions as a kind of fallback identity when the home identity has been full of hatred. It runs the risk of becoming a hyper identity, masking the deeper psychological problems. It can even take on the sense of fighting for the underdog to the point of not being able to see one's own people—like those who are Jewish and yet so utterly pro-Palestinian that they protest too much. When Obama was in Israel, he claimed that the Israelis needed to walk in the shoes of the Palestinians. I wondered to what degree he was remotely able to walk in the shoes of the Jews after spending 20 years sitting in the south side Trinity United Church of Christ in Chicago, where the preacher and controversial pastor Jeremiah Wright spewed anti-Semitism from his pulpit. Yet Obama never said anything about that. He refused to speak out against the anti-Semitism during all that time.

The course in Hebrew prepared me for my first trip to Israel. The Man without Empathy, who had many relatives living there, wanted to go to

Hadassah Hospital for his elective quarter in medical school. I just wanted to become literate in Hebrew.

We landed in Tel Aviv in June 1972, mere days after the Lod Airport massacre on May 30. Twenty-five people had been killed and seventy-one injured in a joint attack by the Japanese Red Army and Popular Front for the Liberation of Palestine. There were other bombings in Jerusalem throughout that summer, including one at the neighborhood supermarket. But it was the pockmarked walls of the Lod Airport (now called Ben Gurion, or Natbag for short), where the massacre had taken place, that made a lasting impression on me. The event became my baptism into political violence and Islamic terrorism. Little did I know that some 30 years later, I would be interviewed for a documentary concerning airport security at Natbag.

I threw myself into my studies once again and after only nine months was placed in *kitah gimel,* the highest level for the study of Hebrew. The course was grueling, but it was led by Chana Shai, another fabulous Hebrew teacher. This kind and generous woman invited the entire class to her apartment to watch the 1972 Summer Olympics in Munich on her black-and-white TV. The games were memorable on two counts, one joyful, the other tragic: the American Jewish swimmer Mark Spitz won a record-setting seven gold medals. We were so proud of him, especially since it took place in Germany, where the former Nazi ideology made the Jew out to be a weakling. But our feelings of sweet sportsmanship and victory were not to last as 11 Israeli athletes were murdered by terrorists in what came to be called The Munich Massacre, perpetrated by Black September Palestinian terrorists. Chaos and confusion reigned during the initial news reports about the first two murders and subsequent kidnappings, then anger and sorrow took over as we learned that the other nine also had been killed .

Of all the events of that summer, it was the final exam for the Hebrew course that I remember vividly. Our class was asked to translate the *mavo* (introduction) to the recently published *BaCur Shel HaMahapecha: In the Crucible of Scientific Revolution* by Aharon Katzir. I have often thought whoever decided to have the class translate the book's introduction made a strategically profound decision. Katzir was a brilliant and gifted scientist who made science accessible to the wider public. His brother, Ephraim Katzir, was then president of Israel. Professor Katzir had been murdered in the terrorist attack at Lod Airport.

I returned to Chicago after an incredible summer, having fallen in love with Israel, my "good" mother. The Man without Empathy promised it would be possible one day for us to have an apartment in Israel and to make *aliyah*—to immigrate to Israel. I had no family there, but it was precisely because of this that I felt at home. Because of my strong, unspoken identification with Holocaust survivors, many of whom had no family, I felt completely comfortable being among my own, and they seemed instantly at ease with me as well. I decided to continue studying Hebrew at Spertus, along with Jewish theology, history, and literature.

Of course, the Man without Empathy never made good on his promise to make *aliyah*. My neighbor Merry would tell me that the promises were part of the seduction lure, a way to hold me captive. She was right.

Terrorism is based on broken promises. Terrorists promote themselves as men of peace but they are not, just like Yasir Arafat and his Nobel Peace Prize. Terrorists make promises to keep you tied in and under control. Whatever you want, they don't want you to have it. They do not want to see you happy and content because they cannot achieve happiness themselves. They envy and attack. It gives them time to regroup, like the Arabic *hudna*—a temporary armistice or a *tadiyah*, a lull in the war, a time to steel themselves for attack next time around—or even for the *sulha,* traditional peace negotiations, They do not seek a permanent peace because they have inherently unstable personalities, and they don't know what peace feels like or means for that matter. They are essentially terrified.

At Spertus I lucked into an excellent course on Jewish thought, taught by Rabbi Byron Sherwin, protégé of Rabbi Abraham Joshua Heschel, the rabbi who walked in Selma, Alabama, with Martin Luther King. President Barack Obama named Rabbi Heschel in one of his speeches in Israel in March 2013. Rabbi Sherwin was the first to explain Judaism in a systematic way, and it was his style of teaching that brought me back to Judaism. He was also the first professor to genuinely encourage my intellect. I wrote a paper on the first novel I ever read in Hebrew, Yoram Kaniuk's *Adam Ben Calev: Adam Resurrected,* and for the first time I was told that my work was brilliant. The main character in the book is a dog. I often identified with both the underdog and real dogs. The image of my father beating our pet dogs in front of me was burned into my memory. Rabbi Sherwin encouraged me to research the Holocaust and literature appearing in Spanish, Portuguese, and Ladino (Old Spanish in Hebrew script). This project led to my first publication in *Tradition: A Journal of Orthodox Jewish Thought.*

I became a colleague and friend of Rabbi Sherwin after graduating from Spertus. At his 60th birthday party, I recalled for his friends and family how he was the first teacher in whose class I had felt safe enough and worthy enough to ask a question. Even though I already held two university degrees, I had never asked a question in class before then. I was too terrified to speak, a crippling effect of having grown up not being allowed to speak unless spoken to. I remember to this day that I asked Rabbi Sherwin a question about Rambam, Maimonides, the great medieval Jewish philosopher and physician, who is also considered an important prophet in Islam! Maimonides was fluent in Arabic and wrote some of his tracts in Judeo-Arabic. The profession of the physician has always been venerated in both Arab and Jewish cultures.

The Recurring Theme of the Prenatal Mother

It was in 1975, during the Man without Empathy's residency in ophthalmology in Portland, Oregon, and before my daughter was born, that I had a spontaneous abortion. It happened five years after the "legal" abortion in 1970. In the middle of a conversation with a friend from medical school days who was visiting from Arizona, I felt an incredibly sharp pain. I rushed to the bathroom. When I saw the blood and the fetal clot, I knew I had miscarried. In a state of shock. I said nothing because I had been taught not to make a fuss about myself or my pain.

A month passed and I was still bleeding. The Man without Empathy, the doctor, never once, suggested that I make an appointment to find out about the bleeding. When I finally went to the gynecologist, he did a D&C on the spot. No one asked if I had someone to drive me home. The Man without Empathy hadn't offered to go with me (perhaps another example of rage against the prenatal mother), so I drove myself to and from the clinic. On the way home I almost passed out at the steering wheel from the pain. It was sudden and sharp, taking me completely by surprise.

I did not understand at the time that to deny something that someone needs, such as appropriate medical care, is a form of sadism and abuse. How could anyone believe that a doctor would deny his own wife such care? Especially when he belonged to an extended family of so many physicians? Who would believe this or me saying that this happened?

Similarly, my own parents had not provided me medical care when needed. This is what is called the repetition compulsion. My parents had laid the groundwork for me to seek out someone like them who would not provide appropriate medical care. Another interlocking link set me up for further abuse: repetition compulsion of the trauma. When I was younger than three, Brother Bully pushed me into a typewriter and split my chin open. My parents didn't take me to an emergency room to have it stitched.

That would have been against Christian Science, so I looked at this scar on my face every day until I finally had it physically removed after many years. A concrete example of being proactive to overcome abuse.

Another time, when I was thirteen and riding my bike fast to the park, I caught my leg on the pedal, flipped over the handlebars, and slid across a gravel road. The police found me and took me home, where then my mother failed to clean the wound properly. It became infected, and I was unable to walk on the injured leg for six weeks.

Becoming a Mother

I became pregnant with my daughter in the late spring of 1975. My friend Lindy made a care package of used maternity clothes for me. In January 1976 my daughter was born. I desperately wanted to be a better mother than my own mother had been to me. I would do anything to make my daughter's life better than what my own had been. I asked the Man without Empathy for permission to go to therapy when we were still living in Portland, but once again he would not agree. I had a wonderful, gorgeous baby girl. I was so happy, but I knew I had issues to work on and that I needed emotional support. I remember one Saturday when the Man without Empathy came home from rounds and asked me what was for lunch. I was exhausted from nursing, which I had trouble with because of scar tissue from a breast biopsy. I turned to him and said, "Tell me, do you do retina surgery?" He said, "Yes." I continued, "Open the cabinet and start reading the labels. I am sure you will be able to find something to eat." One of the few moments of my being assertive. But it wasn't enough, and it didn't last. He would retaliate.

I was studying Biblical Hebrew and Ladino at Portland State University while teaching Spanish at a community college when my teacher for

Biblical Hebrew recruited me to go to Russia. I had been tapped to help the Refuseniks—Jews who wanted to leave Russia—by smuggling names, papers, photos, and documents so that Israel could create immigration documents and help them to leave the gulag of anti-Semitism.

Years later, I would learn from an Israeli Russian student who wrote a research paper on my terrorism writings that the program was called *Nativ*, which means "path" in Hebrew. I was sent into Russia in 1977, ten days after Anatole Sharansky, who now goes by his Hebrew name Natan Sharansky, had been arrested and thrown in jail for his human rights activities, which included spearheading the Refusenik movement for Jews who wanted to leave Russia. On his release from prison, Sharansky made Aliyah and became an elected member of the Israeli Knesset. While in Russia to help the Refuseniks, I was stopped several times by the Russian police. I was sent first to Moscow and then into Muslim Central Asia—Tashkent, Samarkand, and Bukhara. The Man without Empathy tagged along.

My daughter was 14 months old when I went to Russia. The Israelis would not allow me to take her along for fear she would be kidnapped, so I left my daughter with the Man without Empathy's older sister. This was before I thought of the sister as the Weasel. I now deeply regret having done that. My daughter did not speak to me for a week after I came home. I was devastated, but the Man without Empathy thought nothing of it— or if he did, he blamed me.

I published my first article at that time. I had spent four years researching the Holocaust and Sephardic Jewry and felt compelled to try to help others understand the atrocities. I was haunted by the image of Nazis smashing the heads of Jewish babies against walls. I knew that the Amalekites had murdered babies that way in the Bible but that was in ancient times, not 60 years ago. This obsession to murder babies is further evidence of the terrorist's rage against the prenatal and postnatal mother and against what babies represent: complete vulnerability and dependency. While it may be hard to believe, they are envious of babies because developmentally, behaviorally, and emotionally, they are at an equivalent age—infancy.

The Man without Empathy's expectation that I would work to support him continued. Somehow it was my responsibility to keep us afloat. I continued to work even while going to school myself, working toward my doctorate after my daughter and then my son were born. I would say to the Man without Empathy, "But so and so doesn't work," listing our Jewish couple friends whose wives were stay-at-home moms. I knew of at least four of his ophthalmologist colleagues' wives who did not work while they were raising their children. Even my sister-in-law, also married to a physician, had weaseled out of that supporting role. But not once, in all of our thirty-nine years of marriage would he really provide for me. In addition, his terrible problems handling money only compounded the problem.

He was a relentless complainer and criticizer, manipulative for his own gain. He was oppositional, like a baby. Whatever I wanted, he did not want, and he refused to give me. He was withholding. When I had wanted a third child, he would not give in, even though he had forced me into the abortion that had robbed me of a third child. My kids to this day believe that I abandoned them while working and that was my choice. It was not. I had wanted to take time off, but he would not let me. He was a tyrant in his own insidious passive–aggressive way. I was terrified, but everyone loved him. Who would believe me? Who would help me? Ultimately, he pushed me out the door with his rage after all those years of deprivation.

But people never saw this side of him. To the public, the community, his colleagues, friends, and family he was a wonderful guy, cheery and gregarious. He gave the uncanny public appearance of being the obedient, docile Jewish husband.[21] It was all show. He was superficial, a shell of a man. This is exactly how jihadi terrorists and the Muslim Brotherhood are. Their statement that women should be dominated and controlled is their attempt to normalize their insecurities and impotence.

I fended for myself and kept the peace, reminiscent of that Hebrew phrase, *shalom beit*—for the sake of peace within the household. But in our household it was more on the order of *Dar-al Sulh*, an Arabic "house of calm," achieved through utter terror by the revenge-seeking behavior and vicious accusations of the Man without Empathy. But this fragile Arab-like house of cards began to collapse when Lindy was murdered.

Repetition Compulsion to Murder and Terrorize

I rarely talked about having a dead brother, who had been essentially a victim of my parents' selfishness and negligence. I also could not talk to anyone about the rape and the forced abortion for ten long, excruciating years because unconsciously I felt like my brother's murderer. I never told anyone until the brutal rape and murder of my best friend. Lindy was stalked, captured, held hostage, repeatedly raped, released, abducted again, and murdered—shot to death at point-blank range with a Saturday Night Special on April Fool's Day, 1978.

Lindy and I were doppelgangers,—two young Jewish women from the north side of Chicago, both Spanish majors, both married to men who had been childhood friends and were now attending the same medical school. Lindy and I even had had the same favorite Spanish professor, a Cuban Jew who taught first at Washington University in St. Louis, where Lindy had done her undergraduate work, and then was hired by Indiana University, which I attended.

Lindy was taking a break from her doctoral studies in Spanish to become trained in Lamaze childbirth (another echoed theme of the prenatal mother) when a convicted rapist out on parole randomly abducted her at gunpoint in a parking ramp at Northwestern University Hospital. Her assailant, who was out on parole for a series of rapes, stuffed her into the trunk of his car and then drove to his parole hearing. He was the husband of a prominent alderwoman who sat on the Chicago City Council. Again, people said he was such a nice guy. Two days later, after repeatedly beating and raping Lindy, he released her on the south side of Chicago.

Lindy asked for help at the nearest home, which happened to belong to a Chicago firefighter, who assumed that her injuries were the result of domestic violence/intimate terrorism (although what terrorism isn't intimate?). Domestic violence calls are considered the most dangerous in law enforcement. Officers never go alone to respond to such calls; they always go in pairs. This firefighter was no different. He was obviously terrified, but he probably could not have admitted it. For my theory of the Islamic suicide attack, I investigated the prevalence of domestic violence and the deep level of cultural denial on both the part of the West and Middle Eastern cultures. I became interested in domestic violence because of the template of murder–suicide that it shares with the Islamic suicide attack. In addition, I was becoming more and more aware that the Man without Empathy was my perpetrator.

The firefighter made Lindy wait on the front steps of his porch while he called the police for back-up. However, he did not dial the special number Chicago police and firefighters call to ask for immediate help, something like a plea from a comrade in distress. Rather than take her in and shelter her, he made her wait, terrified no doubt, on the front stoop of his home. Had he acted more wisely, perhaps Lindy would still be alive today. During these precious moments, her assailant came back for her, grabbed her and dragged her into an alley, where he shot her in the head and chest. Lindy died instantly.

On the morning of the murder, Lindy's sister-in-law called and asked, "Is anyone with you?" "Yes, my daughter," I said. She then told me, "I want you to sit down. Are you sitting down? Lindy is dead."

Only six weeks earlier, I had had a premonition while standing at the window in what I called the La Brea Tar Pit of married student housing in Iowa City that one of my friends would die. I felt I should have been able to forewarn Lindy because of this premonition. The survivor's guilt was unbearable. It would take me 20 years to stop obsessing about being responsible. I was able to let go only after Lindy's murderer received the death penalty by lethal injection some 19 years after the trial. At the time I was not in favor of capital punishment, but I freely admit that I felt enormous relief when he was finally dead. I vowed never to speak his name—to blot it out from human history, like Haman in the *Book of Esther*.

The murder of my dear friend was shattering. It felt like losing my second "twin," just as I had lost my "twin" brother when he was murdered by the medical negligence of my parents. Obviously, I felt like I had lost part of myself, and my sense of self already was fragile enough at this point in my life. As the weeks passed, Lindy's death was becoming my own. On the surface it appeared as if I was handling it well, but I began to struggle in a way I never had—and I had struggled plenty before.

Shortly after the murder, the Man without Empathy and I moved to Minnesota, where he had accepted a job at a group health practice in the Twin Cities. I was in no shape to look for a house, let alone decide which one to buy, so my sister-in-law, the Weasel, picked one out. It was a dump, not a home.

Phobia set in, but I didn't know it was that; nor did I understand what was happening and why. All I knew was that I could no longer do every day, normal things. I could not grocery shop without panicking midway through the store, leaving behind my half-filled shopping cart. I could no longer be in crowds. Going to the Minnesota State Fair was impossible. I could not imagine myself in public, let alone eating in view of others. It was as if I became voluntarily sequestered, like a woman in an Afghan home. This feeling, though, was not really one of volition; it emanated from feeling completely terrorized and dissociated. I could not go to the cafeteria at the University of Minnesota, where I had transferred to complete my Ph.D. Therefore, I didn't eat lunch and fasted while I was at work. I stopped traveling by plane for five years.

Taking care of two small children with little help was hard for me. It was tough for me to go back to the university and my work while my son was an infant and my daughter was still so young. I was nursing and running back and forth to the university. I had asked the graduate school to postpone my fellowship for maternity leave and they said no, that I had to use it or lose it. This was before issues like women's rights and maternity leave became standard university practices. I had to go back to work in less than one week—before my son's *bris*, the ritual circumcision.

I was now studying Arabic and Islam, and I learned that the prophet Muhammad also borrowed the practice of the Jewish circumcision. However, it occurs later in the life of the male and is considered as if it were a wedding or marriage to the mother. Islamic circumcision occurs from the age of two to seven years, although it may take place as late as puberty. It is a celebrated event, with adult males, as well as little girls, looking on. In eastern Egypt, the celebration is referred to as *ars*, meaning wedding, with the boy who is to be circumcised called the *khatan*, the bridegroom and the circumcision *khitana*. In Morocco the circumcision is considered the boy's first marriage, that is to his mother, his *ummi*.[22]

The Muslim male clearly remembers the pain and the trauma of the attack-like circumcision and its extenuating experiences. Those who are able to recall the procedure remember their fear that their penis had actually been cut off and that they were unable to see their penis until the bandages were removed some days later. It is terrifying. A common custom with regard to male circumcision is the infantilizing of the male child by swaddling him after the procedure as if he were a baby. Mother as omnisexual woman is tangibly present at the circumcision. Moroccans believe that the circumcision needs to be remembered by the child, and therefore it should occur at an age when he will not forget the trauma. The circumcision is explicitly linked to *sharaf,* honor. Both the male circumcision and the suicide bombing share the psychological atmosphere of a wedding celebration, which is used to mark the acquisition of honor.

I had trouble looking at myself in a mirror and repeatedly asked the Man without Empathy for psychological help. But he did nothing, which made matters worse. He kept up his classic behaviors, which now included sleep deprivation. I was never allowed to get enough sleep. He demanded that I wake up when he did. He had so much anxiety that he would get up at 5:45. He made sure that I had no opportunity to sleep in. During the night his tossing and turning would wake me, but he would not permit me to leave the bed to sleep in another room. He would take all the covers and then accuse me of stealing them. Sleep deprivation is a strategy employed to break down terrorists during interrogation. The Man without Empathy just turned the practice around to keep me in check.

Years later, in couple therapy, he would defend his actions by saying he just didn't understand that I needed help. Even now, it is hard for me to know how much of his behavior back then was unconscious, passive–

aggressive, and/or premeditated. The older I get, the more I am convinced that he actually did understand. He made conscious choices. He was aware. He was a control freak who could not have cared less if I were helped. He desperately wanted to appear normal so that people would not suspect or find out that he abused his wife. He wore the mask of sanity, but he was anything but sane.

This is also the hidden life of a jihadi with its external "mask of sanity," a phrase coined by Hervey Cleckley, who was an expert on serial killers and the psychopathic personality. The internal life of a jihadi is a mess of violent psychosexual fantasies. Like the jihadi who does *taqiyyah*, dissimulation, the mask of sanity is a tool of deception. You have to be very skilled to read the body language in order to piece together and decode the deception. You have to be a deception detector.

Who would think it, let alone believe it? Yet this is the nature of terrorism, this is the commonality. The Man without Empathy is a Jew, but he was more like a mafioso, an Arab terrorist. By the way, the word mafia is thought to derive from the Arabic, and its clan structure came into being in Sicily, where the Arab Muslims ruled for 700 years. There are several theories about the origin of the term mafia. The Sicilian adjective *mafiusu* may derive from the slang Arabic *mahyas* meaning "aggressive boasting, bragging" or *marfud* meaning "rejected." Roughly translated, it means "swagger," but can also be translated as "boldness or bravado." In reference to a man, mafiusu in 19th century Sicily was ambiguous, signifying a bully, someone who was arrogant but also fearless, enterprising, and proud, according to scholar Diego Gambetta. In reference to a woman, however, the adjective "mafiusa" means beautiful and attractive. Diego Gambetta is a counterterrorist expert and sociologist who raised the issue of terrorists being schizoid, withdrawn, and antisocial and closely related to malignant high-functioning people with Aspergers.

And that is what the Man without Empathy was. He would say one thing and do another. He would claim he was a man of peace, but he practiced jihad-speak. He was the consummate liar and manipulator whose false disposition always masked his rage.

I could not have put this together back then. I was so traumatized by him that I did not realize I could have picked up the phone, made an appointment with a therapist, and had the bill sent home. I wanted to be proactive, but could not override his decision. I was too dissociated, too paralyzed, too terrorized. I asked him for help and he said no—and I had been taught to take no as a final answer. In the end I was nothing more than a doormat to him.

Yet even when I finally did get help, two therapists would completely miss his chameleon demeanor. This is what people don't get about the terrorist living next door. They are so terrified that they come to identify with the aggressor—and the therapists. Even the majority of counterterrorist experts don't get this unconscious level of being the perennial object of hatred. The psychology used by most counterterrorist experts remains wholly inadequate for terrorism, including an inability to examine the implications of the defective maternal bond. I recently received an e-flyer from one of the most prestigious think tanks for counterterrorism in which there were many pictures of male counterterrorist experts but only one picture of a woman who was characterized as a "friend" of this organization, meaning probably that she was a major donor. The flyer was telling in its disparity of female participants. This same organization held a conference with a special session on suicide bombing, and no women experts were invited to sit on the panel. A young prominent male expert on suicide terrorism told me that he has heard similar complaints by women colleagues over the years who have tried to get their research on terrorism taken seriously. These women confided that there was a lot of gender discrimination. Because of this, male experts have been unable to contemplate the importance of the maternal bonding attachment, which remains a key contributor to understanding the psychological make-up of global terrorism. It is important to keep in mind Halim Barakat's insight that if the family is dysfunctional, you will also have a dysfunctional society.

PART II

THE MATERNAL SURVEILLANCE: HER ACCUSATORY EYE

CHAPTER 5

Identifying With The Agressor

I tried to move forward and provide as best as I could for my children. I finally was "permitted" to go into therapy, which I desperately desired because I did not want my daughter to hate me the way my mother had hated me. I did not want any kind of hatred in my home. By then it was 1980 and my daughter was four. That is late developmentally. However, you must remember that my earlier attempts to get help had failed.

A colleague who became a friend told the Man without Empathy which therapist I should see. It was the friend's psychoanalyst, his shrink—a Jewish male psychiatrist. The analyst was a training analyst, which meant that whoever went into intensive therapy with him could ultimately qualify to train as an analyst provided they had the right credentials. Going into analysis is like being re-parented, with the psychoanalyst at times seeming like a mother and other times a father. It is an attempt to repair the bonding between infant and mother, to fix the maternal attachment as well as attachment with the father. My analysis only took me so far. My analyst missed the degree to which I had been traumatized and my pathological need to please him. I did not understand at the time my deep-seated identification with the aggressor—i.e., my mother— and my need to keep my relationship with my father as somehow more "normal." My analysis slowly became similar to American culture as political correctness overcame a sense of freedom. It was a culture of accommodation and appeasement, the kind of culture that slowly kills you. It was a reflection of the inner workings of a very troubled marriage.

My analyst made me wait eighteen months from the time of the initial consultation intake (the first four sessions of the initial interview process) to having regularly scheduled sessions with him four times a week. In this regard he acted like my father, the Christian Scientist who took his time and failed to heed my urgent call for help. Trained early on to be compliant, I did not question that it was an unreasonable, inconsiderate amount of time to wait when one is in excruciating pain. Once again I experienced the trauma of being denied appropriate, timely treatment even though I had asked for help. It was mean, disavowed aggression and the ultimate passive–aggressive behavior.

I had no real family of my own to turn to at the time, no one from whom I could seek consolation or support. Lindy was dead and Menina, aka Angela, my college roommate, lived far away in Germany during those years. I repeatedly asked for help from others, but they only compounded the problem. Like everyone else they minimized and denied what I was experiencing—the brutality, the banality of it. You can be sure that this happens in Arab Muslim homes, especially those that produce terrorists and are ultra conservative.

I even went to my mother-in-law during this time of waiting, and asked her to please try to get her son to behave. But my mother-in-law minimized his aberrant behavior. Her son, the "golden boy," could do no wrong. She was like the classic Arab Muslim mother-in-law who sides with her son, no matter what. After all, her honor derives from his birth. My mother-in-law was incapable of seeing her son's problems. The Arabs have a saying: "In his mother's eye, the monkey is as beautiful as a gazelle."

One of the first things my analyst said when I finally got into analysis was that I needed to hire someone to do the cleaning. Analysts rarely advise, but in this case he picked up on my exhaustion and wondered out loud why I was cleaning the toilets. (The theme of the anality of terrorism returns.) A good question. Later I saw that it was literally punishment for all the shit I was expected to take.

In retrospect, I probably should have been on an antidepressant during the four-day-a-week analysis. It was that painful. But at that time antidepressants were frowned on by psychoanalysts. So I persevered although the pain I voiced was not heard. My analyst finally did help me greatly with the paranoia I had absorbed while living with my parents; yet my analyst never named the Man without Empathy as having a problem. At least, I never heard him name it as such. Remarkable that such rage could remain so overlooked, so hidden. Yet this is the case with terrorism. The person who has or holds the truth is the real victim but is never listened to because the listener could be the next in line to be attacked. Thus, the truth falls on deaf ears.

Visions of Blindness

I had my own rage, which was why I was phobic. I had turned the wrath inwardly, against myself. In the analysis, I began to unpack my rage. More than once while turning the knob of the door to my analyst's waiting room, I felt like I was walking into a blast furnace because of the white-hot anger I felt. My unconscious rage had finally come to the surface, and I could begin to explore and understand it in order to mourn the loss and let go of it. According to the famous Cypriot Turkish psychoanalyst, Vamik Volcan, the need to hate and the need to have an enemy are in place by age three.[23] I had learned to hate. I hate no one now; nor do I need to fight someone else's battles.

As the analysis progressed, I admitted to having felt so under surveillance as a child that I took to poking out the eyes of smoked fish whenever it was served at home. Those fish eyes were the accusatory eyes of my mother, who scolded and criticized me endlessly because nothing I did was ever good enough.

Eyes carry a special meaning in Arab Muslim culture. The eyes tell. They are the communicators of accusation and shame. Think about it: In both Israeli Jewish culture and Arab culture, the *hamsa,* meaning "five," is often represented as a hand with an eye in it, like on the American dollar bill. The hamsa is supposed to offer protection from the harm-bringing evil eye. There is the Egyptian saying "to break his eye," meaning to humiliate someone, and forced sodomy has been a tool of choice for those in power in the Arab region throughout the ages"[24] The sons of Tamerlane, a conqueror who reigned from 1370 to 1405, blinded one another. An Afghan mother was blinded by her son because he had been shamed by her. And a captive was killed when molten silver was poured into his eyes. An Arab, Afghan, or Pakistani man will throw acid in a woman's face to punish her for shaming him. Such is the power of seeing and admonition.

While some may argue that hearing is more important in Islam, I take issue with that because the eye is intimately connected to shame; hence Arab honor and the spilling of blood. Sharif Kanaana's essay on The Arab Ear and the American Eye: A Study of the Role of the Senses in Culture [25] argues that the Arab ear takes precedence over the American eye. Instead I suggest that vision is key to understanding the violence because nonverbal behavior is created by the horrifying imagery, such as beheadings, that we see, engraving terror into our memories. I was drawn to studying sight because of the chaotic graphic imagery of the suicide attack site. Kanaana does not explore the role of hearing in the suicide attack, which would be of considerable importance. Nor does he draw attention to the fact that in Islam the father whispers the *Shahada,* the proclamation of faith, into the ear of a newborn. His analysis concerning hearing seems to be lacking. Moreover when the baby is first born, he or she smells, touches, and sees a bit. The senses are entwined. The Muslims also cup their hands to their ears as if wanting to be heard during prayer. This simple ritual gesture shows us how terribly complex the role of the senses is. In fact I would argue that smell is even more important than sight, as it results from the first cranial nerve to develop in the brain. Smell can take you back in a flash to a memory or a trauma. However it is extremely difficult to study smell, which as of now cannot be communicated to us through pictures (except for scratch and sniff) or to a limited extent by the computer. You would have to experience a suicide attack first hand to feel the impact of the smell of burning flesh. Perhaps you remember how people described the smell of the Twin Towers attack of 9/11. So the eye continues to be extremely powerful, even though Kanaana claims that hearing is more important.

When a person is "attacking" in attitude or gesture, he is disclosing his envy and overwhelming feelings of being inadequate and incompetent. It is a strategy to protect a fragile self from shaming. Author Nonie Darwish notes that *hasad* or, as she translates it, envy was the one thing that children were constantly reminded of when they were growing up in Gaza and Egypt—that one should never arouse envy in the other; otherwise they would be attacked. The Quran also noted that to cause envy was a bad thing.

In her book *Now They Call Me Infidel*, Darwish gives the following memory to explain *hasad*: [26]

> *On our last train trip back to Gaza—when I was eight years old — the treasure I carried back was a very special birthday gift from my father and mother, a gold necklace and bracelet inscribed with verses from the Koran and blue beads to protect against the "evil eye." As on all the other trips, my mother lectured us about how we must not show off our gifts to other children in Gaza or brag about our trips to Cairo. Any show of pride might provoke envy. My mother and grandmother continually reminded us what the Koran says about*

hasad, which is envy. The evil eye from others, we were told, can take away the good things in life that God gives. I often saw the old men squatting in the marketplace fingering their blue beads. And now I had the blue beads to protect me as well.

The two things we feared most were the evil eye and Jews. As a child, I was not sure what a Jew was. I had never seen one. All I knew was they were monsters. They wanted to kill Arab children, some said, to drink their blood. I was told never, ever, take candy or fruit from a stranger. It could be a Jew trying to poison me."

In shame–honor cultures, accusers and those deeply riddled with shame do not look you straight in the eye. Some politically correct anthropologists claim that it is simply a cultural habit not to look someone in the eye. But refraining from looking into another's eyes also provides a psychological function by which shame can be avoided and denied and perhaps even "normalized" under the obscene term of "cultural practice."'

Arab Muslims have both endorsed and institutionalized honor killing in clan and tribal culture, with certain Muslim clergy on occasion issuing *fatwas*, legal rulings, to justify this form of killing as an antidote to male shame. Arab Muslims and others believe that they invented shame and victimhood. While there are important differences between Arab terrorists and those Arabs who commit honor killing, honor killing is nonetheless domestic violence—intimate terrorism. The top police officer in Scotland[27] was interviewed as stating that there are many parallels between domestic violence and political terrorism. However, he failed to establish how they are intimately linked. Domestic violence and political terrorism are not two separate categories. Rather these violences work together synergistically to compound and enhance the threat of terror. If there were no child abuse experienced early in the bonding with the mother and no misuse of the baby as the mother's pathological narcissistic object, there is a good possibility that we would have a lot less political violence and Islamic suicide attacks. The maternal relationship is the platform for the violence.

Islamic terrorism works well because it taps into the deep, unconscious level of domestic violence, with which Westerners are more familiar, but which they also find very hard to talk about and deal with. It is the complementarity of terrorism that further compounds and horrifies, immobilizing witnesses and transforming bystanders into passive terrorists through identification with the aggressor. It is not just that domestic violence is intimate terrorism and works exactly like political terrorism's suicide attack. The two are synergistic, reinforcing and compounding trauma.[28] They are interlocking terrorisms that cannot be separated into neat, abstract linguistic categories of domestic violence vs. political violence. The unconscious mind does not work that way.

Violence does not care how we humans label it. The shared commonality of being murdered by one of your own—the dovetailing of domestic violence's murder–suicide with the suicide bomber's murder–suicide—is among the deepest of human terrors. In fact, in 2008 the Centre for Social Cohesion published a research essay entitled Crimes of the community: Honor-based Violence in the United Kingdom by James Brandon and Salam Hafez, in which the authors quote Nazir Afzal:[29] "If you had a map of the UK showing the location of Islamist groups—or terrorist cells—and you had another map of honor-based violence and you overlaid them you would find that they were a mirror image; they would be almost identical. It could be that this is simply where the South Asians live—or it could be something else—it could suggest that there is a strong link between these two attitudes."

I followed up by email and asked British Police Officer Afzal, Director of the Division for Honor Killing (which should really be called the Division of Honor Murder), if he saw any relation or connection between honor killing and suicide bombing. He emailed me back: "I recognize the links myself but am wary of discussing them further without hard evidence." I shared his reply with Rachel Pain, an expert on domestic violence, who wrote me that "One wonders what would constitute hard evidence?" Do you have to have dead bodies in order to "prove" the relationship and interlocking connection between honor killing and suicide bombing? Such is the frightening nature of the phenomenon of violence that even law enforcement struggles to consider the similarities in unconscious yet highly concrete lethal behavior. Like coinciding circles, political violence coincides with crimes of the community such as honor killing and domestic violence.

Just like turning on a computer, the Islamic suicide attack boots up these early terrors associated with the maternal bond. This is its hidden global maternal circuit. As *The New York Times Magazine* article said of Zakaria Moussaoui, the Al Qaeda terrorist who wanted to fly planes but didn't care about learning how to take off or land, "Everyone has a mother." [30] By coincidence, Moussaoui had been taking flying lessons in Eagen, Minnesota, about ten minutes from my home.

Ironically, it was shortly after he was detained that I nearly spit out my coffee while reading the morning edition of the *St. Paul Pioneer Press*. The article mentioned a charter school named Tariq Ibn Ziyad, also located near Eagen. I knew few people would recognize Ziyad as the North African Muslim military commander who invaded Spain in 711 AD! The choice of his name to grace this private, though state-funded, Muslim school was not exactly like naming the school after the Islamic equivalent of Horace Mann. It was more on the order of Hitler. Ultimately the school was shut down for a series of violations. Yet his name is still used for some educational institutions in Minnesota.

Tarik Ibn Ziyad had no empathy for his men. And the Man without Empathy persisted in denying his rage as if he were Tarik. Instead it came out sideways in passive–aggressive as well as overt mean-spirited acts. My trauma of having been raised under brutal maternal surveillance and being the obsessive object of hatred fit perfectly with my eye doctor husband. Eye doctors, who are highly venerated in Muslim culture, are notoriously emotionally blind, and in many instances emotionally blunted. Ayman Al-Zawahiri, Al Qaeda's number two man, is an eye doctor. So are Bashar Assad, president of Syria, who has been committing mass murder of his own and pretending everything is fine, and Abdullah Abdullah, the candidate who ran against Karzai for president in Afghanistan. Not all eye doctors are malignant, of course. Abdullah Abdullah was not. However, they often have limited insight. They believe that by knowing the mechanics of vision they themselves can see clearly. This is like thinking that freedom of the body is the same as freedom of the mind. Political freedom is not necessarily psychological freedom. Often they see nothing and remain sadists. Moreover, in jihadi culture they are attracted to one-eyed leaders like Mullah Omar and Belmoktar, one of the most dangerous leaders in the Sahara. In Arabic the term for one-eyed is "laaouar," often given as a nickname. One-eyed leaders have a particular charisma for their followers, who project their own defective selves onto the leader's defect, thus purging themselves of their self-hatred.

Eye infections and blindness aside, it is the hostile gaze of power and control that affects us most deeply. The Man without Empathy once told me in passing that when he was a child he had had an operation to fix his crossed eyes. Some doctor told him he could never be an eye surgeon, but he didn't listen to authority and became one anyway. Yet he never had the capacity to wonder whether his sadism and voyeurism were outgrowths of his rage over his early defective sense of self. Granted, it was a hunch I had, but it certainly seemed to fit. He was filled with shame but denied it, and so he heaped his rage on the closest female to hate, namely me.

This kind of vicious rage exceeds murder itself. Often the body of the female is destroyed in some way. The male perpetrator feels so totally dependent on his mother, and so shamed by his dependence that the mother's stare feels accusatory, causing even more shame. Vision and the maternal gaze even cause some men to blind their victims by gouging out their eyes. How convenient that eye doctors should be able to remove eyes without ever having to deal with their hidden rage.

It struck me many years later that the Man without Empathy's eye department was not really an assemblage of ophthalmologists, but a peculiar kind of group whose bonding seemed cultish. I think now that ophthalmologists and terrorists are trained alike. Both have a narrow way of seeing things. Eye doctors look through a lens the size of a quarter all day long. Like terrorists, they suffer from tunnel vision and are dogmatic and inflexible. While this may be an over-simplification and run the risk of stereotyping, there might be a kernel of truth in this parallel.

They had the charismatic leader who was so stingy and cheap that everyone joked about it, but it was no joke. The Man without Empathy would talk about how the leader would bemoan the fact that he had a "little dick." I was horrified that he would mention this to me; it sounded so perverse on his part. I did not need to know this. The Man without Empathy seemed to feel bigger by putting down his boss, who was allegedly his friend! It did not surprise me to learn that the daughters of this former department chair were divorcing. I surmised it was most likely because of similar issues of power, control, and passive–aggressive, sadomasochistic behavior. They had probably married men like their father, stingy with money, hence stingy with emotions—i.e., no empathy.

Midway through my own analysis, I asked that the Man without Empathy also be given a referral to an analyst. The Man without Empathy had once confessed to me that he thought his psychiatry and burn unit rotations in medical school were the most disturbing he had had. Could his experiences in the burn unit have evoked thoughts of immolation and fire because of his undisclosed, unconscious rage? An obsessed person harbors an extreme terror of death and projects that terror onto his unwitting victim. Did the Man without Empathy sense something was wrong with himself but was either unable or unwilling to seek help?

So the Man without Empathy saw an analyst (not mine), but came back after only one visit and declared that he was fine—that the analyst also claimed I was the problem, not him. I was just too busy. Once again I was blamed. What I did not realize at the time was that my Jewish male analyst had identified with my Jewish husband, and together they denied my reality. In fact, the four psychoanalytic candidates who had the same training analyst as I did all divorced after they ended their analyses. It seemed that the bonding between couples and the earlier maternal attachments were not really addressed in these therapies.

So my analysis became a folie à deux between my analyst and my husband. Years later an expert on violence and abuse told me that there must have been extensive gaslighting going on throughout my analysis, although I couldn't see it at the time. The Man without Empathy blamed me repeatedly as having the same problems my family did, but he was the one creating them. I was in a horrible position.

As psychoanalyst Karl Menninger said, there is a little murder and suicide in each of us. The vast majority would rather vicariously engage in actual murder, or soul murder, through "passive terrorism," as Tawfik Hamid has put it. And Hamid should know as he was a former member of the militant Egyptian *al-Gama'a al-Islamiyya*, an Islamic fundamentalist group that is considered a terrorist organization. He also graciously wrote a blurb for my first book. Like the *ummah,* the Muslim community, my analyst had unwittingly engaged in passive terrorism. Given that he admitted that I had had a truly terrible childhood, he should have wondered how it was possible for me to have avoided repeating the pattern in my marriage, especially since I had married so young. It would have been nearly impossible to have married differently or better. My analyst should have known that I was being abused. He did not want to hear, like all the others. To paraphrase what the bad boy of psychoanalysis, Jeffrey Moussaieff Masson, said about the "talking treatment," an analysis is not like a car, where if there is a problem, you can just recall it. My analysis was effective only to a certain degree. The core problem of early maternal attachment that translated into traumatic bonding in partner relationships was not really addressed. But in defense of the usefulness of analysis, I probably was not ready to "go there." Analysis can only do so much.

An Autistic Memory

In my book *The Banality of Suicide Terrorism,* I surmised, along with my colleague Professor Norm Simms, who is skilled in both literature and psychoanalysis, that terrorists probably suffer from something like a malignant form of Aspergers, that they are autistic. I even wrote about this to Professor Simon Baron Cohen, (a first cousin of Sasha Baron Cohen of the movie Borat fame), a leading expert on autism. He did not wish to address this kind of malignancy in association with autism. It seemed to me that it was too sensitive an issue, if not politically incorrect. Another colleague recently told me that when she mentioned autism in her writing on terrorist behavior she received hate mail.[31] To the best of my knowledge, Cohen does not mention it in his writings, though the Unabomber, Cho, Breivik, Lanza, Loughner, and Nidal Hassan were said to be high-functioning Aspergers, and they murdered a lot of people. This got me thinking about a striking autistic memory I had during my analysis. An autistic memory precedes awareness of language and words. It is a recollection that remains on the periphery of memory, remembered by a sense or a combination of senses. I wrote about the memory in my first book. But it comes up now in the context of being under parental paranoid surveillance and not being completely aware of it, and how being embedded in a household of paranoia tunes one into bodily perceptions in a peculiar way. One is always on high alert and yet it cannot be discussed openly for fear of causing more violence.

And so it was that during one analytic session I had a powerful autistic memory that constituted an early traumatic experience. I recalled the terrifying image of a woman lying lifeless on a carpeted floor with a telephone cord wrapped around her neck. It was a rotary dial phone, and its cord was covered in black fabric. I had not thought about this consciously before, yet I described it in alarming detail to my analyst. After months of working to put the image into context, we surmised that when I was about three years old and barely speaking, my father took me to visit his older sister, Alice, who had attempted to strangle herself with a telephone cord. Alice had been the family scapegoat, the biblical Azazel, ostracized for years for being crazy. In fact, the family was terrified and in denial of its own mental illness. Later I was told that my Aunt Alice was schizophrenic—a common diagnosis back then for women who had been sexually abused. Rather than murder Aunt Alice they created a suicidal zone where she felt unsupported and tried to kill herself.

In my opinion, the Middle Eastern honor killing culture is actually a cover-up for incestuous feelings, if not incest itself. It is common knowledge that many Arabs who are practicing Muslims rape their sisters and then murder them under the guise of honor killings. In Arab culture, the only female boys can touch growing up is their mothers, so they develop an obsession with their sisters, whom they allegedly do not and cannot touch. But the boys are so privileged that they have no physical boundaries. All is fair game.

At the time of the incident I had no idea that Alice was my aunt. I only knew that I looked like her, just as I looked like my dead "twin" brother. I took my aunt's place as the family scapegoat. They tried to make me out to be crazy like Alice.

The theme of the telephone cord ran throughout my life like a tenuous thread or umbilicus, and it manifested as a phobia. I could use a phone only under certain conditions. To call people to ask for something I needed was nearly impossible for years. I also experienced surges of anxiety and would nearly have a panic attack if I had to receive an incoming phone call. I continued to have an ambivalent relationship to telephones and telephone calls. Yet this autistic memory and the telephone cord helped me understand the inherently autistic nature of the terrorist's attachment to hard objects as maternal replacements. They bond to hard objects such as computers. They suffer from an attachment disorder and do not know how to relate to people in a nonviolent way because they are terrified of people.

This is not because, as some psychologists who have talked to terrorists suggest and would like to believe, terrorists are suffering from post traumatic stress disorder and that is what makes them suicide bombers. On the contrary, that is a simplistic reading of the psychopathology that overlooks the nature of the devalued female in their culture and its ramifications for disorganized attachment leading to violence. These researchers are not adequately trained in reading terrorists' nonverbal communication and the graphic, violent psychotic imagery. This violence is, in large part, the result of a very compromised maternal attachment in the earliest years. There is probably a panoply of other issues involved, such as genetics, and even brain development.

When I started my psychotherapy practice in November 1989, I did not have a problem handling the phone when my patients were involved. The phobia harked back to my own maternal separation issues, lack of freedom, and struggle for self-expression. The telephone cord was an unwanted, intrusive connection, which hooked into being forced into a merger with the maternal figure. If I could be in control, in reality or fantasy, of when I wanted to merge, that was a different story. But if it were forced on me, it was terrifying.

It is hard to describe the texture of an autistic memory, perhaps because it is preverbal and because one can become so unconsciously attached to it. I also wrote in a published essay that in addition to the trauma of the autistic memory I experienced a cognitive dissonance within it. What had I actually seen? What had my senses taken in? Was this memory a crime scene? Was the crime a murder or suicide? My father never explained what had happened. The family never talked about it or about Aunt Alice. She was yet another phantom in the family.

Many years later, I began to realize that the experience had also been the seed of my interest in understanding suicide terrorism. Was there something unspoken about this near death, in which a family has its own suicidal zone created by its enmeshed members, with one person designated to be the scapegoat and carrier of the family's rage? Enmeshment means that no one in the family has boundaries, and that they will use the other in inappropriate, abusive ways. Everything has a psychosexual facet, as well. Sexual abuse comes with enmeshment, which is an aspect of traumatic bonding because there are no healthy psychological boundaries. There is no privacy or independence. In other words, could a family create the unspoken conditions under which one of its members is sacrificed through passive–aggressive behavior and denial and create a murder zone? This is what I wondered about my Aunt Alice, and about suicide bombers and their groups. I wondered, too, about the siblings of the suicide bombers and if they understood how their brothers or sisters had been killed off, murdered in cold blood by their very own. Then, again, in Arab culture where Islam has forced out all other religions, one encounters the honor killing. Why is it that the religion of peace has not been able to rein in the perpetration of this crime against its own women? Not to do so is to participate in the problem, at the very least passively.

Vicarious Rage

Because my son played ice hockey, I became a passionate Minnesota ice hockey mom. It has been said that of all sports, ice hockey is the most controlling of its opponent, primarily because the opponent is the feminized other put under surveillance and hemmed in. Ice hockey is also a dangerously aggressive sport. Sharp skates nearly beheaded Canadian goaltender Clint Malarchuk and Florida Panthers star Richard Zednik, whose throats were slit by a blade. Think also of the aggression of Zarqawi, the Al Qaeda leader in Iraq who went on a rampage of beheadings after he observed the Islamic mourning period of forty days for his beloved mother. (In Judaism one mourns for thirty days and, yes, this concept was borrowed by the prophet Muhammad for Islam.)

I readily admit that I could vicariously experience and understand aggression through my son's hockey games. The downside was that as "Mom," I was not supposed to enjoy it. I confess that when my son was in high school, he asked me not to yell during the games because he (and everyone else) could hear me down on the ice. I was supposed to remain in a position of shame, without agency even to speak out, shout, or curse a blue streak. The men and fathers could do that but not the mothers. It was reminiscent of the consequences for unladylike behavior that had been drilled into me growing up. I was to have no life. I was like an enraged Arab Muslim woman venting my rage at the enemies, the opponents at these hockey games, and I was being reprimanded for it. Ranting at ice hockey games seemed to be a way to experience power, paralleling the behavior of the Palestinian women who fight their men's battles. Every time I see Arab women going to protest with their men in Gaza, I think of them having a socially acceptable outlet for their show of rage against the "bad" Israelis. Some enraged Arab Muslim and highly identifiable Palestinian Christian women like Hanan Ashrawi join in fighting the men's battle and in their hatred. This strategy merely deflects rage that is not being dealt with at home, because the women are essentially powerless, though they themselves may believe that they are not. The culture shapes the rage and makes it "socially acceptable" to blame the other. Yet the externalization and projection of the rage doesn't really deal with the core issue of inequality and abuse in the home.

CHAPTER 6

Seeking A Rebirth

My analysis lasted eight and a half years, with sessions four days a week. My analyst said one especially important thing that helped: He told me that I had had my own personal Holocaust. Mine had lasted until I managed to leave home for college, but the effects of the early defective attachment to my mother and its attendant trauma would linger for a lifetime. The perpetration of the abuse by my mother left me nearly psychologically destroyed. To paraphrase the title of a book on traumatic attachment written by psychologist H.L. Schwartz, I survived a peculiar alchemy between a she-wolf, my mother, and me as a sacrificial sheep.[32] The Chechens' national anthem venerates the she-wolf, which I find problematic because the other is free game to be targeted.[33]

I finished the analysis but remained in marital bondage because my analyst had missed the abuse going on in the marriage, and I had not been ready to confront the terrorism of this basic source of murderous rage. Instead, my analyst interpreted nearly everything in light of my childhood. When I told him that my husband had raped me and repeatedly accused me of infidelity and betrayal, always throwing everything back in my face, my analyst did not hear me. The only time I had been with another man was when I had broken up with the Man without Empathy, desperately wanting out of the relationship. The first time I told my analyst about my husband's obsession with infidelity, he tried to put a good spin on the rape, implying that my husband should be flattered that I had returned to him after "checking out the goods of another guy." He did not recognize the traumatic bonding. My analyst completely dismissed the severity of my husband's delusion and that he had the capacity to kill me. Even if I had been unfaithful, which was not the case, how could it justify the Man without Empathy's years of berating me? Years of accusing me of being a whore? And what of his years of broken promises? Were they not the ultimate betrayal?

When I terminated the analysis, I felt I had achieved much from the experience. I was shocked when six months later my analyst was dead—from eye cancer, of all coincidences. He had told me that he had a malignant eye tumor and was undergoing special treatment. The Man without Empathy never bothered to explain that it was a deadly cancer and that most likely my analyst would die in the near future. He probably was privately relieved to have my analyst out of the picture because during my analysis he was somewhat under surveillance as well. A prominent woman analyst told me at a meeting of the American Psychoanalytic Association that I was lucky my analyst allowed me to terminate when he did. It made his death less of a trauma. Still it was a huge loss. It reminded me of the death of my dissertation adviser at the University of Minnesota, which had happened only two years earlier while I was in the midst of writing my dissertation. It compounded my grief.

My dissertation advisor was one of the world's leading authorities on the Moriscos, the Spanish medieval Muslims who were forced converts to Catholicism. It is the topic of a popular novel *The Hand of Fatima*. My dissertation advisor did not want to train me initially because I was a woman and a Jew, but I knew that he had to because I had the credentials and was training at a federal- and state-funded university. He was obligated but he took his time. However, as he lay dying of a blood disorder called primary amyloidosis, which is more prevalent among the Mediterranean gene pool, I took to visiting him every ten or so days. It was what Judaism had taught me, *bikur kholim*, visit the sick.

The prophet Muhammad also borrowed this concept of visiting the sick and called it 'iyaadah. The prophet Muhammed also had borrowed all of the Five Pillars of Islam from the Jews, with the hope that the Jews would convert. When that didn't happen, he launched his new geopolitical strategy called Jihad, or the other face of the religion of peace. The martial shoe dropped. In January 2013, I gave a lecture at the Diplomatic Institute in Bucharest, and when I mentioned this the head of the institute started to protest vigorously that I had it all wrong. Fortunately, the Israeli ambassador to Romania, Dan Ben Eliezer, was sitting on the dais next to him and supported my well-documented assertion. Could unacknowledged indebtedness on the part of Islam to Judaism be another part of the problem? Debt is a reminder of maternal dependency, according to Muriel Dimen, 1994.[34] Are Jews asking too much of Islam and Muslims to recognize their Judaic roots? Allow me to extend the metaphor of mother–son for the sake of argument: Should the Judaic mother demand of her Muslim son such gratitude? But gratitude can never be coerced; it must be of one's own volition. Cast in the role of Early Mother but blind to it, Judaism and Jews may be looking for recognition in all the wrong places.

One day as I was leaving my advisor's home, I turned to his wife and asked if there was a need for me to give blood. He had been undergoing blood transfusions following an amputation. (Think body parts and Sharia law's punishment by amputation.) I gave blood. When I returned the following week, my adviser and his wife practically considered me family. I was a bit stunned because I had not realized what I had intuitively done. Blood, like the eye, has a very special meaning in the Middle East. The concept of *nasab* establishes the relationship with one's father through the bloodline. *Nasab* "determines everything from whom a woman can sit with unveiled to rights of inheritance."[35] In a way, my giving blood had allowed my terminally ill adviser to cleanse his honor from the shame and humiliation of being so sick with "defective" blood, albeit oddly enough with the blood of a Jewish woman. This experience helped me to understand that in Arab culture you must willfully spill blood to cleanse honor because you have been shamed. For Jews it is different. We have moved to the stage developmentally that we do not have to literally spill blood when shamed. There is the Talmud expression that says "Shaming another in public is *like* shedding blood." In Arab culture, there is the saying "Blood demands blood."

Indeed, the gesture that I made by giving blood moved my advisor's family to invite me to eulogize him at his funeral. I was deeply honored. Prior to his death, Professor Chejne asked me to present at a prestigious conference in his place in Tunisia. Unbeknownst to me, the conference was funded by the Saudis, and out of 300 people I was the only Jew. I do remember that the invitation was embossed in gold. The women were assigned hotel roommates since as females we could not have our own privacy. My roommate was a prominent professor of Spanish and a known member of the PLO terrorist organization. She nearly threw up when I said that I had studied at The Hebrew University in Jerusalem. Moreover, her "commandant," Generalissimo Yasir Arafat, was ensconced in La Marsa, a suburb of Tunis a few miles from the hotel. I will never forget the vicious stare of one of the Tunisian conference organizers, who was horrified that a Jew was contaminating the conference. He looked like a member of the Muslim Brotherhood and probably was.

Psychoanalysis Training, Another Cult

After I completed my PhD, I was eligible to apply to the Chicago Institute of Psychoanalysis. Back then, Minnesota did not have its own psychoanalytic institute, and the only two training analysts in the Twin Cities were in the middle of a feud. Another analyst had sued my analyst for restraint of trade. Years later this analyst, whom I always thought was nuts, had a psychotic break and was forced to surrender his license. It was all very sad. By comparison, the Chicago Institute of Psychoanalysis was world renowned. It was founded by Franz Alexander, a Hungarian physician–analyst from the Berlin Psychoanalytic Institute who was a founder of psychoanalytic *criminology* and the study of psychosomatic illness. I stress criminology because I came to decode the Islamic suicide attack site as a crime scene.

When I was accepted in 1984, I became the first non-medical, non–mental health, humanities-trained candidate commuting to the institute from Minnesota. Plus, I was female, Jewish, and a nonresident of Chicago. By definition I had many strikes against me. Mine was a small class of five—three women and two men. The training and supervising analysts at the orientation cocktail party boasted how our class was the first in which women outnumbered men, but in the end only the men prevailed politically. Of the three women, I am the only one who is alive today. That is sobering. The male training analysts were narcissistic and some were downright mean, probably destructive borderlines. I could scarcely believe that they could be therapists! I was very naïve. One or two female training analysts made the males look like pussycats; they were so vicious and envious of other women. These female training analysts gave new meaning to women's inhumanity to women. They had been completely co-opted by the male structure and reminded me of the Arab mothers ululating on the street, fighting their males' gender wars like the destructive queen bees they were.

Training was a long, drawn-out process lasting many years. I commuted between St. Paul and Chicago every other weekend, leaving on Thursday evening and returning on Saturday afternoon. I also taught full-time, was expected to see patients, and was raising my children, then five and eight years old. The Man without Empathy felt greatly humiliated that he had to stay home while I went to Chicago. He always complained about me spending the money even though I worked to pay my own way. He felt infuriated when he would go to the grocery store and run into suburban stay-at-home mothers who would ask him what he was doing there. Yet he recognized that having a wife train as an analyst worked to his advantage because it made him look "normal" mentally; it provided him cover. Besides, he liked that I was still bringing home a paycheck.

While I loved the psychoanalytic training itself, I did not like the politics or the way in which the institute was run. Nevertheless, I enjoyed enormously the intellectual exchange and friendship with my classmates. I am still in contact with the two who are still alive. One is now president of the institute and nurtured our tiny class with a supply of M&Ms. However, it was very hard for a woman. There was no grievance procedure, no ethics committee back then, and every problem was analyzed as the fault of the female candidate in training. The institute was another cult, reminiscent of Christian Science and my pseudo family doctor, Uncle Willy. At that time I could not articulate this ruthless and denied aggression. There was really no venue in which to present a reasonable complaint concerning unjust discriminatory practices because you were summarily pathologized. A real catch-22.

The institute was the consummate good ol' boys club, made worse perhaps because it was dominated by physicians who hated that psychologists, social workers, and even a non-mental health professional like myself (let alone female) were now infiltrating their ranks. In fact, one of the more senior candidates sodomized his control case, a woman patient who was the close friend of his classmate. I reported him to the Minnesota State Medical Board. No one else did. The Chicago Institute investigated independently from the state medical board and allegedly "rehabilitated" this candidate physician. He was allowed to graduate and continues to practice to this day. *Ein Din ve-ein Dayan*, Hebrew for "There is no Judge nor Justice." Here was a glimpse of psychoanalytic politics as its worst, with the female paying the price. If this happens in Western culture one can only imagine that it is twenty times worse in Arab Muslim society where women get sexually harassed on a bus riding to work or raped by a mob.

While the institute was extremely strong in certain areas, especially Heinz Kohut's theory of narcissism (he taught there and was one of the prima donnas of narcissism), it was weak in other areas, especially in the psychopathology of the perpetrator or predator rather than the victim. British Object Relations—the school of psychoanalytical thought founded by the Jewish émigré to Britain, psychoanalyst Melanie Klein, who developed the study of objects to communicate nonverbally and symbolically—was barely taught at all when I went through my training. Klein should be considered the "code cracker" of terrorist behavior, a psychoanalytic cryptologist, so to speak. I am now in the process of writing a dictionary called *The Dictionary of Desperanto* that looks at terrorist behavior from the point of view of her theory—focusing on the symbolic meaning of the terrors of the terrorist, how they use and misuse objects (like confusing hard cooked rice with stones) and how they project their terrors and manipulate verbal language, which is very concrete and literal, in conjunction with their nonverbal behavior. We are nothing more than objects to terrorists.

As I studied Klein's work on my own, I saw that it was perfectly suited to the study of terrorism because it deals with paranoia, delusional thinking that harbors a developmental cognitive deficit, aggression, terrors, and an extreme lack of empathy. Paranoia is about the mother-infant relationship. The mother grew up a devalued female and experiences her baby as attacking her because she feels so depleted. This, in turn, risks a poor maternal attachment, coupled possibly by the developmental lack of mirror neurons necessary for empathy. Counterterrorist experts have given little thought to what Margaret Mahler called the psychological birth of the infant. We often make the assumption that everyone cognates or thinks at the same level. This is not the case. Consider the Bell Curve. Maybe less than ten percent are to the right of it and exhibit fuller, more optimal thinking and feeling, coupled with a sense of empathy.

I came to contemplate and research the terrors of the terrorist in light of early childhood development. I discovered that the early years of development, the most critical for the child's brain and building cognitive capacity, was not on the radar screen in counterterrorism studies. Thus, a blind spot exists that causes the experts to unwittingly collude with the terrorists through countertransference, which is experienced by a psychotherapist during the course of treatment. It is the psychotherapist's reactions to the patient's transference and involves a complex of feelings toward the patient. The idea of countertransference can be applied to the interview, which counterterrorists pride themselves on. Yet they conduct the interviewing process and even their research without an awareness of the workings of the unconscious. The Hebrew term for blind spot is called a "dead field," which aptly points to an area that cannot be explored critically. In short, countertransference causes collusion with the terrorist. It is a critical area in the topology of terror.

Later I realized why Klein understood paranoia so well. Her generation of psychoanalysts experienced war first hand. Fairbairn, another founding theorist of Object Relations, is often pictured in his military uniform; he served under General Allenby in the Palestinian campaign from January 1915 to October 1918, then went on to medical school and psychoanalytic training. He developed the idea of the splitting of the ego. This gives us black-and-white thinking, or people like Adolf Hitler or Eichmann, who could compartmentalize their destructiveness and not deal with paradoxes. Then there was Bion, a great thinker on group psychodynamics and a decorated British WWI tank commander, who came up with the theory of the working group and the regressed, fused destructive clan like terrorist groups, His memoirs demonstrate how he learned to work in groups and understand their unique dynamics. I have been in the closed quarters of a Bradley personnel carrier where you experience group dynamics in a profound way. Some may disagree with that, but when the U.S. Army at Fort Leonard Wood found out about my work, they told me that a British special forces commander for one of the outfit's multinational missions had made the same argument I did—that Islamic suicide terrorism is a form of domestic violence's murder–suicide dressed up in the myth of martyrdom. This commander just never wrote anything about it.

I was the first to propose and develop a link between the devalued female and the Islamic suicide attack and its symbolic meaning vis à vis family dynamics. This culminated in my book *The Banality of Suicide Terrorism*. Other shame–honor cultures, like the Japanese, also produced a similar phenomenon, the kamikazes. (Bin Laden named one of his training camps Islamikaze.) In fact it was written in their pilot manuals that they were not to fear death because when they were within meters of their target, the face of their mother would appear and they would be returning to her. This is a reenactment of the maternal fusion and a classic rebirth fantasy. The mother is over-idealized and the female is completely devalued. It is as if the mother is not even female. The terrorists cannot understand how they could be born from such a denigrated female body. How could a lowly female do something they can't do? Something so life-giving and powerful? Terrorists are terrified of their vulnerability and emotions. They are extremely dissociated from their behavior and traumas. We are only in the initial stages of understanding the phenomenon, but it has a lot to do with the first years of the terrorists' life as they bonded to their devalued abused mothers.

Özbek and Volkan[36] recall the Turkish saying that "Hell and Heaven lie at the feet of the mother." Yet Cebiroglu and his colleagues[37] countered that despite this the mother remains insignificant ". . .she is dominated and suppressed both socially and emotionally. The children are not considered as separate personalities, and complete obedience is expected of them. If they behave to the contrary they are severely punished. On account of the father's unapproachable authority, the children grow up clinging and dependent on their insignificant mother, and all these factors lead to a formation of constricted self."

Interestingly enough, while researching my theory for the suicide attack I discovered that psychoanalysis dealt just as poorly with the subject of domestic violence as it did with the female and gender issues. I realized that when review readers of one of my first articles on Osama Bin Laden criticized me for using the words "domestic violence"to described the shared template of the suicide attack's political violence and the murder–suicide in domestic violence. The elephant was in the room, and they couldn't see it due to denial and their own terrors. It was simply resistance on their part. Ultimately, I was forced to drop the phrase "domestic violence" if I wanted to get the essay published, which I did. It was a moment in which I chose to use "soft" power in the hope that one day I would not be censored. That was the case when I finally published *The Banality of Suicide Terrorism,* in which I used the template of domestic violence's murder–suicide freely.

Years previously, I had won the Eissler Prize for an essay on Freud and his concept of autonomy, which was published in the same journal in which I had been censored. Even then I was preoccupied with separation issues—independence and autonomy. The prize was the second juried prize I had received that carried a monetary award. I had received the Goldenberg Prize for a critical edition of a Ladino text that I had transcribed and written an essay about. Actually, it was the third juried prize for writing if you count the American Legion Prize that I won for writing an essay about experiencing the Abraham Lincoln Memorial in Washington DC. for the first time when I was in sixth grade. I wrote an impassioned twenty-six pager, again on the theme of slavery and emancipation, something to which I could relate. However, rather than congratulate me, my father denigrated my writing. I can only imagine what it must be like for little Afghan girls who want to write. I think it's a miracle I didn't stop writing, like I did speaking.

However, I could not enjoy the Eissler Prize and had to disavow myself the pleasure of the monetary stipend it carried. Rather than indulge myself, I gave my children the money. Back then I was the martyr. Martyrdom becomes engrained in you because the projection of being the chronically hated object becomes identified with doing something bad. You are like a lab rat running around on a treadwheel, having to make grandiose reparations for all those crimes you must surely have committed. While writing helped shore up a budding sense of confidence, it would be years before I would allow myself the pleasure of writing and publishing a book.

I graduated from the Chicago Institute of Psychoanalysis in the early 1990s as a research analyst but had acquired so many clinical hours that I qualified for a license as a marriage and family therapist in Minnesota. I could have chosen to be licensed as a psychologist or a social worker, but I chose family and marriage therapy, which resonated with the deep denial I was experiencing and which I intuitively wanted to understand. In addition, it was a newer field and I felt it would be more flexible concerning the kind of work and research I wanted to pursue.

The politics within the Minnesota analytic community were extremely disturbing, and training was all but impossible back then. I became so accomplished that I was asked to teach and train psychiatry residents in areas such as PTSD and how to listen to patients and understand their pain. I supervised a series of residents in psychotherapy. Having now acquired yet another identity, another academic "hat," I was eager to return to my other research interests and ultimately shifted into the field of counterterrorism. The Israelis have a saying in Hebrew: *Rak dagim metim sokhim im hazerem*, "Only dead fish swim with the current." That became my motto, and it made my life less of a struggle. Clearly I wanted to swim freely. In counterterrorism one has to think outside the box, yet it is equally important to "feel" outside the box. Just thinking persists being in denial through rationalizing. Seeing how I was born outside the box, this kind of thinking and feeling came easy to me. At times it was off putting and threatening to others. Why that was the case I still don't understand, although I feel it stems from their own terrors.

The Utility of Contempt

During my years of commuting between St. Paul and Chicago, the Man without Empathy broke his nose in a car accident he caused. He drove into the back of a truck in stop-and-go traffic on the interstate outside of Milwaukee en route to Chicago. It was a bit like a suicide bomber in an explosive-laden vehicle, only his bombs were his denied unconscious and externalized rage. It was during our first weekend vacation away from the kids in five years, which he always claimed we couldn't afford, and we were staying at a friend's house. Fortunately, I was not in the car. I had always told him he was a bad driver, but he constantly denied it, even blaming me for his bad driving. Because he related to me as an object, I became the garbage can into which he could throw his bad feelings about himself and instead attack me. (The Arabs have merely taken this one step further by pervasively blaming the Jews all the time.) Now I was able to validate my own perception about his driving. I couldn't be blamed for his accident because I wasn't in the car. This was an awakening of sorts.

It will be similar kinds of moments of clarity that will help abused Arab Muslim women regain control of their lives. However, here is the caveat. It is not enough just to stop blaming the other. Middle ground must be found. I say this because I am acutely concerned for my people, the Jews, since we are the scapegoat of the Middle East and at the eye of the conspiracy storm that they circulate. No matter how "emancipated" Arab women become, no matter how many seats they hold in the Consultative Assembly of Saudi Arabia, the Majlis as-Shura, they will never resolve their paranoia if they cannot make peace with us. The intergenerational transmission of hatred will persist. We are too easy to hate.

So the Man without Empathy broke his semitic nose but could not allow himself to fix it. Clearly he was enraged about it. He asked me repeatedly and anxiously if he should have a nose job, and I said it was entirely up to him. It was one of the few things he ever consulted me about. He had to stay locked into his sadomasochism.

I achieved a new-found sense of relief and freedom shortly after his accident because at some level it released me from his complete sadistic control. Sexual pleasure also was a bit better because I had contempt for him. A colleague of mine has written a paper on the utility of contempt. Psychologically, I was beginning to see myself apart from him. The Man without Empathy never once asked me if I enjoyed sex or explained to me what an orgasm was for a female, and he was a medical doctor. It was during the same time that he kept telling me that I could not see a therapist. Obviously, he did not want me to be happy. For the first ten years of the marriage, he just didn't care.

➤➤~ ⊙ ~➤➤

The Man without Empathy was not so different than those who force Somali and Arab Muslim girls, as well as a few Christian Arabs throughout North Africa and the Middle East, to undergo female genital mutilation to ensure they will never experience sexual pleasure. In Somali culture, it is the Isaaq clan, considered the warriors par excellence, that performs the most brutal form of female genital mutilation, taking all of the labia, and leaving almost nothing. The "surgery" is done by the grandmother. Have the women do the dirty work. I was told that it was outlawed by the State of Minnesota in 1994, but that it continues to be practiced illegally. Or the daughters are taken to clinics in Canada or Europe. In 1994, CNN aired an explicitly graphic segment on female genital mutilation, which helped to fight the practice. When I lived in Minnesota, I was told that Somali schoolgirls could tell who had undergone the barbarity of female genital mutilation by the sound of the urine stream in the bathroom stalls. There is no privacy in such a culture. Not being mutilated was a cause of great societal pressure and shaming.

According to El Feki in *Sex and the Citadel*, a 2008 survey in Egypt found that ninety percent of married women are genitally cut during the *tahara*, the purification. In Egypt they say "the circumcised woman is a woman with a broken wing." The clitoris is considered a protopenis and has to be cut out to preserve female chastity.[38] This does not even include discussion of the *dukhla*, Arab for "entry," literally the defloration of the bride's hymen, and how the white bedsheet of honor must be paraded around for all to see that she came to the marriage as a virgin. The *dukhla baladi,* or country style virginity test, is even debated within the culture as family-sanctioned rape. This is the ultimate sadistic control.

Later on when I confronted the Man without Empathy about my trouble achieving orgasm, he blamed me, saying it was my fault. I had been traumatized by the rape and abortion early on in the marriage. It also seemed to me to be cruelly unfair to make it out to be my fault when I finally became orgastic. Still, I was locked into the sadomasochism of the marital relations; it remained perverse traumatic bonding, a reflection and embodiment of traumatic bonding left over from childhood. It is well known that some children become violent through disrupted attachment. While I did not become violent, the Man without Empathy did. He also made a big deal of the fact that I had hit him once early in the marriage. The couple therapist did not put two and two together. After all, he had raped me and forced me into an abortion, then refused to let me see a therapist. None of this counted. I was the violent one, allegedly.

It is still not known what makes someone choose not to become violent. I remember early on in my childhood that I never wanted to be mean like my parents and brother. It was a conscious decision to be kind and generous, even though I did not consider myself naïve or looking at life through rose-colored glasses, despite still being in denial. I knew I was not Anne Frank. My attitude of forgiveness was a bit Christian was a bit Christian, but then again, I was raised that way. Nonetheless I remained vulnerable.

I was not a yeller, but the Man without Empathy accused me of that, too. Others would yell at me, like a long-time younger friend who tried to exploit me through a company she became involved in. I had even given her a bridal shower when no one in her family did that for her. The company was on the order of Tupperware. My friend wanted me to host a party to sell her products to my other friends. That's where I drew the line. I didn't like the idea of doing someone else's work. I found it offensive and pressuring and didn't want my other friends to feel pressured into buying. This young friend raged at me when I told her I would not host a party, although I had already bought several hundred dollars worth of products from her. People somehow had the idea that they could yell at me and try to take advantage of me. Like it was stamped on my forehead.

I often wonder if predators can smell terror. I asked Professor Stuart Firestein, who works on olfactory perception, and he said it was anecdotal. There is some work in counterterrorism on smell. We see it with bomb-sniffing dogs and other animals. There is a woman in Philadelphia named Pam Dalton at Monell Chemical Senses Center who designs "really bad smells to pump into cave hideouts and make them uninhabitable"[39]

The Man without Empathy even pointed out to me that one of my labia was scarred and torn, trying to make me feel defective. He did not say this with any kind of empathy but more on the order that I was damaged goods. Many years later I realized his intention. By seeing me as damaged goods, he could mistreat me. I was only a part-object to him, something for him to hate. He sought to subjugate me through this terroristic strategy: part object = body part.

I vaguely remember being molested by a swarthy handyman when I was very young in the old apartment on Kenmore near Loyola University in Chicago. The subject came up while I was in analysis. Many years later I went back to the apartment building and stared through the wrought-iron-gated courtyard entranceway at the nooks and crannies of the huge apartment building, surrounded by dark shrubbery. I was flooded with feelings and thoughts. My maternal Romanian grandfather, whom I had never known, was an artisan and designer of wrought iron. A family narrative was that he fashioned the wrought iron fence for the Canadian Parliament. He had died long ago and could not have helped me. I recalled the handyman perpetrator and even wondered if his swarthiness had caused me to gravitate toward studying Latin culture.

I knew that no narrative could ever adequately contain all the lessons learned about the psychodynamics of terrorism and its tenets from my lived experience. I did not directly experience a suicide bombing like John Tulloch's *Icons of War and Peace*. But then again even Tulloch didn't experience three suicide bombings like Maliha, the Afghan woman who did. No, it was not the shame of survival that bothered me so much now. Nor was it not being believed. Those feelings had subsided, along with trying to get my head around all of it. Now that I had become a *savta*, a grandmother, I felt more of a permanency to my existence, and it was without shame. It was my legacy.

Yet, it was because of the profound sense of forever being different and having to explain the degree to which I had struggled to become free that *I understand terrorism—through having lived it*. This inevitably differs from the majority of macho counterterrorist experts. Those who do feel they are different are reluctant to reflect upon it and reveal how it has shaped their lives. The Holocaust remains what I can relate to—a life apart filled with memories and the struggle to get out of the terrors. Yet I surmised that many of the macho counterterrorist experts know that they have their own shame of survival and terrors. My hunch is that even with denial there is a faint sense of knowing one's own motivations.

Name Change

Pursuing a name change is like getting a psychological tattoo for the heart. It is to ease the pain of having been denied an identity and hence forging one for one's self. After years of being told by my father that my maiden name was German, which was reinforced with his Nazi-like sadism, I discovered that my surname was actually Dutch Jewish while visiting my college roommate and her in-laws in Germany. Curious, I began to research my roots. The caretaker at the Portuguese Synagogue in Amsterdam told me to go into any bar in Amsterdam and ask for Hartevelt gin (the Dutch invented gin). I found bottles of it at Schipol Airport in the duty-free shop. It took the company several years to respond to my query, but eventually one of its representatives told me that Avraham Hartevelt had bought the distillery from the French in the 1730s. My father's middle name was Abraham.

Could my family be in part of Sephardic origin, descendants of the Spanish and Portuguese Jews who had fled to Holland from persecution in Spain? My father had dark hair and dark eyes and was also tall like the Dutch, rather big-boned and fair-skinned, more like a *Castellano*. I wondered about the *Ancestor Syndrome* of Anne Ancelin Schutzenberger,[40] where knowledge of the past generations' traumatic experience becomes encoded in one's family memory and narrative. I started to follow Dutch news.

My grounding in Sephardic culture proved to be very important for understanding terrorism since it was the point of departure into Islamic, Arab, and Muslim cultures. As I mentioned, the prophet Muhammad borrowed extensively from Judaism and those Jewish tribes living in Saudi Arabia because he wanted to convert them to Islam. Because of this, those Jews who lived in close proximity to the Arab Muslims and the North African Muslims knew Islam well. The intense relationship between these competing identities facilitated gaining access into the mentality of the Jihadis, whom you could characterize as an extreme of Islam. The Jews who lived in Muslim-dominated countries and did not feel safe used aliases to protect themselves. Of course, this is a different kind of name change, not for nefarious means like the Jihadis. There is one similarity about name changing even among Jihadis and Jews: It functions to shore up one's evolving identity, although the purposes behind the name change are very different. Jihadis do it in order to justify their rage within a religious frame, not to gain psychological or emotional independence as a mature adult.

In 1995 I decided to go to court and change the spelling of my maiden name from Hartenfeld to Hartevelt to grasp my ancestral roots, something that my father couldn't deny me, even by carrying through on his threat to disinherit me. Initially, I identified with the tolerance of Dutch history and society. However, now with the engulfment of Dutch culture by Islam this feeling has sadly diminished.

I personally took the name Hartevelt—a heart on a heraldic field—to mean heartfelt and caring. Okay, so it was part of my family romance, as Freud would call it. Yet these kinds of fantasies are common; everyone has a right to a family and a history. The sense of identity is so intimately bound to naming. Yet its obvious meaning can completely be overlooked. It can also provide a clue to a rageful, hostile personality, as in the case of the jihadis. Jews were not called by name but numbers by the Nazis. And while we all have social security numbers or identity numbers, they are not used in a murderous way like the Nazis did. What's in a name? Everything. In Arab culture, upon which Al Qaeda is modeled, the mother is named after the son. In a sense, she is married to him, not the father. It is striking how in Islam people continue to name their kids Jihad. While they might say that jihad really refers to an inner struggle rather than war, I do not buy into the deception. It unconsciously almost sanctifies a self-fulfilling prophecy for the child to grow up and be at war with the world.

It was a relief to modify the spelling of my own surname, to put something right. It was concrete, a piece of the puzzle that allowed me to regain a sense of identity from such facelessness and build a life for myself. I can understand why Muslim terrorists constantly use aliases and especially why terrorists convert to radical Islam. They have such fragile identities that they need to do what I did, but on a much grander jihadi scale. While my quest wasn't exactly the same thing, it was similar. It was my attempt to reconcile not fitting in, a search to achieve a more stable identity after having been fused, misused, and abused, and not being allowed to separate and grow up in a healthy way. The abuse bound me into an enmeshed family, which I carried over into an enmeshed marriage.

My name change was liberating, something of a rebirth. My accident in India the following year nearly cost me my chance at a new life.

CHAPTER 7

Separation From Husband: As Sadistic Father/Suffocating Mother

I went to India, a Hindu Muslim country, in February 1996 to participate in a conference on art and ethics in the third world and the exploitation of artisans by first-world artists who have their workshops in India because of cheap labor. I traveled with my closest friend from childhood, whom I will refer to as "she" rather than expose her by name. When you come from a dysfunctional family, you attempt to repair the primary relationships through friends or those people you have daily contact with outside the clan.

She was the sister I had never had, although in some ways I had gotten along much better with her younger sister, who had died several years earlier from breast cancer and who was loved by my kids. Unlike Lindy, my best friend from adulthood, my best childhood friend was complex, incredibly difficult to get along with, and yet enormously generous at times. I was also terrified and probably perversely fascinated by her ability to rage. But in the end her behavior went beyond the pale. She had been kind enough to host me while I commuted to Chicago for psychoanalytic training, and also did a huge amount of baking for my daughter's bat mitzvah. She had her own catering business before starting to work on her advanced degree. Even though she was considered smarter than I, she lacked emotional intelligence.

I had long feared a confrontation with this friend since she reminded me of my mother. I had known consciously for as long as I could remember that the relationship was my attempt to deal with the reality that my mother never loved me, and had told me so in a moment of calm. It was devastating, but I knew the truth. Not having real loving available parents, I took the Man without Empathy to meet my friend's parents, who knew me well but somehow did not want to intervene on my behalf with my abusive parents. Nobody did back then. They must have been that terrified of my mother, who was known to be "a piece of work." I will never forget what my friend's mother said to me when she met the Man without Empathy: "He is such a nice Jewish boy; you should marry him." And so I did, like an obedient child. I craved approval and was in need of affirmation.

The night before the accident, my friend and I fought for the first time in some 40 years. Throughout the two-week trip, she had thrown a series of tantrums and then had a major meltdown. I tried to go with the flow and did not confront her, but I became so exhausted as the target of her rages that finally I let her have it. She was spoiled and entitled, a real narcissist. She had married a rich, much older man and never had children. She had never once asked about my daughter for the entire year after her birth. Perhaps she was envious since she had no children of her own, but I don't think she really wanted them. Children would have cramped her style; she was still emotionally a child herself.

Almost Dead; Reentry into Life

The next morning, on the way from Mysore to the airport in Bangalore to catch a flight to Delhi, then Amsterdam and home, I was nearly killed in a taxicab accident. It was predawn and the Bangalore highway was known to be dangerous, yet the hired driver would not listen to us when we told him repeatedly to slow down. It was a gender thing; why listen to a woman? In the distance I saw what looked like a glimmering pool, a mirage, but as the cab approached I realized it was gasoline from a tanker that had tipped over on the right side of the road. The taxi driver could not slow down in time. He braked hard in the middle of the pool but the brakes froze and the car spun around, became airborne, and flew off the road—in the opposite direction of the tanker, thank God. As if to ask what he should do, the moment before impact the driver turned his head around to look at me, his face reminiscent of the figure in Munch's *Scream*. The cab hit a stand of trees in a gully at about 65 miles an hour. When I came to and put my hand to my head, there was blood everywhere. I was on autopilot, yet felt a surge of adrenaline I have never forgotten. I wrapped my bleeding head with a tie-dyed scarf that I had bought for a dollar the day before, then stumbled out of the car. It was as if my uninjured self was giving orders to my injured self. Like the good girl scout that I had been, I told myself: "Stay calm. You must make it home to the kids. Wrap your head, find your water bottle. Keep standing. You must stay awake. You must give your own medical history at the hospital. Do not fall asleep."

The accident had taken place in the middle of a desert, yet villagers slowly appeared to watch and help. There was no emergency evacuation equipment, but the Indian people were amazingly kind. They seemed to be accustomed to picking up people injured in road accidents. They stopped a public bus and put the three of us on it. I was placed in the middle of the bus, where the ride would be less bumpy. I felt chilled and realized I was going into shock. I asked to use my best friend's shawl because I had used my own to wrap my head and was so cold, afraid that I was about to pass out. She said yes, but admonished me, "Don't get blood on it."

I disregarded the hysterical fantasies that flew at me one by one, remaining calm while she fell apart. I remember telling myself, "Cut the cord. Take care of yourself." (Here the theme of traumatic bonding reemerges in the image of the umbilicus.) I did not cry or scream. The hardest part was fighting the heavy desire to go to sleep. At the hospital in Bangalore, the doctors told me that had I not stayed so composed, I would have died of blood loss.

My friend had broken her collarbone, and the driver had a small gash on his forehead. My injuries were life-threatening. Years later a sports medicine doctor theorized what had happened. The cab had no seatbelts, and I had flown up into the ceiling of the car, whose roof collapsed like an accordion as it sheared off my scalp behind my hairline like a meat slicer. My skull was chipped, but the brain was not perforated. I had suffered a concussion and was out for a minute or two.

The surgeons thought I was missing my scalp, which had retracted like the top of a convertible. A neurosurgeon was brought in first and then a plastic surgeon—who found my scalp, which was hanging by a thread of flesh—shaved my head. All I could think about was the Holocaust and the humiliation of having one's head shaved. He stitched it back in place. It took over an hour just to irrigate the wound as it had been exposed to the air and they were worried about infection setting in. It then took more than 40 huge sutures to put me back together again, like Humpty Dumpty. What I didn't know at the time was that I had also broken the C-4 and C-5 vertebrae in my neck and had compression fractures in my back.

Never once after I returned to the Twin Cities did the Man without Empathy say I should stay home and get some rest. Never once did he offer to help me. He was angry that I had spent money on myself to go to the conference and that he was left behind, though he couldn't admit it. Instead, I went back to work three days after the accident with my broken neck, a head that was shaved and bandaged, and a face that was black and blue. It was February in Minnesota, with temperatures in the subzero digits, one of the coldest winters in recent memory. And there I was schlepping groceries across an ice-filled parking lot. By then I was brainwashed beyond the imaginable. All I knew was that I had to work, no excuses. I was always to be a good, obedient, submissive wife, mother, friend.

I wrote my childhood best friend three times after the accident but never heard back from her. In fact, she had abandoned me in the

Amsterdam airport to fly back earlier to Chicago. She left me there alone with life-threatening injuries. I had a nine-hour layover. Finally my daughter, wiser than her years, said to me, "Ma, give it up. The rabbis say you only have to try three times. She doesn't want contact with you." The Man without Empathy claimed it was my fault that we had lost contact. It was his vicious attempt to lord the accident over me because I had left him behind. Leaving was always an abandonment issue for him. Was it also because he would miss how my best friend used to flirt with him? Yet she had the nerve to call the Man without Empathy a week after the accident behind my back. That, plus being told not to get blood on her shawl, were defining moments of contempt in the relationship. I finally turned the corner and never regretted it.

To this day, I live with the physical pain of my injuries. But not a day goes by that I don't say the *Shehechiyanu*, the Hebrew prayer giving thanks for having been preserved to this moment, as well as *HaGomel*, the prayer for surviving a near-death experience, "Who bestows goodness upon the culpable, for He has bestowed goodness upon me." I try to cover all my bases. I am not especially observant yet I have a deep sense of faith and gratitude. I say the prayers several times a day. Just going up the stairs reminds me how grateful I am that I can walk. I also made up another prayer voicing my thanks that I am here and my parents are not. And now that I have gotten out of a really bad marriage I say a blessing for that as well. I bet many Muslim women who have been abused and are in recovery have their prayers of gratitude, too, for having survived.

This accident changed my life and began to release me from the bonds of a sick and troubled marriage. Of course, it is regrettable that I had to experience such pain in order to feel entitled to a real life. While head trauma is known to precipitate personality change, I feel the trauma was more on the order of literally knocking sense into me. It would take another fourteen years to give myself permission to let go completely, but the slow thaw in the deep freeze of denial and dissociation had begun. The length of time I needed to escape completely from the marriage bonds speaks to the depth of traumatic experience. This is a function of the terrorism. I contend this is not something most men "get," let alone macho counterterrorist experts.

Sex Discrimination and More

"In the Supreme Court of the United States, October Term, 1997, Nancy J. Kobrin, Petitioner v. University of Minnesota; The Regents of the University of Minnesota, Respondents, On Petition for a writ of certiorari to the United States Court of Appeals for the Eighth Circuit."

This bit of legal work—one of the last Rajender Decree sex discrimination lawsuits—cost a chunk of change and yet my lawyer couldn't even get my name right. The initial "J" belonged to the Man without Empathy. But even though it was expensive, it was something I needed to do on principle. My case initially was taken on contingency, and the Consent Decree under which this was filed was ultimately repealed.

My petition was part of a class action suit over fair hiring practices at the University of Minnesota. Under the decree, the University of Minnesota had been ordered to make every attempt to hire its own female PhDs. The job that was relevant to me was a posting for a tenure-track assistant professor in comparative literature with a specialty in psychoanalysis. What transpired was also a form of emotional abuse, meaning that like the good child who did everything right in the end I was punished.

There were a series of male professors listed in the university's College of Liberal Arts catalog who received their doctorates or just their master's degrees from the University of Minnesota and had been hired without a problem. Yet for female graduates of the institution, hiring remained a significant impasse. I had been invited to stay on at the university after completing my Bush Fellowship and dissertation fellowship. I was appointed director of graduate studies during this time and invited to develop and teach seminars on psychoanalysis and literature, even though I was not regular faculty.

I had received a special grant to develop and teach a course on Sephardic culture, the first for the Jewish Studies Department. Indeed, my studies of Sephardic culture helped me understand the competition and the fear of the identity between Jews and Muslims in medieval Spain, which transferred over to my studies in Islamic suicide terrorism. Furthermore, I was the first and only humanities staff member that had gained acceptance to train as a psychoanalyst at the Chicago Institute of Psychoanalysis. I was actually doing psychoanalysis while the others were just talking about it.

I was writing doctoral exam questions and unofficially advising dissertations for students and had started to see patients under supervision in the Department of Psychiatry. Yet my department hired a man who not only had no experience in psychoanalysis but went on to have sex with a series of graduate students and was sued by one he had impregnated. Although this information was considered inadmissible in court, he was ultimately "canned" by the university. The point was that he had gotten the job over more qualified candidates who were female.

The university did business with virtually every Twin Cities law firm, so it had its pick of who would defend the school. It was like a tightly knit Arab tribe of lawyers. In fact, toward the end of the decree consideration, my lawyer told me that a distinguished alumnus, a major donor to the school, had been appointed court special master and was throwing out consent decree cases left and right.

I won the first round in the Eighth Circuit Court of Appeals. It was ruled that I had a bona fide case of sex discrimination, and the case was remanded for a hearing. I was offered a measly sum to settle, but I decided to persist. I lost, so the case went back to the Eighth Circuit Court of Appeals. Suing was costly, but I felt it had to be done. After all, I had developed the courses on psychoanalysis and literature being taught by the guy who ultimately got fired and then by a senior professor from Germany who not only took over the courses but was rumored to be using my syllabus. He was, in my opinion, anti-Semitic and part of the problem.

I found out ten days after my accident in India that I had lost the appeal. The upshot was that the university did not have to follow the decree. It was a low point for me. I decided, however, that I would petition the Supreme Court for a writ of certiorari. My take on the discrimination was that there was latent anti-Semitism in the department that one couldn't prove. The department was completely pro-PLO back then, and I was a Jew. Worse than that, I was a female who was raising her kids Jewish and therefore did not toe the party line of its armchair academic Volvo Marxist's creed. Even though I had studied Arabic, it didn't count. I could have done somersaults, handstands, and the high vault, and it would not have helped. I talked to my lawyer about it, not knowing at the time that she was very much involved in the Democratic Party, the same party in which the court special master was a big honcho. I later heard from a couple of other clients that she was an incompetent lawyer.

This was a department that venerated Edward Said, the consummate liar who claimed he was Palestinian when he was not. He was brought in to lecture, along with others who were anti-Israel. I could smell the problem, but what could be done? It was okay to be "a Jewish mother" and oversee the caretaking of the graduate students, since the rest of the faculty lacked interpersonal skills. But I was not to be recognized for my intellect. In fact, I was told that I was weak in theory. I didn't agree, but I kept my mouth shut until I sued. Either way, the court did not want to involve itself in university employment matters. What happened to me in academia was pervasive, routine, and represented the unspoken anti-Semitism among faculty. It was and still is politically incorrect to confront it. Martin Kramer wrote about how the Saudis had bought academia in *Ivory Towers on Sand: The Failure of Middle East Studies in America.*[41] There is also the Campus Watch, part of the Middle East Forum, that tracks anti-semitism on campus. However, there was no such entity when I was training. For a counterterrorist expert like myself, with no institutional affiliation or support such as one would have through a professorship, it was particularly difficult to compete. The anti-Semitism in academia has been a way to bully others out of the discussion and shape vulnerable minds. In my opinion, the universities have been lost to the pressure of oil money from the Arab Muslim world and Islam's pressuring strategies to rule academia.

Years later, on April 2, 2009, I went to the University of Minnesota for a lecture on Sharia law. A Muslim woman professor from the University of Wisconsin law school tried to put a good spin on Sharia. There were banners in the auditorium claiming that Islam enhances America, or something to that effect. I regret that I didn't photograph them. They gave away free copies of the Quran and free food—humus and pita bread for starters. I wondered how dhimmitude, the subjugated category of Jews and Christians and other non-Muslims and its pervasive Islamic anti-Semitism in academia, could enhance America. It was a stretch. It is generally not known by the vast majority of the Western public that the Jew is identified as the anti-Christ in Islam. This image and ideology certainly doesn't promote harmony and peace. Moreover, it is said that the Jewess Zaynab bint al-Harith poisoned the prophet Muhammad, making matters worse.

I also found out from the FBI and the Hennepin Sheriff's deputies to whom I taught radical Islam after 9/11, that there was an old Palestinian crime syndicate in the Twin Cities dating back to the 1950s. My dissertation advisor for *Aljamía,* Old Spanish in Arabic script, was an Arabophile. It did not surprise me when I heard that the Muslim Brotherhood had designated Minnesota as a toehold of entry for their endeavors. It seemed to fit with the election of Keith Ellison, the first former Nation of Islam member, to the U.S. House of Representatives, as well as with the huge Somali diaspora beginning in the 1990s. Today one of the most popular names for boys in the State of Minnesota is Muhammad. That is how dramatic the demographic change has been. Minnesota has become like Europe.

Coincidentally, the chair of the department of comparative literature, who did go to bat for me during my court case, just happened to begin studying Arabic at the University of Minnesota. He then moved to Geneva, Switzerland, and his son ultimately became a banker. I always wondered if he became friendly with Tariq Ramadan, the grandson of Hassan al-Banna, the founder of the Muslim Brotherhood. Tariq grew up in Geneva. Quite a few professors of comparative literature traveled to Saudi Arabia and made a lucrative teaching career there.

I met Tariq Ramadan at a closed NATO meeting in Cambridge, England, in February 2006 when I presented a paper on suicide bombing called "Putting the Umm (Arabic for mother) back in Islamic Suicide Bombing." The paper, on the role and platform of the mother in the dynamics of terror, was published in a NATO collection in 2008. Ramadan had to listen to my paper, though it must have been hard for him. He was one of the most charismatic men I have ever seen in action, and very scary. Another malignant narcissist most likely. Ramadan was fired from his professorship at the Dutch Erasmus University and dismissed from his position with the city of Rotterdam as an integrationist because he was caught teaching extremism on an Iran television program. Nevertheless, the United States ultimately granted him a visa to teach at Notre Dame in South Bend, Indiana.

In 2000, I attended the Sixth International Congress for Research on Sephardic and Oriental Jewish Heritage in Jerusalem. It had been four years since the accident in India nearly ended my life. On this trip, I was about to begin a new life, making more progress to get out of the troubled parasitic bonding that the Man without Empathy had forced on me.

At their core, all marriages link to the maternal object and the baby, the experience of love and pain. The first relationship is forged between the baby and the mother, and this pattern of attachment is repeated throughout life. The type of bonding that occurs is the basis for all attachments that are formed thereafter, especially in couples. This was the case in my troubled marriage

The internalization of the sadistic is a symptom of problems with attachment to the mother. From a cultural point of view, the role of the sadistic Islamic father gets played out within the context of the culture, ideology, religion, and abusive child-rearing practices. However, the bottom line is that the sadistic father is also a result of the formation of attachment or, in many instances, detachment from his own mother. In the West we have in literature the famous story of Trilby, who is hypnotized by the charlatan Svengali. It is a master–slave attachment. We can find these relationships across cultures. However, because of the issue of misogyny in Arab Muslim and non-Arab Muslim cultures, the marital bonds form a master–slave attachment. Take for example, Sura 4 of the Quran and wife beating. Women get beaten because they are enslaved. They are owned like a piece of property.

All babies have abandonment terror, which means all adults have residual abandonment terror to a degree that depends on their particular personal histories, which are embedded in their respective cultures. Abandonment terror dwells at the very heart of intimacy. Similarly, the issue of abandonment lies at the very heart of terrorism's paranoia. In Islam the issue of terror of abandonment arises, even though terrorists ironically are velcroed to their mothers. How do we know this? Through the way in which they relate to their objects. They fuse with their objects. They are obsessed with purity and will not tolerate non-Muslim "interlopers" in their allegedly "pure" Mecca. You have to become like them. Terrorists are repeating the bondage with their mothers; they are held hostage by their mothers and a culture that does not permit them to separate. So if someone leaves them, they feel abandoned and do not know who they are. They are confused about their identity because they have an adhesive identity dependent upon the mother.

This can be easily seen if we think of how the Saudis treat little girls, who will one day give birth to little boys, who will grow up to be terrorists. Saudi girls all have guardians, which means they are nothing more than property to their alleged protectors. It is plain and simple ownership. And it is passed from the father or the brother to another man, never a woman. That other man is generally the husband who can, in turn, "own" more than one wife. Women must obtain "permission" to work and or travel. In short, women are objects. From there these men only learn how to relate to an object, not a real person. Moreover, they themselves do not feel like real persons. They lack an authentic sense of a healthy, vibrant self. The Saudis have created the perfect catch-22 for remaining developmentally arrested and challenged. It is an ideal system for producing terrorists.

When I went to Jerusalem in 2000 with yet another girlfriend to present a research paper at a conference on Sephardic and Oriental Jewish heritage, two things happened that were instrumental in uncapping my suppressed life. The first was that this friend perceived that when I called home every day, I wasn't just checking in to say hi but responding to some kind of pressuring from the Man without Empathy. She felt my anxiety and terror. She intuitively understood that my husband was abusing me. I felt conflicted unconsciously because he projected into me his worst possible terror, that I was abandoning him. I had long felt he was suffocating me.

At the conference, my friend introduced me to a psychohistorian. Psychohistory is the specialized field of viewing historical events and persons through a psychoanalytic lens, a subfield of political psychology. He tapped into profound feelings; for the first time in many years I felt alive, intellectually challenged, desirous, desirable. I did not know until later that he was a Don Juan, but for now I felt like I had been awakened from a deep sleep, though I knew I wasn't Sleeping Beauty. It was a mobilized erotic transference, as we say in psychoanalytic parlance. His was an unconscious psychological connection or bonding to me in the guise of a combination of my dead brother MurrayMurphy and my dead Uncle Lenny, who was tall, brilliant, odd as in nerdy, a bit autistic, and a bachelor like this psychohistorian. He fit my psychopathology.

I was so beaten down by the Man without Empathy that I was essentially pushed into the arms of another. Indeed, my analyst had once marveled at how so little attention went such a long way with me but said that this was because I had been so extremely deprived. At times it felt that I was groveling like a dog for a bone in my marriage, which consisted of extreme deprivation and lack of affection. I continued to correspond with this scholar by e-mail after the conference ended. And then, in a way, I began to live out my husband's ranting narrative that accused me of being unfaithful.

Trapped in a bad marriage and desiring more, terrorized unconsciously that his rage and spousal rape would escalate to murder, no longer willing to take the chronic psychological abuse that continued to worsen despite my attempts to get the Man without Empathy to admit that he was abusive and or at the very least apologize, I finally made a significant break in November 2000—about five months after the conference at which I had met the psychohistorian. I sat the Man without Empathy down and told him I wanted a divorce. He was shocked.

I fled later that day, without a plan or a place to go. I called a psychoanalyst colleague, who heard the terror in my voice and urged me to come to her home to sort things out. I was in such turmoil that I got lost on the way. I had to ask a young couple who were out strolling with their baby for directions to my colleague's home. The young father went home to get his "Hudson" (the most popular street atlas in the Twin Cities) and then drove me in my car to my colleague's home, which was only a couple of blocks away. I stayed for three days.

Then I moved in with a different female colleague, paying rent for a month before finding a studio apartment in downtown Minneapolis where I worked. I no longer had to drive to work, something that I did not enjoy in the Minnesota winters, especially after my accident in India. I began traveling back and forth to Israel twice a year, the place where I had always wanted to live and the only place I felt totally at home. Unfortunately, both of the colleagues with whom I stayed during the difficult time of initial separation were anti-Israel and pro-Palestinian, though I had not realized this at first. Neither one had been to Israel though both were well traveled and one was Jewish. They were the typically pseudo-educated left-leaners who knew nothing about Israel, but since Israel was strong they identified with the poor Palestinians who keep shooting themselves literally in the foot as they continue to fire bullets into the air to celebrate a wedding!

When my son came to see my studio apartment, he said, "Oh, Ma, things must have been really bad for you to move here." I was living on less money than my own son had while he was in medical school. My daughter never came to visit, probably because the truth was too terrifying and remained unspoken. It must have been hard for my children to hold me in their thoughts since I had completely exposed the character of their father and the charade of the marriage. As mom I understood, though it was painful. When you are the one to leave, you pay the price, all the more so if you are the female.

I never allowed the Man without Empathy to see the inside of my studio apartment, which enraged him despite his denials. It was as if I needed to carve out a concrete physical space of my own that he could not enter. I came to understand this was my way to keep my abuser from infiltrating my mind, and therefore every orifice of my body, any further. This is how terrorists hold you hostage. This is why it takes six to seven tries on average for a woman to leave an abusive relationship. Men's traumatic bonding with their mothers recycles with their partners. It was hard for me to leave. How much harder it must be for a woman in an unwanted arranged marriage, alone and isolated.

Couple Therapy—Identifying with the Aggressor

That same fall, the Man without Empathy and I began couple therapy. He resented it, but I demanded it so I could work through the trauma of the longstanding marital abuse. I was looking for an apology from him for the rape. It never happened.

Therapy was a disaster. The therapist flirted with the Man without Empathy, just as my mother and my best friend from childhood had done. And, like my analyst, the therapist also missed the abuse completely. Unfortunately, this is a common countertransference problem for therapists in cases where the therapist is manipulated by the abuser. The therapist colludes with the sociopath.

I tried to explain how oppositional the Man without Empathy was, but the therapist put the blame on me. I gave the example of how I wanted to rip up the old carpet in our first home and get the floors sanded. The Man without Empathy had told me no. But when it came time to sell the house and the male real estate agent told him to rip up the carpet, he did it. "Well, why didn't you just pick up the carpeting and have it thrown out?" the therapist said in an accusatory voice. Couldn't the therapist see that I was terrified of his rage? That he could lose it? What kind of a comment is that to make to a patient? So here I was in couple therapy with a therapist absolutely without empathy—a repetition of the trauma and abuse. I even confronted the therapist about yelling at me, not him, but the therapist said nothing. She was mimicking the Man without Empathy's tactic: never say anything and you avoid assuming responsibility.

I tried to explain how the Man without Empathy would terrify me with his bad driving, but the therapist minimized its significance. I gave the example of the time he slowly turned onto a major thoroughfare and into the path of an oncoming semi-trailer truck. I was sitting in the passenger seat. I was sure he was trying to kill me. It reminded me of my father's sadism of wanting to get "a rise out of you." Another example of passive–aggressive behavior. This took place after my taxicab accident in India, so he was well aware of how difficult it was for me to be a passenger in a car. His nonverbal behavior spoke volumes and, of course, when confronted, he denied it. He had a "thing" about cars.

This therapist also happened to sit on the State Board of Psychology. Yet another example of a disturbed person hiding behind a professional title reinforcing and justifying the Man without Empathy's no-boundaries behavior, making it out to be inconsequential when it was full of red flags for abuse. Failing to set appropriate boundaries with the Man without Empathy and passively–aggressively colluding with him, the perpetrator, this therapist compounded the abuse. The Man without Empathy's behaviors worsened, and his rage increased. His rage came out sideways. He redirected his aggression to the therapist's aggression against me. I write this with the hope that people will understand the complexity of a malignant personality and its destructive behavior, which is routinely and pervasively denied. It is the function of terror.

Once again I became the scapegoat, but I was becoming more aware of the dynamics. I had come to expect such behaviors of my husband, but the therapist's aggression and flirting were appalling. I had it on good authority from another source, a woman neurologist, that in her couple therapy this therapist had done the same thing—flirted and sided with the husband and yelled at and ridiculed the wife. She even told me that she had called the therapist after one of their sessions and confronted her about her destructive and unhelpful behavior.

My friends, many of whom were therapists and psychoanalysts themselves, urged me to get out of the therapy, saying that this practitioner had no empathy for me. But I kept working at it. On the one hand, when you have been nothing more than an object in other people's lives it is hard to distinguish the feeling of consistent, real empathy; on the other hand, while you may have the capacity to understand this, it is difficult to grasp that a person can sort of slide along in a chameleon-like way, acting normal but not being normal because they lack empathy. Terrorists lack empathy because they murder in cold blood.

I wanted to understand why the couples therapist didn't believe me and why she didn't have empathy. I couldn't understand why she too hated me. While my friends kept urging me to get out of the therapy, I didn't feel like the timing was right. Also, I didn't want to be told what to do. I had to do it my own way and at my own pace and find out for myself when I felt like I had enough of therapy. The couple therapy mimicked the marriage.

The traumatic bonding was fierce. It had been a very long marriage, and I had been trying to make it all work somehow. I had the lingering hope that somehow the marriage would be salvageable and viable for me, but it was not possible. Most of all, I had wanted an intact family, but he knew that and sought to destroy it. Anything that I wanted, he aimed to destroy. In the end the therapist had identified with his aggression, while finally I was able to disidentify with both him and the abusive therapist. I do not believe that the majority of counterterrorist experts even remotely understand the ferocity of the identification with the aggressor and how complicated it is to uncouple.

CHAPTER 8

Connecting The Dots

An expert on the emotional abuse of high-functioning women, Dr. Joan Lachkar, invited me to participate in a June 2001 seminar for a human rights group on Islamic suicide terrorism. To prepare for my presentation, I sent questions to the International Institute for Counter-Terrorism, a think tank in Herzliya, Israel, part of the Interdisciplinary College (IDC), the first private college in Israel. One of the instructors at that time wrote back. He turned out to be the top Israeli counterterrorist expert, who had identified Osama bin Laden.

As further preparation, I read my psychoanalytic colleague's doctoral thesis in which she interestingly compared the competing narratives in the Torah and the Quran and their psychological meaning for Jews and Muslims, respectively, to a couple's pathological dance. Simply put, the Jews got the land "flowing with milk and honey" (the good breast) and the Arabs got the desert of deprivation (the bad breast).

Im tirtzu, ayn zo agadah, as the Hebrew Zionist saying of Theodore Herzl goes: "If you will, it's no dream." Herzl was no psychoanalyst, but he did get it right. Fantasies can limit what is possible. If you view yourself as eternally deprived, you will remain eternally enraged and vengeful, always the victim like the good borderline. One's narrative about one's self and one's group can limit how one chooses to live. If you get the land flowing with milk and honey, you feel nourished emotionally and psychologically.

I would be remiss if I did not mention in passing that the "maternal" manifests itself in other ways as well. For example, when the King David Hotel was bombed by Jewish terrorists, the bombs were placed in milk containers. So even for Jews there is a risk of acting out the feelings of desperation and deprivation unconsciously vis à vis the symbol of the maternal. The repeated theme of deprivation associated with mother's milk occurs in global terrorism. We are hot-wired to crave warm breast milk. In August 2006 the foiled airplane plot in the United Kingdom led to a concern of liquid explosives being transported in baby bottles. The explosive TATP is called The Mother of Satan.

Take the case of Somalia. The name "Somalia" comes from *somaal*, meaning "go milk the camel." Somalia is a land of harsh deprivation, torn apart by a horrendous clan-cleansing civil war. Indeed the prize-winning Somali novelist Nuruddin Farah wrote *Sweet and Sour Milk*, which fits within this frame of deprivation and violence. The theme of sour milk even surfaced when the Israeli guy who informally recruited me for terrorism studies characterized my work in a disparaging way as "your mother's sour milk theory"! There was truth in the idea of difficulty of the maternal bond and the mother as platform, but he did not realize or value what I was doing. This is when a joke is not a joke but highly aggressive. It showed his own disparaging attitude toward women. The theme of the lowly regarded female in Somali culture is further articulated by several famous proverbs: "Women are like your shadow; they follow at the heels of those who run away from them. They bully and boss and lead those who follow them. They follow those who leave them and run from those who follow them."

In the jihad in Chechnya, all the war trauma has caused nursing problems. "Mothers have difficulty lactating." Paul Murphy relates this in his book *Allah's Angels: Chechen Women in War*.[42] Such difficulties may be devastating for a secure maternal attachment. Similarly, a nursing mother, a chronic object of hatred, compromises the maternal attachment because she is not able to function in a relaxed environment.

The unconscious narrative about violence and the effects of being an object of hatred were what I was interested in framing. That behavior points to primitive mental states as expressed graphically by nonverbal behavior. Terrorists are not able to fantasize and dream; instead they must act out some destructive fantasy. A suicide bomber cannot fantasize about being a bomb; rather he or she literally becomes the bomb. "I am ready to implode; therefore I am the bomb." In psychiatric hospitals, we see patients who may feel cold. Normal patients can verbalize that they feel cold or even express it with their body language—for example by shivering. But the psychotic patient has to *become* the coldness, the iceberg, and sit in a catatonic state.

This arises, in part, because the mother of the baby is abused and devalued. She struggles to have a relaxed, healthy attachment with her baby as the one building the motherboard of the future terrorist's brain. But she is working at a disadvantage and should not be blamed. The stress and trauma of the abuse she experienced inhibit a calm maternal attachment for the baby, who is at risk of failing to develop the proper mirror neurons necessary for empathy. The baby comes to lack an understanding of the other and perceives the other to be a threat. Instead of a calm, secure attachment that enables these children to go out into the world feeling safe, they experience the opposite. Because of this and other intervening influences and factors, they learn to bond with others through violence, in many cases. This is the theory in a nutshell—the only theory to date, to the best of my knowledge that considers neuropsychological factors.

Indeed, one of the top stories in Al Qaeda's English e-zine, *Inspire*, was entitled "How to Make a Bomb in the Kitchen of your Mother." This issue gained renewed interest because of the Boston Marathon Bombing on April 15, 2013, and unwittingly encapsulates how the rage of this autistic-like behavior gets channeled in a way that masks its true target—the mother—as it cavalierly describes where to build the bomb, as if in the womb of the prenatal mother. However, the majority of people do not want to consider this depth of knowledge in order to penetrate the terrorist psyche. It is right under our noses, but it is so terrifying to be in the presence of psychosis that we must remain in denial. If one looks at the diagrams in this bomb-building issue, they look quite autistic and abstract. Picasso was thought to be a bit autistic too.

This is not to say that sectors of the Israeli Jewish community—for example, the extremists and the terrorists like *Tag Mehir* (Hebrew for price tag), as well as those who spit on little girls and attack women from the ultra-orthodox sector Sicarim (also called Sicari'im)—do not also have a similar problem. They have no empathy and have lots of unthought thoughts. Yet the ideologies are also different. As Jews we love life, and we do not seek death. There is a higher frequency of violent ideologies in Islam, and its position as the last Abrahamic faith rather paints it into a corner because it is the religion taken up by shame–honor cultures such as the Arabs and the non-Arab Muslims in Afghanistan, Pakistan, Chechnya, etc. I would add that the black- and-white binary oppositions, such as the religion of peace and the religion of jihad, need to be read functionally together and that it facilitates black-and-white thinking in paranoia. Islam claims that it precedes Judaism and Christianity, which compounds the relationship through its grandiosity and omnipotence. Moreover, the demographics are much different; Islam is the fastest growing religion in the world with1.5 billion adherents, as opposed to the Jewish population of 13 million.

However, in my opinion, Jews also could become suicide bombers if their situation were to deteriorate psychologically. After all Jews, too, experience domestic violence's murder–suicide, which shows flagrantly the problem of traumatic bonding, with poor maternal attachment leading to disorganized attachment disorders. In fact, when the Israelis were withdrawing from Gaza in 2005, the army was on high alert for Jewish suicide bombers. There were none. Yet there were two self-immolations by Jewish settlers. I consider immolation to be the slippery slope in the phenomenon of suicide bombing. Furthermore, being chronically exposed to Islamic violence has degraded Jewish culture, especially in Israel. One cannot be the ongoing, pervasive object of hatred and not have it impact one's sense of self. Such is the case for Judaism in this day and age after the Holocaust.

The concept of a cognitive deficit along with primitive mentalization is often difficult for non-analytic lay people to understand, but it resonated with me. I understood the respective narratives of the Torah and the Quran, to say nothing of the emotional experience as well. It was a kind of mirror image for me, but one that showed contrasting reflections: Islamic terrorists love death, and Jews love life. I would joke that I was half-Israeli and half-Shia. My Israeli half was represented by my near-fatal road accident in India. After Israeli kids serve in the army, they travel the world. Many go to India and South America, where some are tragically killed in road accidents. But my Shiite half was even easier to understand. The followers of Shiite Islam, the second largest denomination of Muslims after Sunni Islam, experienced great deprivation, especially those living in southern Lebanon. Historically, the Shiites did not receive the inheritance from the Prophet Muhammad, just as I did not receive an inheritance from my father. Moreover, I am a great Fatmah—like the Prophet Muhammad's daughter, Fatima, known to serve everyone and to be self-sacrificing and self-effacing, the exemplary wife. Besides, it seemed to me that I had married a Palestinian. Of course, this is not to say that all Palestinians treat their wives so miserably, but the women do live under the death threat of the honor killing. I find that chilling, having lived under one myself, and having a dead brother plus a brother who raped me.

One day after 9/11, I was talking with the Israeli at the Interdisciplinary Center in Herzliya who was then mentoring me in the history of terrorism. He would probably not take credit for this, but he did acknowledge me in the preface of his book for helping him. I mentioned in passing how I had gone into Russia in 1977 to smuggle out papers of Jews trapped in the Gulag. "Oh, so you were recruited," he said in his inimitable Israeli accent. It dawned on me that I had been recruited a second time, for the human rights seminar in Los Angeles.

I saw for the first time how similar my "recruitments" were to recruitment into a terrorist organization. I also realized how unconsciously familiar I was with the psychopathology of a terrorist group—that is, I, too, had had a maternal disturbance in attachment due to my abusive mother and father. We all have an internal terrorist. Depending on our history, it is probably a matter of degree as to how traumatizing this terrorist within us is. This is where traumatic bonding begins, which easily leads to bonding with a nefarious, charismatic leader and being in a cult or a terrorist group. Could my revelation help me explain the violence of Islamic suicide terrorism?

An Expert in Town

After 9/11, my Israeli mentor was scheduled to give a seminar at Lawrence Livermore National Laboratory in California. I suggested that he fly through Minneapolis to see where I lived and meet my husband. Having the Man without Empathy meet the Israeli with whom I was working was my way of trying to protect myself from my husband's rage as I became more deeply involved in terrorism studies.

I thought that I would try to set up some lectures on terrorism for him in the Twin Cities, so I called the Jewish Community Relations Council to gauge interest in having the leading Israeli authority on Bin Laden give a talk. They said no; there was not enough time. There was more than a month, so I figured they didn't want to because the idea had not originated with them. That is the narcissistic truth. I contacted a church group that readily got the word out that he would speak instead to the organization Bridges for Peace.

Before he arrived, I phoned the FBI and said, "I am calling as a concerned citizen. I am Jewish, and the leading Israeli authority on Bin Laden is coming to town. Would you like to meet him?" A lunch meeting was set up near Macalester College in St. Paul. For more than four hours he and I met with Debbie Streibel Pierce, a counterterrorist expert who then headed the Minneapolis FBI office. The FBI had many, many questions. I was still feeling good about being able to facilitate that meeting when I went into my office on Monday morning and answered the phone. On the other end was the secretary of the Jewish Community Relations Council, who screamed at me and asked how I dared go behind their back and contact the FBI. "But I gave you the opportunity to host my colleague," I replied calmly. Why do people feel entitled to scream and to tell me what to do? People scream and yell when they begin to feel terrified that they are losing power and control. They are terrorized because they actually feel vulnerable. In particular, they sense those they envy as having genuine power and independence. Therefore they must attack and destroy. Yelling is the adult equivalent of throwing a tantrum.

Linking the Political and Domestic

In couple therapy I had talked openly about my desire to take a kind of a sabbatical for one month to write on Islamic suicide terrorism. In January 2002, I went to Jerusalem and stayed at A Little House in Baka, a neighborhood B&B, and there I began to write. During this time, I was still separated from the Man without Empathy. My abusive couples therapist even said to both of us during a therapy session that whatever happened while I was separated was my own business. The Man without Empathy could not accept that.

In Jerusalem, the words flowed. And suddenly the plot line of *Othello* hit me in the face, and I said to myself, "Oh wow, so that's what it is—nothing more than murder–suicide." It was my "aha moment" of clarity, when the underlying, girding image of conjoint murder–suicide in Islamic suicide bombing snapped into focus. Shakespeare portrayed his perception of the clash of civilizations through the intermarriage of Othello, a North African military Muslim, and Desdemona, the daughter of an Italian senator, and through Othello's murder of Desdemona and his subsequent suicide.

It seemed that I had discovered what was so obvious about the banality of the suicide attack: It was a form of murder–suicide routinely seen in domestic violence in the West, only on a broader, grander scale. It made this kind of political violence complementary to domestic violence—or intimate terrorism as it is euphemistically labeled—and hence synergistic, carrying a powerful impact and horrific punch, all the more to terrorize and tap into the earliest terrors we have from childhood. At the same time, the shared sadomasochism and violence of murder–suicide in both kinds of attacks had an uncanny appeal for Western converts to Islam, who became radicalized, for example, in jail. I had met some of the jailhouse converts while doing prison interviews in the Hennepin County Jail in Minneapolis. Some were former Nation of Islam members who told me that they "upgraded" to Sunni Wahhabi Islam. The majority of the interviewees were Somalis and a few Sudanese.

My first experience interviewing the prisoners recalled the interviews I had conducted many years earlier on the locked ward of a psychiatric hospital. Of course, there are differences between a prison and a locked psychiatric ward, but the singular commonality is that it they are locked places in which the inhabitants do not live of their own volition. The staff of the prison brought me five detainees at the same time. I had not intended to do "group therapy," but I went along with those that the prison staff had brought. Halfway through the initial interview I felt a heaviness come over me, a deep desire to sleep. I immediately realized that this was a result of the somatic impression that these inmates were making on me, a kind of body countertransference. I discussed this with a colleague after the session, and we both concluded that it was my countertransference to a kind of group psychosis.

There is some question, too, that because I was there listening to them in a profoundly empathic way that my bodily response was linked to mirror neurons and automatic somatic empathy, as shown by current research conducted by Booth, Trimble, and Egan in Ireland concerning therapist's response to their trauma patients.[43] As psychoanalysts we use our bodies' response and track our somatic experiences in relation to what is being aroused in us by the patient's verbal and nonverbal communication. One psychoanalyst has likened it to using the analyst's body as a tuning fork that resonates with the patient. It is this deep level of encounter related to the maternal bond that is often missed in the interviews conducted by counterterrorist experts. Hence, because an entire dimension of this bond is missed in the interview, there is diminished understanding of the internal psychic world of the jihadis. While it is true that interviewing is a tricky business and one must be very careful to disentangle one's own lived experience and trauma from that of those being interviewed, being aware of the problem is central to the effort.

I have given careful thought to all the issues involved in understanding terrorism on many different levels. Some critics may say that I am projecting my experiences and my processing of these experiences onto suicide terrorism. Yet, one's life experience always contributes to how one understands the world. The ability to turn the corner and take a hard look at one's self is crucial in order to obtain a better understanding precisely through such subjectivity as life experience, which leads to insights that may not otherwise be accessible and knowable. I am grateful that I have been able to undertake this task, as painful and as destructive as the suicide attacks have been. I also am fortunate that I have met such good, competent colleagues and scholars along the way who have shared with me their special knowledge. Putting the genie back in the bottle from whence suicide terrorism has come is next to impossible, precisely because it is imitative behavior. Like the emperor in the story, it is my hunch that the other sheikhs who remain alive yet follow bin Laden's path of jihad also know they are naked, and that this is an unbearable, shameful humiliation. Nonetheless, only they and their community can stop the charade, which will relieve, in part, their own shame and humiliation.

Here are glimpses of several conversations I had while listening to detainees. I had been going into the jail for a while to listen closely to the stories of these detainees in order to learn about their early childhoods and their pain. After several months, at the end of one such session an African American Muslim detainee who had "upgraded" from Nation of Islam to Sunni Islam while in jail asked what my religion was. I was taken aback since this had never happened before. I responded with another question: "What religion do you think I am?" He answered: "Buddhist or Hindu." At first I was startled, and then immediately realized that he probably didn't know many Jews, let alone Jewish women, and that he couldn't read me "ethnically." I had to think on my feet. Should I disclose that I was Jewish or not? I felt it was important to be honest and said I was a Jew. He then asked, "What do Jews believe?" Again, I had to think fast to answer this question, for which I was totally unprepared. But I said: "Love thy neighbor as thyself; all the rest is study."

The prisoners now knew that a Jewish woman came to listen to them. Jewish women are the lowest on the totem pole in Islam. They are considered concubines and identified with the alleged poisoner of the Prophet Muhammad, the Jewess Zainab bint al-Harith. A Jewish woman is perhaps scary to Muslims who don't know any, but I didn't think of that at the time. I intuitively felt it was important to be honest and to show that there was a woman, albeit Jewish, who was concerned about their life experience.

I then met a young Somali detainee, whom I will call Muhammad. When I asked him what clan and tribe he was from, he told me Hawiye on his father's side. He talked about the clan and I said; "I get the clan thing, Muhammad; you're talking to the female baby of the clan." He didn't laugh because he knew that I knew that the shit, or *zift* as they say in Arabic, rolls downhill. We both knew that it was not "fun" to be a female in a Somali clan; in fact it is quite brutal. It was as if I had caught him in recognizing the insidiousness of clan relations, especially for the female. My heart sank as I realized that he was the same age as my son. Here was this nice-looking, smart young guy in prison for his second drunk-driving offense, while my son was on the verge of graduating from medical school. Moreover, my daughter had just tragically buried a close girlfriend, 25 years old, who had been hit by a drunk driver the previous week. This young woman had done more good in her short life than the majority of us will ever do. I told him about my daughter's dead friend.

Muhammad then began to describe his childhood, and my heart sank further as I realized that he had been a child soldier, seized and taken hostage from a refugee camp in Kenya, taken back into Somalia and forced to fight. At least that is what he told me. I had no way to verify his narrative and I accepted it as a possibility.

I asked, "Do you understand why people drink?"

He answered: "No"

To which I replied, "People have a tendency to drink when they have seen or experienced too much violence when they were too young—too much trauma."

He sat back in his chair and mulled over this new idea. He then started talking about his dead brother. I tried to express my condolences in af-Somali, but I totally mispronounced it.

Muhammad understood nonetheless and said, "No big deal. He's dead."

I told Muhammad that it was a big deal. "Your older brother is dead. Even though you will see him in paradise, he is not here now to advise you, to guide you as a big brother does. It's very sad and a big loss, especially now when you could use a big brother to help you." I did not tell Muhammad that I, too, had a dead big brother whom I think about and miss to this day, even though I had never met him. I could relate to Muhammad's loss, a loss so profound that one never really gets over it. Rather one learns to cope with it at best. I also worry about the siblings of the suicide bombers because it is a big loss to them most especially, and they are not permitted to genuinely grieve and mourn the loss. That is why, in part, they have so much rage and then must externalize it. Because they are taught that dependency needs are scary and they are not suppose to feel vulnerable, they are impelled to destroy that which is good.

Muhammad then leaned forward and said to me, "So explain to me about the Arab–Israeli conflict and why the Jews hate us?"

I nearly fell off my chair. No prisoner had ever asked me this.

"Muhammad, we don't hate you," I told him.

He said, "There are one billion Jews in Palestine."

I was incredulous. "What????!!! There are only 13 million . . .

He interrupted me, "In Israel?"

"No—in the entire world."

He said: "No way, how can that be?"

I told him that we do not proselytize, that we believe less is more. Muhammad sat back, and I could see him digesting this new idea. Then he launched into a diatribe on behalf of Israel!! "Israel, it's the only democracy in the Middle East; it's the only country where there is real freedom!! All the Arab countries, they're worthless and their leaders are tyrants, dictators, corrupt!!"

Really, I thought to myself, who is going to believe me when I relate this conversation? Muhammad did not say this in order to please me or to curry favor with me. I could tell that his outburst was genuine and spontaneous.

"Yes," I, said "it's true. Israel is a democracy. But it's not perfect, you realize, and Israel is working to make it better for all of its citizens—Jews, Christians, Muslims, Druzes, even atheists. Israel tries, the Israelis try, and we as Jews try." The session was up and he had to go back to his cell. I shook his hand, wished him good luck, and thanked him in af-Somali.

I left feeling that I had connected with at least with one detainee. I did not anticipate what would happen next. The following week I returned and two detainees voluntarily came to speak with me. One was Somali and the other Sudanese. I had spoken with each one before, so I was surprised that they had come back. The Somali said to me, "If we find out that what you are doing is not good for Islam, you'll be sorry." I thought but did not say aloud that what I might think is good might be different from what they thought is good. I also realized I had just received a death threat to be taken seriously. These guys were vicious but also terrified of the truth, and they didn't even know it.

I realized why I had been threatened. It was because I had made progress and had connected with Muhammad. He must have gone back to his pod and spoken to the other guys about what we had discussed. What else is there to do in the jail? It's a pretty boring place. The group must have been alarmed by this talk. These two detainees were terrified thinking about the violence they experienced during early childhood, which had had great impact on their lives and their subsequent violent behavior. I had upset their "mental" apple cart about how they thought about the world and how it should work. It was a threat to their fused group mentality, all the more so because a middle-aged Jewish woman could understand their pain and empathize with what they might have been through as children.

I also recalled the words of Ayaan Hirsi Ali, the Dutch Somali parliamentarian who lost her colleague and friend Theo Van Gogh to murder by a jihadi: "Jew is the worst term of abuse in both Somali and Arabic. Later, when I was a teenager and living in Somalia and Kenya, from the mid-eighties onward, every prayer we said contained a request for the extermination of the Jews. Just imagine that: five times a day. We were passionately praying for their destruction but had never actually met one."[44]

These Muslim detainees were no different. They were terrified of me, so they tried to threaten me, to get me to feel the terrors that they themselves could not feel. Rather they had become the terror and the rage. They had been socialized to hate, even though they did not know Jews. This is a form of emotional abuse.

Similarly, the Islamic suicide terrorists and all their accessories to the crime (the engineer bomb maker, the recruiter, the sender, the escort, the charismatic leader, the mothers and fathers, the uncles, the clan, the tribe, the Umma) are terrified because they too have been "neotenized." They are like neonates, raised to stay immature all their lives. They have never been allowed to grow up, to mature, to be free and to become independent, self-sufficient, confident, and competent human beings. This has been done through terrorizing, shaming child-rearing practices. This has also happened because the bad has become accepted as normal by the clan. They have become habituated to death, making it easier to become a jihadi in general and a suicide bomber in particular. Terrorists have been lied to in an insidiously infantilizing, humiliating, and shaming way until they have become enraged and seek an outlet for this rage. It is estimated that 1% of the 1.5 billion Muslims are violent jihadis.[45] This should come as no surprise; in fact, the numbers have to be much higher than that.

Murder–suicide is so terrifying and simple that few want to consider it a possibility, especially in this era of political correctness. In Arab Muslim culture in the Middle East, murder-suicide is not yet as common as honor killing of females who have allegedly brought stain upon the family honor. The category of political violence used to define terrorist attacks also acts as a hindrance because it does not allow for inquiry into childrearing practices, which inform the very heart of culture. If you are going to claim that terrorism is shaped by culture, it is mandatory to examine childrearing practices and domestic violence. Thus, I expanded the template of murder–suicide, describing it as a hybrid of three instances of lethality: Western-style domestic violence, Middle Eastern honor killing, and serial killing by proxy, which is known to both the East and the West—i.e., mass killings that include those by serial murderers and by the bomb makers and the handler escorts of the suicide bomber.

There is much talk about the body parts after suicide attacks in the reports by journalists. Body parts also occur in serial killing. We know from serial killing that the killer often makes a tableau by cutting up and dismantling his victims. The body parts of serial killing or the suicide attack represent the psychologically immature, unintegrated picture of the mother's body, or what psychodynamic theory refers to as "part objects." There are instances of serial killing where the crime scene's body parts are chaotically strewn, such disorganized attachment rage indicating an even more psychotic mind. Body parts may be graphically arranged and displayed to send a message to the police, the killer's way of taunting them to find him. These serial killers are bullies but they are also mama's boys, having never separated from their mothers. Recently we actually saw a "twinned" jihadi serial killer in action when Michael Adebolajo and Michael Adebowale hacked to death in cold blood Drummer Lee Rigby in Woolwich, England. The killers warned that they would murder more kufars or infidels in the future. They were producing body parts as they murdered Drummer Rigby. At the end of the day, the lowest common denominator for the Islamic suicide attack is the template of domestic violence's murder–suicide.

There is the Arabic saying that *Heaven lies beneath the feet of the Mother.* This is the hidden black hole in the jihadi's "body" armor. The extremist ideologies become like the glue for a fragile violent personality. When *ummi* dies, her death functions like a tripwire, unleashing the lethal rage that leads the radical Islamist to become an operational terrorist. Abu Musab al-Zarqawi mourned his mother for 40 days according to Islam and then went on his beheading rampage. Bouyer, who nearly decapitated Theo Van Gogh in Amsterdam, had lost his mother only months earlier, which, according to his sisters, was why he was so rageful. And then there was Nidal Hassan, the U.S. Army Medical Corps officer responsible for the 1990 Fort Hood slayings, who had lost both his parents and had a pet bird. Adam Lankford, author of *The Myth of Martyrdom,* intuitively noted that the bird was his only meaningful attachment. Like a mother, he chewed food for the bird and then let it eat from his mouth. This is a child-rearing practice in the Middle East and Africa and other developing countries where there is no Gerber's baby food. Then one night Hassan rolled over in bed while sleeping and killed the bird. Like a traumatized child, he reversed roles and psychologically killed his mother. Could this have been a tripwire for his shooting rampage? It is rightfully suggested by Lankford as a contributory factor in uncapping his rage, though he did not specifically link it to the bird as a symbol of mother and the maternal attachment. I had an email exchange with Lankford, who is a criminologist, about this particular incident, and he said that he found my interpretation of interest and importance since it took the discussion to an earlier and important developmental level.

In the movie *Zodiac*, the serial killer was finally found by the police. Where? Living in his mother's basement. The basement literally signifies the unconscious "foundational floor" of his psychotic mind and its primitive behavior. He was fused to his mother, and being murderously enraged at not being able to live apart from her, he murdered others as if they were his mother. A murderer cannot tolerate dependency needs and must destroy what is perceived as good and innocent, or what Melanie Klein would call the good breast.

In Arab culture, boys growing up can touch no female other their mothers, but we know many abuse their sisters, some sexually. This has to mean something. The Arab street is always full of raging males who vilify the West because they envy our freedoms and can't compete. They are terrified of modernity, which means free and independent females. All this male testosterone rage was once described as a "wargasm," the Arab equivalent of an orgasm, intimating that such rage shows their impotence, their immaturity.

In the Quran Surah 4, wife beating is mandated in order to "educate" the female. Arabic proverbs help to reinforce this highly ambivalent relationship to the mother, who is also a female: "Woman is shame." "Shame is worse than hell." "Better to die with honor than to live with shame." Related to this matter of controlling the female, in Somali culture they have the custom of a special bridal whip called the Jeedal. So we see that cultural practices are intertwined and inseparable from religious ideologies.

The Arab Muslim community generally condones the behavior associated with suicide bombing, and thus participates in it vicariously in a sadomasochistic way. Have they not created their own unique suicidal zone? The female has merely internalized male rage of the female as self-hatred, and essentially has been co-opted into the psychotic drama of Islamic suicide attacks.

It is true that the Arab father is sadistically tyrannical and makes life miserable for the family in many cases. He is the classic absent father focused on his harem of polygamy rather than on the internal psychic stability of his children. Ruth Stein, the well-known Israeli psychoanalyst, wrote *For the Love of Father,* which concerned religious terrorism,[46] but she failed to take into account the abused mother. Anecdotally, I was told by a New York psychoanalyst that Stein's mother was extremely critical, and whatever Ruth did was never good enough. She was the chronically, relentlessly hated object in her mother's bonding. Ruth, unfortunately, did not give us her inside take on the maternal relationship. The Arab father is a symptom of the problem, not the cause. The problem according to the psychoanalyst and the leading authority on the history of child sacrifice, Dr. Sander Breiner, is "the denigration of the female child from birth on. Everything else is a result (direct and indirect) of this underlying serious pathology."[47]

When I was researching domestic violence and post-traumatic stress disorder, few insights on domestic violence were available in psychoanalytic writing. It was generally not taught at psychoanalytic institutes. But as an increasing number of women psychoanalysts broke through the glass ceiling in the mid-1990s, more literature began to appear. Most of the good scientific literature on PTSD victims was coming out of Israel. Indeed, under the direction of Harold Kudler, M.D., I had helped review the psychodynamic literature on short-term therapy for a chapter in the first edition of *Effective Treatments for PTSD*, which has become a critical text for the disorder through the International Society for Traumatic Stress Studies.

As a psychoanalyst, I had been pondering this kind of aberrant behavior since the Hezbollah Shiite suicide truck bombings in Lebanon back in the early 1980s. The 1993 Hamas suicide bombings took place on my birthday—April 16—which made me want to understand it all the more. There is an Israeli song—*Aretz, aretz, aretz, lanu he em ve-av,* "Our land, land, land is our mother and father"—that illustrates why so much gets wrapped up in land disputes because of the bonding to the mother, which lies buried deep in the unconscious and influences the way people relate to nationalism and "freedom." I am not in favor of a blood and soil kind of nationalism because it psychologically reinforces the maternal fusional link in a potentially violent way. Fusions obviously have their downsides. The suicide attack is emblematic of this unique pathology.

I knew that the destructive behavior of the suicide attack would continue to morph and escalate, that unchecked aggression breeds more aggression and more psychotic behavior. But I did not yet understand what it was about, how it worked psychologically, and how to piece it together. I had not yet recognized its simple underlying pattern of murder–suicide as a common denominator and its significance for group psychodynamics because it was too close to home. I was living it. It was *unheimlich*—uncanny, as Freud would say.

Like the suicide bomber who ultimately kills himself and takes out others by murdering them, the victim–victimizer suicide bomber is nothing more than a pawn, a scapegoat. The family and the public are manipulated by their hysteria, and the perpetrator gets away with murder. Indeed, the suicide bomber concretely acts out a projective identification of the handler and bomb maker and all others in the group.

Isn't this how domestic violence works? When there has been pervasive abuse along with rape, it is not about words, it is about terrors, images, behavior, and senses. This is the essence of manipulation. More than ninety percent of what we communicate, we do so nonverbally. The nonverbal behavior is so horrifying that it blinds us from the craziness and its regressive pull into paranoia, forcing us to side with the aggressor–perpetrator, who claims to be the victim.

Recently a young Haredi girl from the ultra-orthodox Jewish world wrote about her experience of witnessing the abuse and rape of her best friend by her best friend's brother. This occurred in a large "secretive" Hasidic family. Her young friend committed suicide in the bathroom of her home. It is as if the traumatized, abused girlfriend knew that her friend would be strong enough to confront the insular patriarchal hasidic community about this kind of sexual abuse, often rampant within paranoid families. And indeed she was. Her aptly titled memoir *Hush*[48] confronts a similar kind of terror and coercion—that segments of the Jewish community, too, are at risk for increased violent behavior. This is terrorist behavior and that is why it spreads so rapidly and easily across cultures and religions, though some religions are more at risk than others.

Similarly, Deborah Feldman, in her somewhat controversial memoir *UnOrthodox*,[49] writes about escaping from the oppressive Satmar Hasidic community, delving into the unspoken coercive destructive group behaviors grounded in implicit terror due to profound ignorance. It should not come as a surprise if we can see parallels in mentality and behavior between the ultra-orthodox Israeli Jews and, say, the Taliban: engaging in autistic rock throwing rather than trying to negotiate through language, defacing posters of women, refusing to listen to them sing, lacking any sense of aesthetics, etc.

When I watched the first CNN footage of the Twin Towers falling in Manhattan, I immediately associated it with two little boys in pre-school building towers with wood blocks and then knocking them down with a toy airplane. I realized that the terrorists had impaired thinking and that they did not have an early childhood that encouraged play. Like Tom Hanks in the film *Big* they were playing, but in a lethal, destructive way. It was as if these adults were mentally and emotionally stuck at the level of a two-year-old in comprehending how the world works. They just smashed through it, without regard for others.

Even the jihadis or radical Islamists' demand for the burqa speaks volumes about the male since this piece of clothing is a peculiar nonverbal cry for help—that they are trapped in a kind of autistic bubble that they don't know how to get out of and must make the female "feel" what they can't feel. Hence, they shroud and bully their women. When these men who live behind a glass wall come crashing through, they momentarily are free with their bombings, in which they quite literally shatter a lot of glass. I call it jihaditism. It is a kind of malignant autism that no one wants to talk about because it is not politically correct. But just maybe we should begin to think of political correctness as a mask for our own terrors. By turning away, we are participating in the terrorism. It is a process of dehumanization. "Some women who only started wearing the burqa during the Taliban were so unaccustomed to their muffled sensory perceptions and vision, they would stumble and fall."[50]

I understand the burqa as an artificially induced autistic environment. This is what Ayaan Hirsi Ali wrote about it: "The debate that rages over the veil, particularly the *niqab*, which covers most of the woman's face save for the eyes, goes to the very heart of the matter of liberty for Islamic women. Not just freedom for its own sake, but from a life of repression, subordination and violence." Yet an important point of the discussion has been completely missed—namely, that the burqa and niqab are strategies to induce sensory deprivation. Where else is sensory deprivation also found? In torture. Ayaan Hirsi Ali also described sensory deprivation upon seeing Saudi women in black for the first time as a little girl:[51]

> *And all the women in this country were covered in black. They were humanlike shapes. The front of them was black and the back of them was black, too. You could see which way they were looking only by the direction their shoes pointed. We could tell they were women because the lady who was holding our hands tightly to prevent us from wandering off was covered in black, too. You could see her face, because she was Somali. Saudi women had no faces.*
>
> *We pulled away and ran over to the black shapes. We stared up at them, trying to make out where their eyes could be. One raised her hand, gloved in black, and we shrieked, "They have hands!" We pulled faces at her. We were truly awful, but what we were seeing was so alien, so sinister, that we were trying to tame it, make it less awful. And what these Saudi women saw, of course, was little black kids acting like baboons.*

There are counter terrorist experts who describe their interviews as "talking to terrorists." The shortcoming is that they tend to overlook listening closely to them, and are not trained to discern the unconscious communication of these terrorists. The emphasis on "talking" to terrorists misses the point of critical, in-depth "listening" to terrorists. You will learn little from them if you do not detect the deep splitting in their psychological makeup, which is covered over by their slick speech. Some experts assert that the cause of terrorism to a large extent is post traumatic stress. I disagree, as a PTSD trauma expert myself. And while I agree with

Adam Lankford's assessment that suicide bombers are in fact suicidal, the problem arises much earlier in childhood through the traumatic bonding whereby the personality is formed. The personality and developmental disorders that arise are like cognitive deficits. It is a multi-layered affair of trauma compounding trauma that starts in the womb.

Listening and exploring emotional reactions, including somatic or body-centered responses, is key to understanding the terrorists' dissociated minds and their life experiences. In therapeutic lingo we talk about transference and countertransference—the unique bonding experience, albeit temporary, between interviewer and interviewee. Attachment and attunement are indispensable to gleaning exceptional information about the terrorism's communication, about their pantomime of terror. Just as Sun Tzu, the famous ancient Chinese military commander, wrote we must know the mind of the enemy; so too we must know their deepest terrors. Why? Because such insight will lead to better profiling, earlier interventions, along with more effective solutions to counter the kind of violence that exceeds murder itself. Better to play offense than defense.

Terrorists themselves are unaware of their own terrors and are living in deep denial. They are highly dissociated. This does not mean that we simply turn the other cheek; nor do we have to stoop to their level of violent behavior.

I felt myself to be intuitively fluent in the symbolic language of terrorists, having been raised by and wedded to terrorists and having lived the horror. However, little of this could I put into words, It would take time, more moments of realization, and a significant effort on my part to deal with the ebb and tide of my emotions and anxieties plus all of my formal studies. For example, it hit me one day that I needed to read the victim together with the perpetrator as a dynamic, dysfunctional relationship. It wasn't enough to contemplate the pain of the victims. What about the mind of the perpetrators? I began to flip the victim–perpetrator relationship to study the mind of the perpetrator–terrorist systematically.

I enjoyed my mini-freedoms—my travel to Tunisia and Madrid to finish my dissertation and the month in Jerusalem writing and researching. I was also invited back to Madrid after the Al Qaeda train attacks in 2004 to speak on Islamic suicide terrorism. I remain in contact to this day with Isaac Martin Barbero, who was serving on a European Union committee on domestic violence and was one of the few who got the connection to the devalued female. From Madrid I traveled up to Basque Country and met with one of the leading lawyers for civil rights. I asked him if the Basque ETA terrorists could become suicide bombers. He said yes. You can see that religious ideologies do not in and of themselves cause suicide bombing. ETA is interesting because, while Roman Catholic, it is a shame–honor culture and reminded me of the Chechens. Both are mountain people with large patriarchal families and control over the female, and are not particularly modernized, though that has changed for the Basques more than the Chechens. The point here is that the universality of maternal attachment and early childhood development is a much more influential determinant as to who might be drawn to suicide bombing and its violence.

I also was invited to speak in Sri Lanka and traveled to Colombo in March 2005, where my colleague Arjuna Gunawardena, a counterterrorist expert, arranged the lecture, "The Psychodynamics of Islamic Suicide Terrorism: Its Hidden Key & Taproot for The Violence," hosted by Protect Risk Management Solutions Ltd. I also took a brief trip to Tamil Territory. The Tamils and Prabhakaran, their nefarious charismatic leader, recruited child soldiers and females for suicide bombing. The devalued female again played a role. While the Tamils were a nationalist ethnic separatist movement, counterterrorists missed the fact that they were nearly all exposed to Hinduism early in their childhood , where the custom of wife burning on the funeral pyre of the husband had been practiced. This is a fusional image to be sure. Global terrorism has these repeated common threads and interlocking links, yet it is played out locally in culturally specific ways. There were Muslims, too, who were involved in the LTTE, the Liberation Tigers of Tamil Eelam, but Prabhakaran threw them out of the terrorist group in the early nineties. When I was there, I saw areas of Sri Lanka that were almost entirely Muslim and men who seemed to be sporting jihadi attire and the full henna beard venerating the prophet Muhammed. It remains to be seen what radical Islam has in store for Sri Lanka.

As interesting and as helpful as these trips were, they were also hard on me. I was in conflict and terrified about separating myself from the Man without Empathy and from the marriage and allowing myself permanent self-chosen pleasure free from terrors. Why was I terrified of leaving him? Why the phobia? The answer was simple, but it would take years to understand: Since he had raped me, his implicit message was that he could murder me too. It was common knowledge in his family that his increasingly paranoid uncle went after his wife with a butcher knife. I didn't want to wind up that way and saw it coming. After all, many women leave their abusive relationships and are murdered. The excruciating pain of living under a death threat isn't talked about much, or understood.

The death threat under which I lived also dovetailed with the clan culture of the Arabs or even the Somalis. Like Ayaan Hirsi Ali, who received a death threat from her father's clan for writing about her abuse in the movie *Fitna* and in her books *The Caged Bird, Infidel* and *Nomad,* I, too, had been captured early and trained by my clan to be submissive and dominated. I was not supposed to have pleasure. I was like the well-known comical stereotype called "Fatma An-Nabulsiyah," Fatima from Nablus in the West Bank, the ultimate submissive, terrified, dispensable Muslim wife, one of many in the polygamous culture. Fatima or Fatma is the name of the prophet Muhammad's obedient daughter.

Recaptured

I remained separated from the Man without Empathy for only one year. I slid backward into the relationship once again and ultimately returned, as I did after Brazil. However, I was more conscious of the repetitious behavior. By going back, I was repeating the familiar pattern of traumatic bonding with my husband and with my parents, especially my mother. If you haven't lived with terrorism, it is hard to understand it. You are like a mouse caught in the paws of a cat that tosses you back and forth playfully. But it is not play. The intent is lethal. Some of my friends couldn't understand why I went back. But what they also didn't understand is that everyone has a unique sense of timing for exiting a relationship. The timing was simply not yet right for me to permanently cut the cord. With each escape attempt, one gains a bit more ground for the final leaving. The most recent separation had constituted my fourth attempt.

For the first few months after I returned to the Man without Empathy, he scurried to open doors for me and even bought me flowers. But his was nothing more than a foxhole conversion. He was mimicking classic maneuvers in Islamic warfare: the *hudna*, a truce or armistice, and the *tahdiya*, a calming or quieting lull in attacks. He practiced *taqiya*, dissimulation in order to regain the upper hand, while concealing his real intentions. His viciousness then returned tenfold, and he once again raged at me. But this time I was moving forward, gaining strength, as I worked my way out of the marriage. I realized I was married to an emotional infant.

Like an electrical cord slowly becoming unplugged, he was losing his energy source, along with his fantasy of power and control. He never understood that his terror of abandonment and death was like a self-fulfilling prophecy. I surmised that he must have been abused and abandoned in childhood, but he routinely denied it as he began to push me away all the more, enraged that I was gaining freedom. Actually, he had abandoned himself, by not being willing to know and understand his "unthought thoughts," his paranoid accusations, as the famous psychoanalyst Bion so aptly put it. As he became more of a shell, I was becoming more whole. Even though my analysis and the couple therapy failed to deal with the rape and his paranoia, I managed to shore up some solid ground for myself, writing as I went.

PART III

LIBERATION FROM MY "SAUDI ARABIA"

CHAPTER 9

Ending the Delusion
from the Marital Maternal Fusion

In 2006 the Man without Empathy and I were in Tel Aviv. "Menina," my college roommate, and her husband, who live in Nicosia, came for a visit. Menina, which means "girl" in Portuguese, was the nickname my roommate Angela and I had for each other during our third year of college, when I was getting ready to go to Brazil, another attempt to separate from my abusive family and my boyfriend, the Man without Empathy.

One evening, while walking together along the Mediterranean in Tel Aviv, something most remarkable happened. Menina, who had known the Man without Empathy since college, turned to him and started calling him on the carpet: "How could you be so mean to my friend? She doesn't deserve to be treated like that!" I was in awe and couldn't even integrate what Menina was doing on my behalf.

Just like a criminal who has been apprehended, he said nothing. That was always his defense, refusing to speak. He did it in therapy. too, when he was asked questions point-blank. He would say nothing until the therapist changed the subject. Mr. Miranda personified. What I had wanted all along was to have someone throw the Man without Empathy up against a wall and crack his pseudo-defensive shell, although I doubted that his phony exterior could be cracked. But Menina was the first, and the only person, who got his "number" and called him on his grossly abusive behavior. Menina had always considered the Man without Empathy's "sunny" disposition as phony. She was my second source of support after my dead brother MurrayMurphy and could see that the

Man without Empathy was not this wonderful doctor that everyone thought he was.

One other person also bore significant witness to the Man without Empathy's abusive behavior: Ruth Hayden, the Money Lady. During the six years of couple therapy, a friend encouraged me to take Ruth's course on money for couples. The Man without Empathy had actually violated the marriage contract, the *ketubah*, because he never provided for me according to its terms. So my Jewish marriage was a complete sham. The history of money problems was long. For years the Man without Empathy would create credit card debt and then shift the debt around by transferring the balance to new credit cards. I never really understood what he was doing. He was secretive about money. Finally, I realized that he took out home equity loans that ultimately gutted the house of any accumulated worth. He denied me access to money, even the money that I earned, which, out of my own guilt and because of his relentless pressuring, I would hand over to him like a whore to her pimp. After all, he called me that, as did my mother. What was mine was his and what was his was his. He was like a boulevard grand master playing a shill game of walnuts and peas where you had to guess under which shell the money was hidden.

The Man without Empathy had no patience for the Money Lady. But for the first time in the marriage we had a budget, and he finally had to be accountable to someone. Now *he* was under surveillance and he didn't like it. Plus he had to give me money, and I was entitled to keep my own. I made a small contribution to the monthly household budget. And at the end of the six years of seeing the Money Lady once a month, this wonderful woman and accomplished financial adviser said to me in the Man without Empathy's presence, "I want you to know that I see what he is doing." The Money Lady realized that he was a con man. To hear it from another source made me hopeful that not everyone saw me as crazy and knew I wasn't making all of this up.

Calling It Quits

Another turning point came at the wedding of his cousin's daughter in San Antonio. I was having fun with the music and dancing. I've always loved to dance. But the Man without Empathy ordered me to stop. "You're a narcissist!" he shouted at me. His words were a classic example of projection. His was a clever strategy: accuse others of what you do or are. In other words, he was the narcissist who could never think of himself as having a major problem. He then projected his defective narcissistic self on to me, and I became the narcissist. I am not even sure he knew what the word meant. He would pick a fight and then accuse me of starting it. He was like the Taliban—no dancing, no music, no pleasure for females. Since he couldn't obtain pleasure for himself, he had to destroy mine. Pure envy.

He also accused me of being an alcoholic. Even my kids began to assume this was true when it was not. I realized that they had been brainwashed through the chronic insidious exposure of him devaluing me in their presence. This was such a devastating realization on my part that I still have trouble writing about it. Another unspoken effect of living under such compromising conditions.

In 2006, after six years of on-off couple therapy that had failed to help me keep the family intact in a nonviolent threatening environment for me, I decided to divorce the Man without Empathy. I also decided to go back to the couples therapist for three sessions alone. I had felt traumatized by the experience and I needed to figure out for myself why this psychologist would yell at me but not him. I needed to figure out how the therapist could miss the Man without Empathy's abusive behavior and its significance.

At the first session the therapist said to me, "You are so easy to talk to without your husband here." I thought, "What a bizarre thing to say to a client." In retrospect she was telling me that she felt some kind of unconscious pressure to collude with him, that she was terrified of him too. As I was leaving the third and last solo session—it is well known some of the most important things in therapy are said spontaneously at the door knob of the consulting room—I said: "By the way, I have been meaning to tell you that I bit my brother in the chest to get him off of me." It was a spontaneous comment related to Brother Bully's rape. The therapist replied, "Oh, some people would call that amorous lovemaking."

I realized in that moment that the therapist had never believed that I had been raped by my brother or, for that matter, that my husband had raped me as well. It had been the reason for seeing the therapist in the first place—to have my perception of reality validated. I had wanted the Man without Empathy to own his responsibility for the rape, the abortion, and the persistent accusations of being unfaithful, the alleged betrayal. He had repeatedly abused me, and emotionally battered me and yet he avoided responsibility and showed no remorse.

But then again, hard-core rapists would never admit rape. Their defenses are so ingrained and their personalities so poorly developed. This, coupled with the fact that they never developed a sense of empathy, make them incapable of apologizing or, for that matter, making restitution or reparation. They have one-dimensional personalities and can only seek revenge. That fits, too. The couples therapist had made it worse by colluding with the Man without Empathy and participating in his gaslighting. It was too surreal to believe that this happened to me again, and that this therapist treated me unprofessionally and without empathy. I was no longer in denial.

I then saw a therapist who specializes in clergy and therapist abuse. While very perceptive, he made a particular comment to me that showed he just didn't understand the nature of traumatic bonding. He asked me, "Why did you stay so long?" His question should have been, "When did you feel safe enough to leave?" The answer to his question was that I was paralyzed. I was consciously aware that I was grappling with my own grandiosity that somehow I could change things. But deep down I knew I couldn't, and that also complicated the paralysis.

Delusional jealousy is a precursor of homicide. From rape it escalates to murder. That is what is known about domestic violence, and that is why I was too terrified to make a move. When I finally understood this, I felt I was breaking the surface, coming up for air. It's obvious that in a Western therapeutic setting with all its alleged psychological sophistication it is still hard to tackle the nature of delusional jealousy and its paranoia, along with its accompanying dissociation and identification with the aggressor that parallels the honor killing and the mythic delusion of martyrdom. The honor killing occurs because of delusional jealousy. The myth of martyrdom, as Lankford[52] has shown, covers over suicide and depression because one doesn't know how to extricate oneself from all the pain and craziness in the dysfunctional families who have created suicide zones to get rid of their disavowed rage and the scapegoat. It is so terrifying that its reality is repeatedly denied.

Shaking Off the Denial

Like a dog shaking water off its body, I finally was able to shake off the psychological shackles of the marital bonds. I deliberately use the metaphor of "shaking off" because it has a specific meaning to the intractable Israel-Palestinian conflict, as it has been characterized.[53] The "shaking off" of a conqueror is the translation for the Arabic word intifada. It had been a more than 40-year personal intifada for me.

So much of the language surrounding marriage and divorce articulates the bonds of the maternal fusion and the traumatic couple attachment. Psychologically, separation is an attempt to extract oneself from a maternal merger or fusion and regain a new sense of identity. The process of divorce is much more complicated and reflects the struggle for freedom. Divorce also includes the reactions of others to the change in the status quo. There is significant identification with the aggressor when there has been domestic violence. The lawyers are duped into identifying with the stronger horse, so to speak, and take a dim view of the female, especially the older female, who becomes invisible in their eyes because she has nothing exciting to offer, so they think. Often the female lawyers have been co-opted by the patriarchal power structure of the court system, which is like one big clan.

Divorcing is like cutting the cord or splitting an atom with a nuclear reaction—fission versus fusion. In 2000, the year I fled from the marriage, I chose the first divorce lawyer I saw from *Women and the Law*, edited by an acquaintance who was a gifted lawyer and whose husband was also an ophthalmologist. I told Lawyer 1 about the domestic violence, and she told me that I would fare poorly in the divorce proceedings because I had been married for so long and my husband had created debt and was a power and control freak. Lawyer 1 did nothing to help me, and it seemed as if I were doomed to more years of abuse. The encounter increased my terror of divorcing.

In 2004 or 2005 I was referred by a friend to Lawyer 2, who could not or would not take the case for reasons that were unclear. Probably because the assets weren't that lucrative. It went to one of her underlings, who ultimately left the firm. The case reverted to Lawyer 2, who seemed both competent and nice. But things fell apart at the temporary spousal maintenance hearing. The court referee hearing divorce cases, many of which involve domestic violence, had been accused by his ex-wife of being abusive. The Man without Empathy smirked like the Cheshire cat during the hearing as the referee sided with my husband's argument that the spousal maintenance payment should be lower than I requested because he (like the court referee) was close to retirement. That the Man without Empathy had taken a huge pay cut in order to diminish spousal maintenance payments didn't seem to matter to the referee. Lawyer 2, distressed after the disastrous hearing, told me to go out and create credit card debt to show the court that I could not meet my budget! I refused and told Lawyer 2 that I could not trust her. My anxiety soared.

Older women pose a particular threat to lawyers and the legal system because most of such divorces are not amicable. The majority of women probably divorce out of desperation. The older woman who initiates divorce proceedings shows that she is bucking the system of submission. She does not want to exist as if she were living in Saudi Arabia. The system and its players did not seem to want to help me get out of the marriage in a financially viable manner; nor had they communicated to me that I was believed. It was as if because I was an aging female psychoanalyst they could act very poorly and treat me disrespectfully behind closed doors. They hurled their transferences at me, the projections of their own rage and unhappiness.

This projection put me in mind of what it must be like in a very strict Muslim society like Saudi Arabia, Afghanistan, Iraq, Pakistan, and even parts of Indonesia where Wahhabi Salafi ideologies rule. It even reminded me of the Shiite-infused Iranian mistreatment of women. I thought of the Iranian movie *A Separation* (2011), in which the Iranian woman struggles to divorce. There is also a subplot of a prenatal woman suffering a miscarriage. It is an upside down world with limited rights for women and the female is rarely believed. Life seemed to me to be stranger than fiction as I struggled through the ordeal.

In 2006 another friend referred me to Lawyer 3, who, it turned out, had trained Lawyer 2. He assured me it would represent no conflict of interest and that all would be fine. It was not. He was reputed to be one of the Twin Cities' best divorce lawyers, but I later was told that he was a big talker and earned little respect from his colleagues. I thought about looking for someone else, but I knew the court would not look favorably on my changing lawyers again. Not only did Lawyer 3 not have me sign a legal retainer, he lied to me. He promised me that I would get at the very least what I had gotten for temporary spousal maintenance. In fact, the final settlement was railroaded through. I sensed that some kind of deal had been cut behind my back.

In 2008, I sought a legal consultation with a fourth lawyer, who helped walk me through the remaining process of the divorce. Lawyer 3 didn't like being under surveillance, but eventually he got the job done. All of this speaks again to the layers of paranoia wrapped around the control of the female who seeks freedom. The process of divorcing became for me more and more complicated each step of the way. And this was America. If it is hard to pursue this in America, imagine how much more complicated and difficult it must be for a female in the Middle East, Afghanistan, or Pakistan.

We tried two separate sets of mediations. I knew it would be useless, yet I also knew that if I didn't participate, the court referee would hold it against me should the divorce go to trial. The entire experience made me understand why mediation is unsuccessful between the Israelis and the Palestinians despite repeated attempts. Since they don't have a viable partner, it just doesn't work. Similarly, I did not have a viable partner because the abusive personality is bent on revenge.

Arab Muslim and non-Arab Muslim families are predicated on only giving an "appearance" of peace. Since Islam continues to claim it is the religion of peace and denies its doctrine of jihad and accompanying violent ideologies, this means that Muslim families really only know war. The majority of women who are devalued must go along with the program; otherwise they will be killed. Because they do not know inner peace, they cannot achieve peace with others. They are constantly embattled because being in opposition to the other through battle provides them the boundaries they otherwise don't have. They lack a psychological infrastructure and have a cognitive deficit. For the terrorists this is just multiplied many times over. They are a hyperextension of these troubled, highly paranoid societies that kill their own, which exposes the major deficit in their thinking: Why would you want to kill your own children and women?

Terrorism is a destructive bond. To gain distance from terrorists, one must find transitional objects and concrete activities involving new experiences that help destroy the destructive bond and allow one to break free of their power and control. The objects function as place-holders, and map out new space. By being proactive and choosing freely what you want to do, you put something solid under your feet. These new experiences and objects, like buying a pair of ballet slippers or changing one's name, are often the first time that the abused woman gets to decide for herself what she wants to do. The terrorists can't stand to see people embrace freedom because it reminds them momentarily of what they lack. They must have power and control. The terrorist's destructive bond is his half of the traumatic bond. He wants bondage; the other person wants to be free of the imposition of being dictated to. The bondage/bond harkens back to the issue of maternal attachment, the first bond in life. That is why terrorists misuse people. They unconsciously experience and relate to people as objects.

The lawyers and mediators never set limits with the Man without Empathy. They allowed him to continue his abusiveness. At one mediation session, he started ranting at me that I had to give up going to ballet because it was an extravagance and too expensive. My ballet lessons cost about $15 for an hour and a half. It wasn't the money; he just couldn't stand that I enjoyed myself. Going back en pointe forty-eight years after my mother had stopped me from studying ballet was a personal challenge in celebration of my sixtieth birthday. I wanted to reclaim my relationship to the arabesque, to seize control of my own take-off into a new life. I practiced hard, hoisting myself up to the barre, bursitis and all. Ballet had always been special, magical and gave me a tiny taste of what it meant to be free.

The arabesque (arab-esque) became my initial and ultimately concrete kernel of interest in Arabic. Studying Arabic was my attempt to understand and walk in the shoes of the other. This was part of my spirit, too—this desire for liberty and justice for all. So why not for myself? I wanted to know the roots of the dance position, its beautiful movement, its sense of extension of self and openness. My fascination with this word began when I learned about the Golden Age of Spain. To an eight-year-old, the Golden Age sounded glorious, like a fairy-tale time when Christian, Jews, and Muslims lived together allegedly in peace, *convivencia*. As I learned about periodization, narrativity, genres, national literature, and power relationships, the Golden Age became tarnished. It was nothing more than an engineered narrative of the 1950s, produced by the Arab world to whitewash what was essentially the spread of Islam into the West in A.D. 711, by three things—the sword, forced conversion, and making a lot of babies. Once again an obsession with spreading one's seed, an impregnation fetish!

The old narratives were disproved by Bat Ye'or, a leading authority on dhimmitude, the protected class of Christians and Jews under Islam who are never really free. The root of dhimmitude means to blame. The Christians and especially the Jews are always blamed. They are the female in a terrorist's mind's eye. And although it shouldn't have, Anton Shammas' Hebrew novel *Arabesque* rocked Israeli society, primarily because Israeli Jews were terrified to think that a non-Jew, let alone an Arab Christian Israeli Palestinian, could write so beautifully in Hebrew—and that Israeli Palestinian Muslim and Christian Arabs existed and mattered.

I also was inspired to study Arabic by the Man without Empathy's great aunt Yocheved. We stayed with them during the 1972 summer in Israel. They had lived in Rana'ana since 1942, way before it was completely built up and settled by the "Anglos," English-speaking immigrants. I was gratified by Yocheved's kindness to and patience with me. Yocheved was fluent in Arabic even though she was not formally educated. This made an impression on me, and she became a hidden role model, so to speak. I learned much later at a family celebration that she had been unhappily married for years. She was an orphan and the larger clan insisted that she marry the man whom they had chosen for her. She had been in love with someone else. There are many women in the Haredi community like that and many millions more in the Arab Muslim and non-Arab Muslim world.

In both the Haredi world and much of the Muslim world, marriages are an arranged affair. The more ultraconservative the group, the more the young woman is stripped of the ability to make her own decisions. She does not have that prerogative and has been trained early through subtle and not-so-subtle terrorist practices, threats, innuendos, and accusations that her behavior is not acceptable. She is worn down, and in the end submits. There is always an undercurrent of terror and anxiety surrounding the issue of "who is going to take care of me?" And in the end women are emotionally abandoned in horrible marriages. The promise in the marriage contract that they will be "taken care of" is obviously never fulfilled where there is abuse.

Enough

At some point in the divorce and mediation proceedings and the couple therapy, I finally threw the Man without Empathy out of the bedroom. His reaction was like a two-year-old throwing a tantrum. I wished I had had a video camera to tape his behavior and bring it to therapy. There it was again, the importance of the nonverbal communication that many never see because it happens behind closed doors. It made me wonder how devalued his mother must have been as the fourteenth baby of an Ultra Orthodox Haredi family. In retrospect, I am convinced she was also abused. The Man without Empathy refused to leave the house and said I would have to call the police to get him out. I told him I would not do that. Restraining orders often don't work, and besides I did not want any more high drama. It took him four days to move out. That he would want to stay when I didn't want him revealed more of his adhesive identity and traumatic bonding to me, behavior that I regretted others did not see.

My good friend Meira, one of Israel's leading psychiatric nurses, who met the Man without Empathy on a medical mission in Odessa, told me years later that she was profoundly relieved when I finally divorced him. Meira had seen and felt his rage once when she innocently offered him her massage appointment at the hotel. It fascinated me that he became enraged over something so blatantly erotic—a massage. She had never told me this before. Few ever saw this rage, and his family, friends, and colleagues would defend Dr. Jekyll to the max, not knowing that he was Mr. Hyde, too. He was that clever.

Terrorism is hype. People are always surprised to discover that a terrorist is a doctor or dentist, like Al Qaeda's Ayman Al-Zawahiri, or an eye doctor, or a Nazi physician like those that Robert Jay Lifton wrote about.[54] Robert Louis Stevenson got it right when he created Dr. Jekyll and Mr. Hyde. Some doctors hide behind the mask of their profession, predicated on the Hippocratic Oath to do no wrong, yet behind closed doors, or in the case of the terrorists, commit violent, violating acts. Doctors are not humanists. There will always be people like Nonie Darwish, Wafa Sultan, and Ayaan Hirsi Ali who will continue to speak out and refuse to be terrorized. And they will bring along others, who will begin to understand how terrorism works.

The Man without Empathy was told by my lawyers not to contact me. He did anyway. He hated that I would not e-mail him or speak to him, that I ignored him. Even at the divorce proceedings he had the audacity to speak without permission, and the judge did nothing. On a limited income I had saved money and had not created debt, even in the face of mounting legal bills. Because the Man without Empathy had never paid off a mortgage and kept borrowing against the house, there was no equity as part of the settlement. He then stuck me with half of the undergraduate loans for the children, who had been sent out East to school. He made four times what I made, which was not factored in by my lawyer. After I moved to New York to spend some time with my kids and grandsons, I was told that doesn't happen in New York divorces: the husband pays for the educational loans.

As soon as the divorce was final, I went back to the Money Lady and told her that I could not have divorced without the knowledge that she had given me. The Money Lady understood my dilemma. She also taught me a most important thing: that everybody has a dream, and you have only one chance to live your dream. Your dream is your own—no one else's—and it is not to be put down or disparaged. My dream was to live in Israel. Since my first visit in 1972, I had wanted to live there and have my children born and raised there. I harbored other smaller fantasies that were like the placeholders for shoring up my fledgling sense of self in trying to figure out how to pursue my dream. I still had to get out from under the remnants of The Man without Empathy's obsession with me, the focus of his hatred.

Concrete Identity Change

I had dark hair and was fair, like my father. In my quest to piece together a sense of freedom, a sense of self, I intuitively went blond. It was another "concrete" act of doing something different rather than just thinking about it. Concrete behavior is not necessarily a bad thing if it is emotionally understood. Terrorist behavior is concrete. However, it is dissociated. Think of the planes flying into the Twin Towers. To use planes as missiles with innocent people on board shows that terrorists are deeply disturbed and detached from reality. To attain a sense of reattachment requires literally bonding through violence that creates death. They do not know how to be, to live. They are out of touch with reality and exist in a violent dream world. But if confronted, they will deny it.

When I first became a blond, I thought that I was trying to master something about my mother, who was a natural blond terrorist. Then I wondered if I were simply trying to fit in with Minnesotans. Both my kids were blond when they were little, but I didn't look like the typical Minnesota Scandinavian. Back in 1978 Minnesotans prided themselves on their historical roots and ties to Sweden and Norway. In fact, the bond is so strong that it written in the charter for the University of Minnesota that Swedish will be taught in perpetuity. This ethnic tie proved to be the back door through which the Jewish community made the argument in the early 1960s that if Swedish could be taught at the university, so should Hebrew. It opened the door to diversity and minority language studies, including af-Somali, which is now taught there. And, of course, I was able to study the dead language of Aljamia, Old Spanish in Arabic script.

However, there were downsides to this identification with Scandinavia and other Germanic cultures. Minnesota, like Sweden and Norway, was pathologically in love with what I called the "erotic, exotic other of the sadomasochistic bondage"; à la Lawrence of Arabia, they loved the Arabs and by extension Somalis. The other was the "slave," and the "Aryan" blonds remained the masters. Yet this love masked a history of well-known anti-Semitism in the state. I generalize here and run the risk of stereotyping, but it is important to make the point that the Aryans and the Arabs/Muslims could unite in hatred against the early mother—the Jew. Bottom line: they did not want to accept that the Jews came first in terms of religious history and still struggle with their failure to accept their Judaic roots.

Neighbors, colleagues, and especially strangers would inevitably ask if I were from New York, implying, "Are you Jewish?" Some asked that outright. I finally realized why I had gone blond after a conversation with my Jewish Argentinian neurologist, who trained in Buenos Aires, which has the largest per capita number of psychoanalysts in the world. "Your husband has an obsession with you," the doctor told me. "We marry our psychopathology." That seemed to be an obvious fit, yet I had to hear it from another person whom I trusted, and the timing had to be right. I don't ever remember my analyst saying that; he had been too focused on my childhood, perhaps because he, too, feared the aggression of the Man without Empathy. I was now ready to integrate what my neurologist said. The Man without Empathy had an obsession with dark haired, brown-eyed women. As if to prove the point, within the same time frame of me throwing him out and going blond, he found a girlfriend—a woman with dark hair. Perhaps they had even been together before then.

The girlfriend was the perfect prey: a widowed physician in administration in his clinic system: not particularly attractive but smart, someone he could hide behind; financially well off, someone he could also pimp; non-Jewish, someone who wouldn't pressure him about providing for her the way a Jewish woman might; single, someone he could use to evoke sympathy for having rescued her; widowed, so he would have no sexual competitor.

I was told that the divorce would cost me personally, that I would lose friends. Indeed, several turned on me. They did not believe I had been raped. I asked a female friend how it was possible to be friends with him knowing all that he had done to me. She was shocked at being confronted. I felt sorry for her. The Man without Empathy went running to everyone he knew, trying to win over our mutual friends, including one of my closest analyst friends. He even told my cousin that he was the victim in the marriage. But when he visited old friends back in Portland, they could see that he was evasive and could not establish eye contact with them. His shame was so great.

While terrorism is always lethally malicious, maiming and murdering, it is also repetitious, boring, and monotonous. This is part of its banality. Repetition tries to wear down the victims. But every now and then terrorists escalate and perpetrate an act that is new and shocking, a twist—like ramming airplanes into twin towers. There was a paradigm shift after 9/11, but the underlying template is the same old, same old, revolving around the terror of abandonment and the terror of murder. The key is the maternal platform of the early bonding experience, which makes or breaks terrorists.

CHAPTER 10

When East Meets West:
The Unmarriage of Two Minds

The divorce was finalized by the Minnesota courts on December 31, 2008. I also got a Jewish religious divorce, called a *get*. The process takes about six months, and the husband has to give the divorce. Judaism and Islam share this in common. The divorce is given by the male, not the female. The complicated nature of obtaining the *get* falls within the parameters of religious law and offers yet another point of departure on how Islam borrowed from Judaism and its Middle Eastern culture but expanded and upped the ante to arrive at a more grandiose fixation on marriage and divorce. In this regard the female is at a disadvantage and does not have the power or control. She loses financially and socially. In Islam divorce is even worse.

In Islam divorce is called *talaq*; the husband grants the divorce like in Judaism, but all he has to say is "I divorce you" three times and, poof, you are divorced. This speaks to the similar speed with which a suicide bomber works: Poof, you are gone! The impetus is the inability to tolerate anxiety and the rapid rise of rage. In Islam like Judaism it is true that the wife can initiate a divorce, a *khula*, but it is much more complicated. She doesn't just say "I divorce you, I divorce you, I divorce you." It is not quick and immediate as it is for the man, who can say it on the spot in a moment of rage, and the marriage is history. So the woman is always at risk of being divorced if her husband becomes enraged. She has no genuine stability in the marriage and is constantly walking on eggshells.

There is also the category of temporary marriage in Islam that works at this same lightening speed. A jihadi can decide that he wants to have sex with a woman. This is known as jihad al nikah, or sex jihad, which permits extramarital sexual relations with multiple partners during battle. If he is married and off fighting, he can opt for a "quickie" marriage in order to fulfill his sexual urges. How does a woman's initiating a divorce and temporary marriages fit with the mentality of jihadis? They show that the woman always pays the price. Her circumstances are much harder and asserting her will is nearly impossible. Moreover, treatment of the female as an object to be controlled shows that the terrorists are terrified of the female. Otherwise why would they need to control her? Also, it shows that terrorists have very poor impulse control since their personalities are fragile—that is, they are borderlines.

In conservative sectors of the Muslim population, those that are producing the terrorists, they practice polygamy. Because they can take up to four wives, they never really have to emotionally invest in one stable relationship, so the men have many female "objects" to relate to. This causes instability in relating to people in general, or poor object constancy, and problems with boundaries. If you don't like someone, you just "divorce" them. There is no sense of genuine commitment. It is hard to make peace with someone like this as they are always ready for war—i.e., divorce.

Jewish divorce is also patriarchal. The Jewish Agency, the *Sokhnut*, the pre-state organization for Israel that subsequently took on the operation of immigration to Israel, also requires a *get* for *aliyah*, the right of return for Jews to Israel. *Meshane makom, meshane mazal*—change your place, change your luck—is a favorite Hebrew saying. I value my Judaism, but I look forward to the day when Judaism becomes less patriarchal. For now, I was willing to go along with the rules as they stand. Another instance of using soft power, picking and choosing one's battles.

I knew two of the three male rabbis who were at the ceremony formalizing the *get*. The first was a rabbi that the Man without Empathy demanded for both the *get* and the ceremony. He was not my rabbi, but I had respect for him. I did not know the second rabbi. I had sought out the third rabbi, Rabbi Shavit-Lonstein, to start the *get* process going. He was the proverbial *mensche*, Yiddish for a person of integrity and honor. He was the rabbi of our former congregation, the synagogue in which my kids were raised. Following my first separation from my husband in 2000, in the time of my crisis, I had felt abandoned by the synagogue.

When I went to start the *get* process, Rabbi Shavit-Lonstein asked a series of questions and took notes. At the very end I asked if it were permissible to speak, as I had been long taught. I said, "Rabbi, I am sixty years old, and I want you to know what happened because I don't want another Jewish woman to go through what I have gone through." I told him the whole saga about the rape three months into the marriage, and about being forced into an abortion, which was terrifying. I told him about the repeated abuse I had received at home from my parents and brother. And that I had thought because my husband came from a traditional Jewish home he would be kind to me.

Rabbi Shavit-Lonstein looked me in the eye and said, "I want you to know that when we learn about domestic violence, we are taught that there can be one instance of violence early in the marriage that shuts it down until the person can get out. You are the success story." I had come for the *get*, but I received something so much more precious: I was believed and understood. Rabbi Shavit-Lonstein did not know how much he had helped me, although I did not feel like a success story. It had taken too much out of me to free myself from the marriage. Moreover, a good friend of mine, Amy Erani, brought to my attention that according to Jewish law if a husband is not willing to make aliyah, to immigrate to Israel, the wife can automatically obtain a divorce. He had made promise after promise but never acted on them, and I came to believe that once again he was manipulative and uncooperative. Whatever I wanted not only did he not want, he sought to inflict harm.

When you go into a public bathroom, for example in a university or in a synagogues, stickers on the door of the stall often advertise an 800 number to call if you are being abused. A sticker is not enough. There is too much passive terrorism in the Jewish community, which has never really wanted to deal seriously with the issue of domestic violence and sexual abuse.

It is said that one-fifth of all Jewish women experience domestic violence. According to The Centers for Disease Control, one-quarter of all women in America experience domestic violence. El Feki reports that in Egypt one-third of all women are victims of domestic violence,[55] and goes on to say that "Intimate partner violence is a common problem across the Arab world and what statistics do exist undoubtedly underestimate the scale of the problem." It is not known, to the best of my knowledge, what the rate is for domestic violence among immigrant groups in America. But sheriff's deputies from the domestic violence unit whom I accompanied on ride-alongs have told me that the number is high, especially among the Somali community in Minnesota. When I interviewed prisoners in Minneapolis about their early childhoods, violence, and their mothers, the Somali men told me why they hated America— because the minute they lifted their hands to strike their women and children, the kids would call the police. Thank God, at least the kids get that it is wrong to be hit and abused.

Hitting one's children is not acceptable in American culture, unlike in conservative Muslim cultures, where wife beating is routine. The attitude that you can treat your wife and children like pieces of property and just smash them is the same attitude of the political terrorists who strike the infidels. By age three, learned violence in the home becomes fertile ground for the males, and even the females, to grow into terrorists.

It is impossible to fully describe what it took to get out of such a bad relationship and marriage. It had taken me more than forty-two years. People still saw the Man without Empathy as the good guy, but I could no longer worry about it. When they asked me why it had taken so long and told me that if I had really wanted to I could have divorced him sooner, I knew they were voicing their own terrors about how threatened they were by me—someone who knew terror in its smallest, most minute details but managed to finally extricate herself from it.

Not long after the *get* was finalized, Rabbi Sherwin, my mentor from my days at Spertus College of Judaica, called one night to ask for my help. He had another former student and now friend whose marriage was in crisis. He said his friend's story was nearly identical to mine and told her that she should speak with me. "She is a psychoanalyst and she has been there. She will understand you." It was late and I was exhausted, but I felt morally obligated to speak with this woman. We talked long into the night. Our husbands, coincidentally both from Indiana, were both control freaks and terrorists. For me it was gratifying to help another woman. I could tell her what to expect and how to stay strong.

My naïve fairy tale narrative had been that by marrying a man from a traditional Jewish family I would be safe. Slowly, over the years—when I felt safe enough to see and face the truth, when I was less dissociated, I finally understood that I had been living with someone who was incredibly like an Arab terrorist. If I had been told that good would come from crying myself to sleep every night, year after year, how all that pain and contemplating suicide would help me understand the psychology of the Islamic suicide attack, I would say it still wasn't worth it.

On the Move

I was ready to try out my new freedom and signed on as a contractor for BAE Systems, headquartered in Rockville, Maryland, to begin training with a human terrain team that would go to Iraq or Afghanistan. I had met General M. C. Meigs, founder of JIEDDO—the Joint Improvised Explosive Device Defeat Office (for roadside bombs) under which the Human Terrain System program is housed—in Israel and had mentioned my desire to go to Iraq or Afghanistan. My training required that I return to Kansas City, the scene of the traumatic forced abortion that followed my rape. This time, I was no longer filled with terror, the terrain of which I now knew well.

I made a trip back to Chicago before I went to Kansas. I had not been there since the mid-1990s, when I commuted to Chicago from the Twin Cities for my psychoanalytic training. It was spring, and Michigan Avenue was abloom with thousands of tulips. As I flew into O'Hare, I thought of my Uncle Lenny, Mayor Daly's chief contract lawyer, who had drawn up the contract for O'Hare after World War II. The visit was healing, something of a bittersweet victory tour. I thought about how I had managed to survive all those years of living in my parents' home, under a kind of Sharia law as the littlest of the *hamula*, the clan. In the worst of times, I experienced fragile but genuine moments of connection with people who cared about me, moments that were buried deep within me for such a long time: moments with Uncle Lenny (my father's eldest brother, whom my parents were united in hating because they believed he was the favorite son) and "Aunt" Florence, moments with my grandmothers, with whom my parents never allowed me to develop a relationship.

Returning to Chicago also reminded me of visiting Lincoln Park Zoo, where I fell in love with Bushman, the zoo's famous gorilla. We silently communicated with our eyes, sort of flirting, and I felt loved by him in an unqualified way. Years later, I read the memoirs of Donna Williams and other people who are autistic and wrote of their revelations about how humans communicate through their relationships with other primates. Other than the Saudis, gorillas are the only primates that have harems. This seemed to fit with the idea of the Saudi man's need to have a harem of females at his disposal in order to spread his "selfish genes," as neurocriminologist Adrian Raine put it in his book *The Anatomy of Violence*.[56] Reproducing and having many babies has nothing to do with the betterment of the social group. It involves pure power and control, with the biological imperative to function like a sperm donor.

In my naïve childhood personification, Bushman was big and strong, and would take care of me. This fantasy helped me understand the nonverbal behavior and imagery of Saudi terrorists—predatory and animal-like, a fall-back position of primitive behavior. I believe that the Saudis themselves at some unconscious level are uncomfortable with apes because they feel that they mimic their behavior. Throughout the Quran, Jews are referred to derogatorily as apes and pigs. This is nothing more than a projection. The terrorists split off what they don't like about themselves and project it onto the other in order to handle feelings that they find hard to admit. It is as if they cannot stand the idea of imperfection in themselves. They have to be perfect, pure, and clean at all times in the shame–honor society in which they live. It is dirty to have messy needs and emotions.

Finally, I visited the pond in Hyde Park, where I fondly remembered children sailing miniature sailboats. Imagining that pond and those sailboats had been my refuge in chaos, a place of calm whenever I became anxious. (As

I write this, I reflect upon the choice of a boat as a hiding place for Dhzokhar Tsarnaev in the aftermath of the Boston Marathon Attacks.)

On a Saturday in June 2009, I returned to Kansas City. I had not been back since the abortion. It is startling how life recycles, including its emotions and trauma. I lived in Kansas City but trained in Leavenworth, participating in the controversial Human Terrain Program created by TRADOC, the teaching arm of the U.S. Army. As a social scientist for BAE systems, I was attached to an interdisciplinary team of seven as part of the counterinsurgency effort of the Army to connect with the local population. In short, I was to be a kind of cultural interpreter for the Army.

BAE Systems was a disaster. They did not protect their employees. They backed the retired military. I suppose in retrospect that this should not have surprised me. Essentially we had no rights. A psychoanalyst and professor of sociology, Jennifer Hunt, dropped out of the program because she felt that the program was so paranoid she couldn't trust anybody if she went down range into the war zone. She is now writing a book about HTS and is conducting extensive investigative interviews. I predict that this book will become a crucial textbook for COIN, counterinsurgency, and what went wrong during the Afghan war in particular. In the meantime Vanessa Gezari published her book on the Human Terrain Program titled: *The Tender Soldier: A True Story of War and Sacrifice.* While the book tells the story of Paula Loyd, an accomplished member of the Human Terrain Program, who was immolated to death by an Afghan, Gezari investigated some of the abuse and corruption that went on in the program. But she failed to research anti-Semitism and hatred of Jews and Israelis in the program as well as within the war zone. One can not really understand Muslim cultures and Islam if one does not honestly explore the use of the Jew and the female as objects of chronic hatred and blame.

I wanted to gain an understanding, if possible, about how the Army conceptualized fighting, as well as to see and experience how the enemy operated.

I have a particular interest in IEDs, improvised explosive devices, better known as roadside bombs. This interest came about after working on the problem of the psychodynamics of suicide terrorism. It seemed to me that IEDs were the next area that I needed to understand. I am trying to conceptualize the IEDs from a psychosexual perspective and the primitive mental states of terrorists. They have an obsession with impregnating the ground with bombs, a fertility fetish if you will. I am also interested in the networks and the "emplacers," those who literally seed the ground with the bombs. The IEDs are cousins to landmines and much work still needs to be done to understand this level of brutal symbolic communication. Indeed, almost no work exists explaining how terrorists choose and use objects unconsciously and what they are really communicating about their internal terrors. For example, in the case of 9/11 they didn't just strategically choose the Twin Towers; they were also communicating to us unconsciously that they feel inferior and rageful and cannot compete in the modern world.

I never got to go to Helmand Province, Afghanistan , where I was slated to deploy as a social scientist. The Human Terrain System program turned out to be a dysfunctional cult, a cross between Jonestown and Lord of the Flies. If you weren't willing to drink the Kool-Aid, you paid the price. There were, however, lots of aspects of the program that I enjoyed. For example, I opted to go to Arabic class, although I was slated for Afghanistan, because I had never really studied Iraqi Arabic. I love Arabic as I do Hebrew.

After months of hard training. I was graduated from the program in January 2010 at the top of the class with security clearance at the level of secret. I was, however, asked to leave. I had confronted my team leader, a Roman Catholic lieutenant colonel, about the intolerable work conditions he had created and his gay-baiting the other social scientist on my team. I also blew the whistle on the program when I was told to contact Tim McClees, a congressional staffer who had been investigating the program for the U.S. House of Representative's Subcommittee on Arms. The program

PENETRATING THE TERRORIST PSYCHE

would not even let me take off for Yom Kippur. I have the email to prove it. They were anti-Semitic, as well as racist, sexist, and homophobic.

Our team had been sent up from Leavenworth Kansas to do the Afghan Immersion program at the University of Nebraska. This is the oldest program in the country; even the Brits and Canadians send their leaders there to learn about Afghanistan, as if it could help. One teammate characterized it as a boondoggle. The teaching was poor and the presentation of Islam was appalling. Everything was given a good spin and white washed. Also, the language instruction was at a ridiculously low level. I had studied Persian and some Pashto, the language of the Taliban, on my own during the preceding subzero winter in St. Paul, Minnesota, which was adequate, although they speak Dari, the Eastern dialect of Persian. I wondered what others really brought away from the program.

During this time in Omaha I had the first of two interviews for U.S. security clearance. The second took place on my return from the National Training Center at Fort Irwin. I ultimately obtained security clearance at the level of "secret." We were told that it cost about a quarter of a million dollars to obtain such clearance, and that it is good for ten years.

Our team was also sent to the National Training Center at Fort Irwin California, to participate in war games. Fort Irwin is larger than the state of Rhode Island. Fifteen hundred troops amassed to begin the games with a lot of big toys. We had to schlep 65 pounds of body armor, but I had trained for it at the YMCA in Kansas City.

When they decided to summarily throw me out of the program, it happened fast, without warning, while I was at Fort Irwin. The poisonous seminar leader told me to pack my stuff, threw my duffle bags in the back of his pickup truck and did not allow me to speak. He drove me to the outskirts of NTC, about twenty minutes away, where there were warehouse-like structures for assembling the troops before war games.

This allegedly professional former military seminar leader shoved a paper and pen at me and said "Sign this. It's counseling."

I refused to sign anything, which enraged the seminar leader, who deposited me in one of the structures, told me I was flying back to Kansas the next day, and drove off. He left me stranded. You never ever abandon a soldier, or even a POW. The sun set. It is cold at night in high desert. I had no food with me and nowhere to sleep. I used my cell phone to call my seminar leader in Virginia, where part of the program is housed. He started screaming at me over the phone, too. Again, blame the female. He finally told me to find the control center, where soldiers drove me to the women's facility, which the seminar leader should have done in the first place. The next day the seminar leader came back to take me to the airport, where I was picked up by one of my classmates, Tim Sweemer, the only one who really stood by me. I am still in contact with him today.

The ultimate irony was that when I got back to Kansas City there was a message on my hotel answering machine from John P. Galligan, the retired U.S. Army Colonel who was the defense lawyer for Army psychiatrist and Islamist terrorist Major Nidal Malik Hassan of the Fort Hood Massacre on November 5, 2009, in which thirteen were murdered, including one pregnant soldier. Hassan had stood up and shouted Allahu Akbar, the jihad battle cry, before he began to spray his victims with gunfire. Hassan was described as socially isolated, which fits with my theory that the behavior of terrorists is autistic-like. Anders Breivik, Cho of the Virginia Tech Massacre, Jared Lee Loughner, the Unibomber, and Adam Lanza who perpetrated the Sandy Hook Elementary School Massacre have all been described as high-functioning autistics, often diagnosed as having Aspergers. Galligan had found my work on line and asked me to be an expert witness at trial of Nidal Hassan. I had to decline the offer because I was working with the Army at that time, and it would have compromised my "neutrality." Gallagher's invitation to be an expert witness spoke to the fact that I had the "right stuff," but within the Human Terrain Program my talents were attacked rather than embraced and sought after.

The episode involving the Human Terrain Program demonstrates yet another tenet of terrorism, that when counterterrorists or military personnel who are supposed to be tracking and dealing with terrorists begin to act like terrorists they have taken the poisonous bait. They do not realize they are terrified themselves, and attack those who discern truth from fascistic falsehood.

This was a program tasked to connect with the local population for COIN, which could not even connect with its own students. A further irony is that HTS and COIN were going into cultures like Iraq and Afghanistan, where the leading problem remains the devalued female and the violence stemming from that hatred. I felt an overwhelming despair that the military refused my help in Afghanistan and Iraq. The program was not the best part of the Army. To this day I remain in contact with the best part of the U.S. Army—some military colleagues, Scott Jansen Cheek and Dr. Steve Lawhead, at Fort Leonard Wood. In July 2012 a former HTS graduate, Michael Gonzalez, wrote to me saying that they were using my work in psyops in trying to reintegrate the Taliban. I was gratified to learn about this and feel that I was making some impact. This has always been my hope and my goal.

Going Forward

In my first book, *The Banality of Suicide Terrorism: The Naked Truth About Islamic Suicide Bombing*, I devoted an entire chapter to what we should do in order to solve the problem of violent terrorist attacks. I stated unequivocally that we must make every effort to support the females, including the little girls, in all these shame–honor cultures that turn to violence. It is really a human rights issue. No child should be simply an object to a parent or family, and, worse than that, an object to be hated. Such abhorrent treatment guarantees the tragedy of transmitting the trauma across generations, furthering acts of terror. I repeat—this is not to blame the female.

Obviously we cannot control global terrorism. We can only be aware of it, try to understand it, attempt appropriate military interventions, and recognize the cultural implications—the differences between East and the West, where terrorism and violence towards women and children is considered not only deplorable but a human rights violation. In the West children are encouraged to express their feelings, to think independently, to be open and free. Creativity, play, and fantasy that support this individualism play a big part in contributing to a child's development. In contrast, in Muslim cultures individualism, freedom of speech, creativity, and play are not only inhibited, they are considered shameful and subject to humiliation. One must conform to the group.

We must understand that domestic abuse and violence are inextricably linked to early childhood deprivation, repression of thoughts and sexuality, and realize that this can escalate to the out-of-control violence of the terrorist. Part of the solution to terrorism involves not addressing it head on, but encouraging integration and bonding through art, music, food, fashion, joint programs for children, learning the other's mother tongue, be it Arabic or Hebrew, and continuing contact through the Internet and Facebook. The internet does not have to be a dreaded tool of recruitment for jihadi activities. It can play a positive role in bringing peoples from different cultures together.

Epilogue

As my psychological anthropological journey comes to an end, I hope I have been able to foreground one of its leading ideas—that each and every one of us has our own internal terrorist. We must discover, understand, and own these intimate connections because they can hook us into global terrorism in general and Islamic suicide bombing in particular. Identifying such links will help us further identify the specifics of the projected terrors of the terrorists. Only then can we defuse the murderous rage and maiming violence they inflict upon the innocent.

We must remain proactive. We must not give in or give up hope. Just because their females and mothers have been misused and abused as longstanding objects of hatred, which in part has fueled the rage of the terrorists, does not mean that we have to unwittingly participate in perpetuating the seemingly never-ending cycle of violent abuse. Nor does this mean that we have to be interpolated into their hysterical drama allegedly concerning political violence. Violence is violence; it does not care how terrorists seek to justify their attacks against the innocent.

By identifying intimate interlocking links to global terrorism, we create a transitional space to unlock, delink and crack global terrorism's code, which is the code of the maternal—if you will, the maternal drama. By doing so, we become like the child in the story of the Emperor's New Clothes. We realize the king is naked—and that he is married to his mother.

"My Arabesque"

Endnotes

1 Psychological anthropology is an interdisciplinary subfield of anthropology that studies the interaction of cultural and mental processes. This subfield tends to focus on ways in which human development and enculturation within a particular group—with its own history, language, practices, and conceptual categories—shape processes of human cognition, emotion, perception, motivation, and mental health. It also examines how the understanding of cognition, emotion, motivation, and similar psychological processes inform or constrain our models of cultural and social processes. Freud, Kardiner, Devereux, Spiro, Obeyesekere, along with Nandy and Kakar, are but a few scholars who have engaged in this genre, although they did not specifically focus on terrorism.

2 Van der Kolk. B. 1996. Trauma and memory. In *Traumatic Stress: The Effects of Overwhelming Experience on Mind, Body, and Society,* ed. B. van der Kolk, A. McFarland, O. van der Hart & L. Weisaeth, p. 293. New York: Guilford Press.

3 Howell, E.H. 2005. *The Dissociative Mind,* p. 3. Hillsdale, NJ: Analytic Press.

4 Barakat, H. 1993. *The Arab World: Society, Culture, and State.* Berkeley: University of California Press.

5 Matusitz, J. https://www.youtube.com/watch?v=l4qFw6SGI_s., accessed 28 June 2013. See also Kornman A., Dr. Matusitz humiliates Islamic Intimidation Group CAIR and http://www.familysecuritymatters.org/publications/detail/dr-matusitz-humiliates-islamic-intimidation-group-cair?f=must_reads, accessed 28 June 2013.

6 El Feki, S. 2013. *Sex and the Citadel: Intimate Life in a Changing Arab World,* p. 91. Toronto: Pantheon.

7 Dr. Kathy Seifert, 23 April 2013, "Is the Maltreatment of Women and Girls at the Core of the Terrorist Culture?" http://www.americanchronicle.com/articles/view/300978.

8 Lachkar, J. 1998. *The Many Faces of Abuse: Treating the Emotional Abuse of High-functioning Women.* Northvale, NJ: Jason Aronson.

9 Honest Reporting, 2013, Al Qaeda vs. Hezbolla, http://honestreporting.com/israel-daily-news-stream-03172013/, accessed 7 March, 2013.

10 From the book *Tahrir ol wasyleh,* Volume 4, published by Darol Elm, Iran, 1990, and verified for me by Reuven Paz, PhD, former director of research for the Shin Bet, Israel's equivalent of the Federal Bureau of Investigation.

11   Lankford, A. 2013. *The Myth of Martyrdom: What Really Drives Suicide Bombers, Rampage Shooters and Other Self-Destructive Killers.* New York: Palgrave MacMillan.

12   Hamid, T. 2005. *Roots of Jihad: An Insider's View of Islamic Violence,* p. 18. New York: Top Executive Media.

13   Zeid, A. 1974. Honour and Shame among the Bedouins of Egypt, in *Honour and Shame: The Values of Mediterranean Society,* ed. J.G. Peristiany, p. 257. Chicago: University of Chicago, Midway reprint.

14   Ali, A.H. 2006. *The Caged Virgin: An Emancipation Proclamation for Women and Islam,* p. 179. New York: Free Press. See also Pryce-Jones, 1989. *The Closed Circle,* p. 35. New York: Harper & Row.

15   Fernea, E. Childhood in the Muslim Middle East, http://isc.temple.edu/neighbor/world/muslim-childhood.pdf, pp.4–5, accessed 21 May 2013.

16   Breiner, S. J. 1990. Some Interesting Child-Rearing Practices in the Arab Moslem World, in *Historical and Psychological Inquiry,* pp. 121-39, ed. Paul Elovitz. New York: International Psychohistorical Association, 1990. Sander Breiner, M.D. was a professor of psychiatry and a psychoanalyst who treated many Muslims and Arabs in Detroit, Michigan. He was also author of *The Slaughter of the Innocents* New York and London: Plenum, 1990, the authoritative volume on the history of child sacrifice Dr. Breiner became my mentor, and I was very fortunate to have had his support over the years—including his encouragement to pursue the publication of this volume.

17   Bouhdiba, A. 1998. *Sexuality in Islam,* p. 277. London: Saqi Books.

18   Davis, S. and D.A. Davis. 1989. *Adolescence in a Moroccan Town.* New Brunswick, NJ: Rutgers University Press.

19   Lawrence G. Sager, The Free Exercise of Culture: Some Doubts and Distinctions, in *Engaging Cultural Differences: The Multicultural Challenge in Liberal Society,* pp. 168-69, ed. Richard Allan Shweder, Martha L. Minow, and Hazel Markus. New York: The Russell Sage Foundation, 2004.

20   http://www.familysecuritymatters.org/publications/detail/the-mosque-as-mother#ixzzzMprogR00.

21   Shukert, R. What happens when the myth of the obedient, docile Jewish husband gets busted, http://www.tabletmag.com/jewish-arts-and-culture/136386/myth-of-the-jewish-husband?utm_source=tabletmagazinelist&utm_campaign=f70073889e-6_28_2013&utm_medium=email&utm_term=0_c308bf8edb-f70073889e-206680929, accessed 28 June 13.

22   Westermarck, E. 1926. *Ritual and Belief in Morocco,* Vol. 2, pp. 424, 426. New York: Random House Publishing.

23   Volkan, V. 1985. The Need To Have Enemies and Allies: A Developmental Approach. *Political Psychology* 6:219-47. See also Volkan, V. 1988. *The Need to have Enemies and Allies: From Clinical Practice to International Relationships.* Northvale, NJ: Jason Aronson.

24   El Feki, S. 2013. *Sex and the Citadel: Intimate Life in a Changing Arab World,* p. 220. Toronto: Pantheon.

25   Kanaana, S. 2005. The Arab Ear and the American Eye: A Study of the Role of the Senses in Culture, *Cultural Analysis* 4, pp. 29-45.

26   Darwish, N. 2006. *Now They Call Me Infidel,* p.3. New York: Sentinel.

27   Gareth, R. http://www.scotsman.com/news/domestic-abuse-like-terrorism-says-top-scots-policeman-1-2776241, accessed 7 February 2013.

28   Pain, R. 2012. *Everyday Terrorism: How Fear Works in Domestic Abuse,* pp. 3-38. Center for Social Justice and Community Action, Durham University and the Scottish Women's Aid. I agree with Professor Pain that there are differences between the two kinds of violence. While somewhat parallel, the grandiosity and omnipotence of, say for example, Hezbollah or Al Qaeda's destruction is on a different magnitude. This does not, however, diminish the profundity of the destruction of the family unit. The family is the psychological microcosm of civic society, with similar disfunctionalities.

29   Brandon, J., and Hafez, S. Crimes of the community: Honor-based violence in the United Kingdom, p. 85: http://www.civitas.org.uk/pdf/CrimesOfTheCommunity. pdf, accessed May 2013.

30   http://www.nytimes.com/2003/02/09/magazine/everybody-has-a-mother. html?pagewanted=all&src=pm.

31   K. Seifert, personal communication, 25 June 2013.

32   Schwartz, H.L. 2013. *The Alchemy of Wolves and Sheep: A Relational Approach to Internalized Perpetration in Complex Trauma Survivors.* New York: Routledge.

33   Schwartz, H.L. 2013. *The Alchemy of Wolves and Sheep: A Relational Approach to Internalized Perpetration in Complex Trauma Survivors.* New York: Routledge.

34   Dimen, M. 1994. Money, Love and Hate, *Psychoanalytic Dialogues*, 4, pp. 69-100.

35   El Feki, S. 2013) *Sex and the Citadel: Intimate Life in a Changing Arab World*, p. 82. Toronto: Pantheon.

36   Özbek, A. and V. Volkan. 1976. Psychiatric problems within the satellite-extended families of Turkey, *American Journal of Psychotherapy*, 30, pp. 576–582.

37   Cebiroglu, R, E. Sümer, Ö. Polvan, K. Aydogmus, S. Onaran, and G. Mocan. 1973. A survey on the distribution of psychiatric syndromes seen in children in three major groups of changing Turkish culture, *Acta Paedopsychiatrica: International Journal of Child & Adolescent Psychiatry*, 39(6), pp. 155-161.

38   El Feki, S. 2013. *Sex and the Citadel: Intimate Life in a Changing Arab World*, pp. 103, 108, 115. Toronto: Pantheon.

39   Firestein, S., personal communication, 7 April 2013.

40   Schützenberger, A.A. 1999. *The Ancestor Syndrome*. Trans. A. Trager. London and New York: Routledge.

41   Kramer, M. 2001. *Ivory Towers on Sand*. Washington, DC: Washington Institute for Near East Policy.

42   Murphy, P. 2010. *Allah's Angels: Chechen Women in War*, Annapolis, MD: Naval Institute Press, Loc4882 of 5865.

43   Booth, A., T. Trimble and J. Egan. 2010, October. Body-Centred Counter-Transference in a sample of Irish Clinical Psychologists, *Psychologist*, http://hse. openrepository.com/hse/bitstream/10147/121271/1/BodycentredCounter.pdf

44   Ayaan Hirsi Ali. 2006. *The Caged Virgin: An Emancipation Proclamation for Women and Islam*, p. 98. New York: Free Press.

45   R. Paz, personal communication, 2005.

46   Stein, R. 2010. *For Love of the Father*. Stanford, CA: Stanford University Press.

47   Breiner, S., February 8, 2010, personal communication.

48   Chayil, E. 2010. *Hush*. New York: Walker Publishing Co.

49   Feldman, D. 2012. *Unorthodox*. New York: Simon and Schusterman.

50   Tang, A. 10 June 2007. Veiled Threads, *St. Paul Pioneer Press*, p. 6e, www.twincities.com

51   Ali, .A.H. 2007. *Infidel,* p. 40. New York: Free Press.

52   Lankford, A. 2013. *The Myth of Martyrdom: What Really Drives Suicide Bombers, Rampage Shooters, and Other Self-Destructive Killers.* New York: Palgrave MacMillan.

53   Bar-Tal, D. 2013. *Intractable Conflicts: Socio-Psychological Foundations and Dynamics.* Cambridge: Cambridge University Press.

54   Lifton, R.J. 2000. *The Nazi Doctors.* New York: Basic Books.

55   El Feki, S. 2013. *Sex and the Citadel: Intimate Life in a Changing Arab World,* p. 83. Toronto: Pantheon.

56   Raine, A. 2013. *The Anatomy of Violence: The Biological Roots of Crime,* pp. 15-18. New York: Pantheon.

Selected Bibliography

Ablow, K. 2011. *Inside the Mind of Casey Anthony*. New York: St. Martin's Press.

Ablow, K. 2007. *Living the Truth: Transform Your Life through Honesty and Insight*. New York: Hachette Books.

Ablow, K. 2005. *Inside the Mind of Scott Peterson*. New York: St. Martin's Press.

Ablow, K. 2004. *Murder Suicide*. New York: St. Martin's Press.

Ablow, K. 2004. *Psychopath*. New York: St. Martin's Press.

Ablow, K. 2002. *Compulsion*. New York: St. Martin's Press.

Ablow, K. 1999. *Projection*. New York: Pantheon.

Aghaie, K.S. 2004. *The Martyrs of Karbala: Shi'i Symbols and Rituals in Modern Iran*. Seattle/ London: University of Washington Press.

Ahmed, A.S. 2003. *Islam Under Siege*. Cambridge, UK: Polity.

Akhtar, A. Ed. 2008. *The Crescent and the Couch: Cross-Cultural Currents between Islam and Psychoanalysis*. New York: Jason Aronson.

Akhtar, S. 1984. The Syndrome of Identity Diffusion, *American Journal of Psychiatry*, 141:11, 1381-1384.

Ali, A.H. 2006. *The Caged Virgin: An Emancipation Proclamation for Women and Islam*. New York: Free Press.

Ali, A.H. 2007. *Infidel*. New York: Free Press.

Ammar, N. 2007. Wife Battery in Islam: A Comprehensive Understanding of Interpretation. *Violence against Women*, 13(5): 516-26.

Ascherman, L. I. & Safier, E.J. 1990. Sibling Incest: Consequence of Individual and Family Dysfunction. *Bulletin of the Menninger Clinic*, 54: 311-322.

Asman, Oren. 2004. Abortion in Islamic Countries—Legal and Religious Aspects. *Medicine and Law* 23:73-89.

Bader, M. 2002. *Arousal: The Secret Logic of Sexual Fantasies*. New York: St. Martin's Press.

Baird-Windle, P. and E. J. Bader. 2001. *Targets of Hatred: Anti-Abortion Terrorism*. New York: Palgrave.

Balsam, R. 2013. *Sons of Passionate Mothering*. International Psychotherapy Institute E-Books, www.freepsychotherapybooks.org

Barakat, H. 1993. *The Arab World: Society, Culture, and State*. Berkeley: University of California Press.

Baron-Cohen, S. 2011. *The Science of Evil: On Empathy and the Origins of Cruelty*. New York: Basic Books.

Bat Ye'or [Gisèle Littman]. 2001. *Islam and Dhimmitude: Where Civilizations Collide*. NJ: Fairleigh Dickinson University Press.

Bat Ye'or [Gisèle Littman]. 2005. *Eurabia: The Euro-Arab Axis*. Madison/Teaneck: Fairleigh Dickinson University Press.

Biggs, M. 2002. Dying without Killing: Protest by Self-Immolation. In *To Die For: Making Sense of Suicide Missions* ed. Diego Gambetta. Oxford: Oxford University Press.

Bin Laden, C. 2004. *Inside the Kingdom*. London: Virago.

Biven, B. M. 1997. Dehumanization as an Enactment of Serial Killers, *Journal of Analytic Social Work,* 4(2) 23-49.

Booth, A., T. Trimble and J. Egan. (2010, October). Body-Centred Counter-Transference in a sample of Irish Clinical Psychologists, *Psychologist,* http://hse. openrepository.com/hse/bitstream/10147/121271/1/BodycentredCounter.pdf

Bouhdiba, A. 1977. The Child and Mother in Arab-Muslim Society. In L.C. Brown and N. Itzkowitz, eds., *Psychological Dimensions of Near Eastern Studies*. Princeton: Darwin.

Bouhdiba, A. 1998. *Sexuality in Islam*. London: Saqi Books.

Bowlby, J. 1969. (3 vols.). *Attachment and Loss*. New York: Basic Books.

Brazelton, T.B., A. Bergman and J. Simo 1991. Simbiosis, Individuación y Creación del Objecto. México, D.F., México: Instituto de Investigación en Psicología Clínica y Social, A.C.

Breiner, S. J. 1990a. *Slaughter of the Innocent*. New York and London: Plenum.

Breiner, S. J. 1990b. Some Interesting Child-rearing Practices. In The Arab Moslem World, in *Historical and Psychological Inquiry,* ed. Paul Elovitz, pp. 121-139. New York: International Psychohistorical Association; also posted online 2004: http://www. state.sc.us/dmh/forum6.htm

Brisard, J-C. with D. Martinez. 2005. *Zarqawi: The New Face of Al-Qaeda*. New York: Other Press.

Brooks, G. 1995. *Nine Parts of Desire: The Hidden World of Islamic Women*. New York: Anchor Books.

Cartwright, D. 2002. *Psychoanalysis, Violence and Rage-Type Murder: Murdering Minds*. Hove and New York: Brunner-Routledge.

Cashdan, S. 1999. *The Witch Must Die: The Hidden Meaning of Fairy Tales*. New York: Basic Books.

Chayes, S. 2006. *The Punishment of Virtue: Inside Afghanistan after the Taliban*. New York: Penguin.

Chayil, E. 2010. *Hush*. New York: Walker Publishing Co.

Chasseguet-Smirgel, J. 1996. Blood and Nation. *Mind and Human Interaction,* 7: 31-36.

Davis, B. 2013. I survived three suicide bombings, http://livewire.amnesty. org/2013/03/20/i-survived-three-suicide-bombings/, accessed 20 March.

Dominus, S. 2003. Everybody Has a Mother, *New York Times Magazine*, February 9.

Dundes, A. ed. 1992. The Evil Eye: A Casebook, in *From Game to War and Other Psychoanalytic Essays on Folklore*. Madison: University of Wisconsin Press; 1997. Lexington: University of Kentucky Press.

Duran, K. And A. Hechiche. 2001. *Children of Abraham: An Introduction to Islam for Jews*. Hoboken, New Jersey: Ktav Publishing House.

Dutton, D.G. 1998. *The Abusive Personality: Violence and Control in Intimate Relationships.* NY: Guilford Press.

Dutton, D.G. & S.K. Gollant. 1995. *The Batterer.* New York: Basic Books.

Dutton, D., & Painter, S.L. 1981. Traumatic Bonding. The Development of Emotional Attachments in Battered Women and Other Relationships of Intermittent Abuse. *Victimology. An International Journal,* 6, 139–155.

El Feki, S. 2013. *Sex and the Citadel: Intimate Life in a Changing Arab World.* Toronto: Pantheon.

Emerson, S. 2002. *American Jihad: The Terrorists Living Among Us.* New York: The Free Press.

Fairbairn, R. 1952. *Psychoanalytical Studies of the Personality.* London: Tavistock.

Falcones de Sierra, I. 2010. *The Hand of Fatima.* New York: Doubleday

Feldman, D. 2012. *Unorthodox.* New York: Simon and Schuster.

Fonagy, P. 1999. Male Perpetrators of Violence Against Women: An Attachment Theory Perspective *Journal of Applied Psychoanalytic Studies,* 1: 7-27.

Fornari, F. 1974. *The Psychoanalysis of War.* Bloomington, Indiana: Doubleday.

Freud, A. 1936. *The Ego and the Mechanisms of Defense.* New York: International Universities Press.

Freud, S. 1919. The Uncanny. *The Standard Edition,* 17: 219-256.

Freud, S. 1932. The Acquisition and Control of Fire. *The Standard Edition,* 22: 187-193.

Galdston, R. 1981. The Domestic Dimensions of Violence, *The Psychoanalytic Study of the Child,* 36: 391-414.

Gambetta, D. 2005. *Making Sense of Suicide Missions.* Oxford: Oxford University Press.

Gaylin, W. 2003. *Hatred: The Psychological Descent into Terror.* New York: Public Affairs.

Gezari, V.M. 2013. *The Tender Soldier: A True Story of War and Sacrifice.* New York: Simon and Schuster.

Gilman, S. 1993. *Anti-Semitism in Times of Crisis.* New York: New York University Press.

Glazov, J. 2009. *United in Hate.* New York: WND Books.

Gorkin, M. and R. Othman. 1996. *Three Mothers, Three Daughters: Palestinian Women's Stories.* Berkeley/Los Angeles/London: University of California Press.

Grandin, T. 2006. *Thinking in Pictures: My Life with Autism.* New York: Vintage.

Grandin, T. and C. Johnson. 2005. *Animals in Translation: Using the Mysteries of Autism to Decode Animal Behavior.* New York: Scribner.

Guileyardo, J., J. Prahlow J. and J. Barnard. 1999. Familial Filicide and Filicide Classification, *American Journal of Forensic Medicine and Pathology,* 20(3): 286-292.

Gunaratna, R. June 2005. Khalid Sheikh Mohammed, The Brain, *Playboy Magazine.*

Gunaratna, R. 2002. *Inside Al Qaeda.* New York: Columbia University Press.

Goldhagen, D. 1996. *Hitler's Willing Executioners: Ordinary Germans and the Holocaust.* NY: Alfred A. Knopf.

Haj-Yahia, M. M. and R. Shor. 2001. Battered Brides in Israeli-Arab Society, *National Council of Jewish Women Journal,* 24:3, 27.

Haj-Yahia, M.M. 1995. Child Maltreatment as Perceived by Arab Students of Social Science in the West Bank, *Child Abuse and Neglect*, 19:1209-1219.

Haj-Yahia, M.M. and S. Tamis 2001. The Rates of Child Sexual Abuse and Its Psychological Consequences as Revealed by a Study Among Palestinian University Students, *Journal of Child Abuse and Neglect*, 25:1303-1327.

Hamid, T. 2005. *Roots of Jihad: An Insider's View of Islamic Violence*. New York: Top Executive Media.

Harris, E. 1995. *Guarding the Secrets: Palestinian Terrorism and a Father's Murder of His Too-American Daughter*. New York: A Lisa Drew Book, Scribner.

Hashemite, A. 2013. Anti-Semitism Is Why the Arab Spring Failed, http://blogs. timesofisrael.com/pro-semitisim-the-road-to-a-prosperous-democratic-middle-east/.

Hass, A. 2013. http://www.haaretz.com/opinion/the-inner-syntax-of-palestinian-stone-throwing.premium-1.513131.

Hekmat, A. 1997. *Women and the Koran*. New York: Prometheus Books.

Herman, J.L. 1993. *Trauma and Recovery: The Aftermath of Violence From Domestic Abuse to Political Terror*. NY: Basic Books.

Heydayat-Diba, Z. 1997. Self-object Functions of the Koran, *International Journal for the Psychology of Religion*, 7:211-236.

Holinger, P.C. 1987. Suicide in Adolescence, *American Journal of Psychiatry*, 134(12): 1433-1434.

Holmes, R. M. and J. De Burger. 1988. *Serial Murder*. Newbury Park: Sage Publication.

Howell, E.F. 2005. *The Dissociative Mind*. Hillsdale, New Jersey: The Analytic Press.

Hughes, T.P. 1994/1885. *Dictionary of Islam*. Chicago: Kazi Publications.

Hunt, J.L. 2010. *Psychoanalytic Aspects of Fieldwork*. London: Sage.

Huntington, S. 1998. *The Clash of Civilizations and the Remaking of the World Order*. New York: Touchstone Books.

Iacoboni, M. 2012. *Mirroring People: The New Science of How We Connect with Others*. New York: Picador/Farrar, Straus and Giroux.

Inamdar, S. 2001. *Muhammad and the Rise of Islam*. New York: International Universities Press.

Israeli, R. 2003. *Islamikaze*. Portland, Oregon: Frank Cass Publishers.

Jefferis, J. 2011. *Armed for Life: The Army of God and Anti-Abortion Terror in the United States*. Santa Barbara, CA: Praeger.

Johnson, I. 2010. *A Mosque in Munich: Nazism, the CIA, and the Rise of the Muslim Brotherhood in the West*. New York: Houghton Mifflin Harcourt Publishing Company.

Jones, J.L. 2010. Countering Islamic Radicalization and Al Shabaab Recruitment within the Ethnic Somali Population of the United States: An Argument for Applying Best Practices for Stemming Youth Gang Recruitment and Initiation. Naval Postgraduate School, Monterrey, CA, Thesis.

Jones, S.G. 2009. *In the Graveyard of Empires: America's War in Afghanistan*. New York: W.W. Norton and Company.

Jureidini, R. 2013. *Domestic Workers in the Middle East: Status, Enhancement and Degradation in Arab Households*. London: Routledge.

Kanaana, S. 2005. The Arab Ear and the American Eye: A Study of the Role of the Senses in Culture, *Cultural Analysis* 4, 29-45.

Kandel, E.R. 2012. *The Age of Insight: The Quest to Understanding the Unconscious in Art, Mind, and Brain from Vienna 1900 to the Present*. New York: Random House.

Karr-Morse, R. & M.S. Wiley 1997. *Ghosts from the Nursery: Tracing the Roots of Violence*. New York: The Atlantic Monthly Press.

Khosrokhavar, F. 2005. *Suicide Bombers: Allah's New Martyrs*. Ann Arbor, MI/London: Pluto Press.

Khuri, F.I. 2001. *The Body in Islamic Culture*. London: Saqi Books.

Kimble Wrye, H. 1997. Projections of Domestic Violence and Erotic Terror on Film Screen, *The Psychoanalytic Review,* 84:681-700.

Klein, M. 1984. *The Writings of Melanie Klein*, 3 vol. New York: The Free Press.

Klein, M. 1952. Notes on Some Schizoid Mechanisms. In *Developments in Psycho-Analysis*. London: Hogarth Press, pp. 292-320.

Klein, M. 1948. Mourning and Its Relation to Manic States. In *Contributions to Psycho-analysis 1921-1945*. London: Hogarth Press.

Kobrin, N.H. 2012, 30 May, http://www.familysecuritymatters.org/publications/detail/the-mosque-as-mother.

Kobrin, N.H. 2010. *The Banality of Suicide Terrorism: The Naked Truth about Islamic Suicide Bombing*. Dulles,VA: Potomac.

Kobrin, N.H. 2009. Uriel Acosta, J.M. da Costa, M.D. What's Freud got to do with it? or How Ladino and Sephardic culture inform psychoanalysis and trauma studies, Conference Languages and Literatures of Sephardic and Oriental Jewry, ed. by David M. Bunis, Yaakov Benttolila and Efraim Hazan. Juried Proceedings of the Misgav Yerushalayim's Sixth International Congress, June 11-16, 2000. Jerusalem: The Hebrew University of Jerusalem Press, 306–318.

Kobrin, N.H. 2008. Jihaditism? Parallels between Autism and Terrorism, *Mentalities/Mentalités*. November, Vol. 22:2, 1–47.

Kobrin, N.H. 2008. Putting The Um (Mother) Back Into the Ummah's Suicide Attack. In *Suicide Bombers: The Psychological, Religious and Other Imperatives*. ed. M. Sharpe. NATO Science for Peace and Security Studies Series, E: Human and Societal Dynamics, vol. 41, 151–159, Amsterdam: IOS Press.

Kobrin, N.H. 2003a. Psychoanalytic Explorations of the New Moors: Converts for Jihad, *Clio's Psyche*, 9(4),171–187.

Kobrin, N.H. 2003b. Political Domestic Violence in Ibrahim's Family: A Psychoanalytic Perspective. In J. Piven, C. Boyd, & H. Lawton, eds., *Eroticisms: Love, Sex, and Perversion: Psychological Undercurrents of History*, vol. 5, 104–139. New York: iUniverse Inc.

Kobrin, N.H. 2002c. The Death Pilots of September 11th, 2001: The Ultimate Schizoid Dilemma. In J. Piven, C. Boyd, & H. Lawton, eds., *Jihad and Sacred Vengeance: Psychological Undercurrents of History*, vol. 3, 76–98. New York: Writers Club Press.

Kobrin, N.H. 2000. The Psychoanalytic Psychotherapy of PTSD (contributor to this chapter). In E. Foa, T. Keane, and M. Friedman, M.D., eds., *Effective Treatments for PTSD*. New York: Guilford Press.

Kobrin, N.H. 1992. Freud's Concept of Autonomy and Strachey's Translation: A Piece of the Puzzle of the Freudian Self , *The Annals of Psychoanalysis*, vol. 21: 201–223 (recipient of the juried Eissler Prize for psychoanalysis).

Kobrin, N.H. 1989. Freud y Sus Fueros: Una Semiótica Preliminar de la Transferencia Psicoanalítica. *MmActas del VI Simposio de la Sociedad Española de Literatura General y Comparada*, Granada, 361-367.

Kobrin, N.H. 1988. Die Psychoanalytische Ubertragung al Historisches Symptom: Freud und seine Fueros. In Hans Ulrich Gumbrecht, ed., *Materialitat der Kommunikation*, 94–105. Frankfurt am Main: Suhrkamp Verlag.

Kobrin, N.H. 1987. Freud and his Fueros, *Stanford Literature Review*, 4:2, 193-210.

Kobrin, N,H, 1986. Aljamía - Lebenstil und Gruppenbindung am Rande des Christlichen Europ, transl. by Ludwig Pfeiffer. In Hans Ulrich Gumbrecht, ed., *Stil: Geschichten und Funktionene eines Kulturwissenschaftlichen Diskurselements*, 463-474. Frankfurt am Main: Suhrkamp..

Köse, A. 1996. *Conversion to Islam: A Study of Native British Converts*. London: Kegan Paul.

Kramer, M. 2001. *Ivory Towers on Sand*. Washington, DC: Washington Institute for Near East Policy.

Kressel, G. 1986. *Prescriptive Patrilateral Parallel Cousin Marriage. Ethnology*, 25(3): 163–180.

Kressel, G. 1996. *Ascendancy through Aggression*. Wiesbaden: Harrassowitz Verlag.

Kugel, S. and S. al-Haqq. 2011. Honor Killing in the Middle East and North Africa: A Systematic Review of the Literature, *Violence against Women*, 17(11):1442-64.

Lachkar, J. 1983. The Arab-Israeli Conflict: A Psychoanalytic Perspective. Unpublished PhD thesis. Los Angeles: International University.

Lachkar, J. 1992. *The Narcissistic/Borderline Couple: A Psychoanalytic Perspective to Marital Conflict*. New York: Brunner/Mazel.

Lachkar, J. 1993a. Paradox of Peace: Folie à Deux in Marital and Political Relationships. *Journal of Psychohistory*, 20(3), 275–287.

Lachkar, J. 1993b. Political and Marital Conflict. *Journal of Psychohistory*, 22(2), 199–211.

Lachkar, J. 1997. Narcissistic/Borderline Couples: A Psychodynamic Approach to Conjoint Treatment. In *The Disordered Couple*, ed. J. Carlson & L. Sperry, pp. 259–282. New York: Brunner/Mazel.

Lachkar, J. 1998. *The Many Faces of Abuse: Treating the Emotional Abuse of High-functioning Women*. Northvale, NJ: Jason Aronson.

Lachkar, J. 2002. The Psychological Make-up of a Suicide Bomber. *Journal of Psychohistory*, 29(4): 349–367.

Lachkar, J. 2008. Psychopathology of Terrorism. Paper presented at the Rand Corporation, 3rd Annual Conference on Terrorism and Global Security, May 9, Santa Monica, CA.

Lachkar, J. 2012. *The Disappearing Male.* New York Jason Aronson.

Lankford, A. 2009. *Human Killing Machines.* Lanham, MD: Lexington Books.

Lankford, A. 2013. *The Myth of Martyrdom: What Really Drives Suicide Bombers, Rampage Shooters and Other Self-Destructive Killers.* New York: Palgrave MacMillan.

Lansky, M. 1992. *Fathers Who Fail: Shame and Psychopathology in the Family System.* Hillsdale, New Jersey: Analytic Press.

Laing, R.D. 1969. *The Divided Self.* New York: Random House.

Levy, M., D. Sanders, & S. Sabraw. 2002. Moms Who Kill: When Depression Turns Deadly. *Psychology Today.* November/December, 60-95.

Lewis, B. 1998. License to Kill. *Foreign Affairs,* November/December,14-19.

Lipshiz, C. (2013). http://www.timesofisrael.com/french-jews-slam-tv-portrayal-of-school-killer/?utm_source=The+Times+of+Israel+Daily+Edition&utm_campaign=71ce15636c-2013_03_16&utm_medium=email, accessed 16 Mar 2013.

Mahler, M. S., F. Pine, and A. Bergman. 1975. *The Psychological Birth of the Human Infant.* New York: Basic Books.

Manji, I. 2004. *The Trouble with Islam,* pp. 9-10. New York: St. Martin's Press.

Markovits, A. 2012. *I Am Forbidden: A Novel.* New York: Hogarth.

Masking, J. 2013. A fig leaf is dropped in Islamic Societies, *The New York Times,* http://www.nytimes.com/2013/04/08/books/sex-and-the-citadel-by-shereen-el-feki.html?nl=todaysheadlines&emc=edit_th_20130408&_r=0&pagewanted=print, accessed 8 April 2013.

Masterson, J. 1982. *The Narcissistic and Borderline Disorders.* New York: Brunner/Mazel.

McBride, J. 1995. *War, Battering, and Other Sports: The Gulf Between American Men and Women.* Atlantic Highlands, NJ: Humanities Press International.

McCrary, G. O. 2003. *The Unknown Darkness: Profiling the Predators Among Us.* New York: HarperCollins Publishers Inc.

Mernissi, F, 2011. *Beyond the Veil: Male-Female Dynamics in Muslim Society.* London: Saqi.

Meyer, C. L. & M. Oberman, with K. White, M. Rone, P. Batra, and T. C. Proano. 2001. *Mothers Who Kill Their Children: Understanding the Acts of Moms from Susan Smith To The "Prom Mom."* New York: New York University Press.

Mitscherlich, A. & M. Mitscherlich. 1975. *The Inability to Mourn.* New York: Grove Press.

Momen, M. 1985. *An Introduction to Shi'i Islam.* New Haven/London: Yale University Press.

Moore, B. and B. Fine, Eds. 1990. *Psychoanalytic Terms and Concepts.* Binghamton, NY: Vail-Ballou Press.

Morgan, R. 2001. *The Demon Lovers: The Roots of Terrorism.* New York: Washington Square Press.

Morrison, A. 1997. *Shame: The Underside of Narcissism.* Hillsdale, NJ: The Analytic Press.

Morrison, A. 1998. *The Culture of Shame.* Northvale, NJ: Jason Aronson.

Mulligan, S.E. 2009. Radicalization within the Somali-American Diaspora: Countering the Homegrown Terrorist Threat. Thesis, Naval Postgraduate School. Monterey, CA.

Murray, S.O. & Roscoe, W. Eds. 1997. *Islamic Homosexualities: Culture, History and Literature.* NY: New York University Press.

Nacos, B. 2003. *Mass-Mediated Terrorism.* Lantham/Boulder/New York/Oxford: Rowman & Littlefield.

Naipual, V.S. 1998. *Beyond Belief: Islamic Excursions among the Converted Peoples.* New York: Little, Brown & Company.

Nesci, D. A. 1999. *The Lessons of Jonestown: An Ethnopsychoanalytic Study of Suicidal Communities.* Roma: Società Editrice Universo.

Newell, K.S., E. Ross, C. McVicker and J. Cromwell. 2000. *Discrimination Against the Girl Child: Female Infanticide, Female Genital Cutting and Honor Killing,* Booklet No. 6 in a Series on International Youth Issues. Washington, DC: Master Print, Inc.

O'Ballance, E. 1979. *Language of Violence: The Blood Politics of Terrorism.* San Rafael, CA: Presidio Press.

Orgel, S. 1974. Sylvia Plath: Fusion with the Victim and Suicide, *Psychoanalytic Quarterly,* 43:272-273.

Özbek, A. and V. Volkan. 1976. Psychiatric Problems within the Satellite-extended Families of Turkey. *American Journal of Psychotherapy,* vol. 30, 576-582.

Pain, R. 2012. *Everyday Terrorism: How Fear Works in Domestic Abuse,* pp. 3-38. United Kingdom: Center for Social Justice and Community Action, Durham University and the Scottish Women's Aid.

Pape, R.A. 2005. *Dying to Win.* New York: Random House.

Patai, R. 2002. *The Arab Mind.* New York: Hatherleigh Press.

Pedazhur, A. 2005. *Suicide Terrorism.* Cambridge: Polity.

Pedahzur, A. 2009. *The Israeli Secret Services and the Struggle against Terrorism.* New York: Columbia University Press.

Pickthall, M.W. 1936. *The Life of Muhammad.* London: Amana Publications.

Peters, F.E. 1982. *The Children of Abraham: Judaism, Christianity and Islam.* Princeton, NJ: Princeton University Press.

Reid Meloy, J. 2002. *Violent Attachments.* New York: A Jason Aronson Book.

Potamianou, A. 1993. En exil de Langue Maternelle: Exiled from the Mother Tongue, *Canadian Journal of Psychoanalysis,* 1:47-60.

Pryce-Jones, D. 1989. *The Closed Circle: An Interpretation of the Arabs.* Chicago: Ivan R. Dee.

Ressler, R. K., A.W. Burgess, and J.E. Douglas. 1988. *Sexual Homicide.* New York: Lexington Books.

Robins, R. S. & Post, J. M. 1997. *Political Paranoia: The Psychopolitics of Hatred.* New Haven, CT: Yale University Press.

Robinson, A. 2001. *Bin Laden: Behind the Mask of the Terrorist.* London: Mainstream Publishing.

Rosenbaum, M. & J. Richman. 1970. Suicide: The Role of Hostility and Death Wishes from the Family and Significant Others. *American Journal of Psychiatry,* 126: 128-131.

Rushdie, S. 2002. *Step Across This Line.* New York: Random House.

Ruthven, M. 2002. *A Fury for God.* New York/London: Granta Books.

Sabbah, F. 1984. *Women in the Muslim Unconscious.* New York: Pergamon.

Sawyer, F. 2002. The Death Pilots of September 11th, 2001. MS-NBC, National Geographic documentary aired March 10, 2002.

Schmitt, A. and J. Sofer, eds. 1992. *Sexuality and Eroticism Among Males in Moslem Societies.* New York/London/Norwood (Australia): Harrington Park Press, an imprint of The Haworth Press, Inc.

Schwartz, H.L. 2013. *The Alchemy of Wolves and Sheep: A Relational Approach to Internalized Perpetration in Complex Trauma Survivors.* New York: Routledge.

Schiffer, I. 1973. Toronto/Buffalo: The University of Toronto Press and The Free Press.

Schützenberger, A.A. 1999. *The Ancestor Syndrome,* A. Trager, transl. London and New York: Routledge.

Schweitzer, Y. and S. Shai. 2002. *An Expected Surprise: The September 11th Attacks on America and Their Ramifications.* [Hebrew]. Herzliya, Israel: ICT.

Schweitzer, Y. and S. Shai. 2003. *The Globalization of Terror.* New York: Transaction Press.

Searles, H. F. 1962. The Differentiation Between Concrete and Metaphorical Thinking in the Recovering Schizophrenic Patient, *Journal of the American Psychoanalytic Association,* 10: 22-49.

Sears, D. J. 1991. *To Kill Again.* Wilmington: Scholarly Resources Inc.

Sennot, C.M. 2003. *The Body and the Blood: The Middle East's Vanishing Christians and the Possibility for Peace.* New York: Public Affairs.

Shay, J. 1994. *Achilles in Vietnam: Combat Trauma and the Undoing of Character.* New York: Atheneum.

Simon, R.I. 1996. *Bad Men Do What Good Men Dream: A Forensic Psychiatrist Illuminates the Darker Side of Human Behavior.* Washington, DC & London: The American Psychiatric Press, Inc.

Souad [pseudonym] in collaboration with M.-T. Cuny. 2004. *Burned Alive.* New York: Bantam Press.

Speckhard, A. 2012. *Talking to Terrorists: Understanding the Psycho-Social Motivations of Militant Jihadi Terrorists, Mass Hostage Takers, Suicide bombers and "Martyrs."* McLean, VA: Advances Press.

Spillius, E.B., J. Milton, P., Garvey, C. Couve, D. Steiner, and R.D. Hinshelwood. 2011. *The New Dictionary of Kleinian Thought.* New York: Routledge.

Steiner, L.M. 2009. *Crazy Love.* New York: St. Martin's Press.

Stern, J. 2003. *Terror in the Name of God.* New York: Ecco.

Stern, J. 2010. *Denial: A Memoir of Terror.* New York: Harper-Collins e-Books.

Stoller, R. J. 1974. Symbiosis Anxiety and the Development of Masculinity. *Archives of General Psychiatry,* 30: 164-172.

Stoller, R.J. 1995. *Perversion: The Erotic Form of Hatred.* New York: Karnac Books.

Stout, M. 2005. *The Sociopath Next Door.* New York: Broadway Books/Random House.

Tauber, Edward S. 1981. Symbiosis, Narcissism, Necrophilia: A Disordered Affect in the Obsessional Character. *Journal of the American Academy of Psychoanalysis,* 9:1, 33–49.

Timimi, S. 2002. *Pathological Child Psychiatry and the Medicalization of Childhood,* p. 22. New York: Brunner-Routledge.

Todd, J. & Dewhurst, K. 1959. The Othello Syndrome: A Study in the Psychopathology of Sexual Jealousy. *Journal of Nervous and Mental Disease,* 122: 367-374.

Trexler, R.C. 1995. *Sex and Conquest: Gendered Violence, Political Order and the European Conquest of the Americas.* Ithaca, NY: Cornell University Press.

Volkan, V. 1988. *The Need to Have Enemies and the Need to Have Alliances.* Northvale, NJ: Jason Aronson.

Wangh, M. 1962. The 'Evocation of a Proxy,' *Psychoanalytic Study of the Child*, 17:451- 472.

Watt, W. Montgomery. 1976. *Muhammad.* London: Oxford University Press.

Weimann, G. 2000. *Communicating Unreality: Modern Media and the Reconstruction of Reality.* Thousand Oaks, CA/London: Sage Publications, Inc.

Welldon, E.V. 2000. *Mother, Madonna, Whore.* New York: Other Press.

Wohlrab-Sahr, M. 1999. Conversion to Islam: Between Syncretism and Symbolic Battle," *Social Compass*, 46:351-362.

Wurmser, L. 1994. *The Mask of Shame.* Northvale, NJ: Jason Aronson.

Wrye, H.K. 1997. Projections of Domestic Violence and Erotic Terror on the Film Screen, *Psychoanalytic Review*, 84(5): 681-699.

Ze'evi, D. 2006. *Producing Desire: Changing Sexual Discourse in the Ottoman Middle East 1500-1900.* Berkeley: University of California Press.

Zeid, A.A.M. 1974. Honour and Shame Among the Bedouins of Egypt. In *Honour and Shame: The Values of Mediterranean Society*, ed. J.G. Peristiany. Chicago: University of Chicago, Midway reprint.

Zonis, M. and C.M. Joseph. 1991. Unpublished paper, cited in D. Pipes, 1996, *The Hidden Hand: Middle East Fears of Conspiracy.* New York: St. Martin's Press.

Zonszein, M. 2013. http://972mag.com/watch-israeli-journalist-discusses-her-article-defending-palestinian-stone-throwing/69192/.

About the Author

Nancy Hartevelt Kobrin, Ph.D. is a psychoanalyst, Aljamiadist (specialist in Old Spanish in Arabic script with a focus on Islam) and counterterrorist expert. She studied romance and semitic languages, including Ladino (Old Spanish in Hebrew Script), along with semiotics and translation theory, before training as a psychoanalyst at the Chicago Institute of Psychoanalysis. In addition to writing numerous publications on trauma and terrorism, she is the author of *The Banality of Suicide Terrorism: The Naked Truth about the Psychology of Islamic Suicide Bombing*, Potomac, 2010, which has been translated into Hebrew. The book is being used by the US military, and elsewhere, as a textbook.

Dr. Kobrin has taught and lectured on law enforcement and counterterrorism in the United States and abroad. She has presented at Rand, Santa Monica, on the Somali terrorist network Al Shabaab. She predicted six months before it happened that America's first suicide bomber would come from this community, and such was the case in October 2008 when Shirwa Ahmed, a Somali American detonated in Puntland, Somalia.

Dr. Kobrin is a fellow of the American Center for Democracy in Washington, DC. She has been a clinical member of the International Society for Traumatic Stress Studies and is an emeritus member of The American Association for Marriage and Family Therapy. She was also a clinical professor of psychiatry in Minnesota, where she was in private practice with a specialty in PTSD for over twenty years until she left in June 2009 to train with the U.S. Army's Human Terrain System program.

Dr. Kobrin has two grown children and five grandchildren. She lives in Tel Aviv with her life partner, Professor Yitzhak Reiter, one of Israel's leading scholars on Sharia law, Islam, and the Arab minority. Together they have seven grandchildren and another on the way.

www.ingramcontent.com/pod-product-compliance
Lightning Source LLC
Chambersburg PA
CBHW070853290526
45795CB00001B/107